OPTIMUM

Collection dirigée par Fabien Fichaux

CW01612927

Burning Issues

vocabulaire anglais de l'actualité

Jean Max Thomson

Agrégé d'anglais

Diplômé de Sciences Po Paris

ellipses

Du même auteur :

The Big Picture, vocabulaire de l'actualité en anglais, 2e édition, Ellipses, 2012

The Big Picture, exercices de vocabulaire, Ellipses, 2012

An Apple a Day, Ellipses, 2e édition, 2012

Anglais : Thème[s] d'aujourd'hui, Vuibert, 3e édition, 2010 (en collaboration)

Vocabulaire anglais : économie, politique, société, Armand Colin, 3e édition, 2009

How to write in English, Nathan, 2002

Anglais : Thèmes suivis, Vuibert, 1999 (en collaboration)

Savoir-faire : la traduction au CAPES, Éditions du Temps, 1998 (en collaboration)

Anglais : QCM d'aujourd'hui [Exercices méthodiques], Vuibert, 1997

Anglais : QCM d'aujourd'hui [Annales corrigées], Vuibert, 1997

From & Into English, Dunod, 1993 (en collaboration)

Anglais Sciences-Po, Dunod, 4e édition, 1993 (en collaboration)

Legal English Vocabulary, Dunod, 1991 (en collaboration)

ISBN 978-2-7298-7883-2

32, rue Bargue 75740 Paris cedex 15

www.editions-ellipses.fr

To Marjorie

As hands doe shut…

SYMBOLES PHONÉTIQUES

La transcription phonétique suit les mots dont la prononciation peut être difficile pour un francophone.

Dans cette transcription, l'apostrophe indique que la syllabe qui suit porte l'accent tonique. Certains mots pluri-syllabiques comportent un accent tonique secondaire, indiqué par une apostrophe basse.

Voici l'explication des symboles phonétiques dont la lecture n'est pas évidente.

voyelles brèves

ə	an
ɪ	pig
e	pet
æ	cat
ʌ	bus, hub
ɒ	dog
ʊ	wood

voyelles longues

iː	sea
ɑː	car, father
ɔː	war, law
ɜː	bird, firm
uː	moon

diphtongues

aɪ	eye, die
ɔɪ	boy, toy
eɪ	snake, wait
əʊ	boat, low
aʊ	cow, now
ɪə	beer
ʊə	poor
ɛə	air, wear

triphtongues

aɪə	fire
aʊə	power
əʊə	slower, mower
eɪə	player

consonnes

θ	think
ð	this
h	hit, heat
j	you, yes
w	west, wow
ʒ	vision
dʒ	judge, jealous
ʃ	shoe, shy
tʃ	church
ɲ	long, king

REPÈRES

 **Citation**

 **Definition**

 **Do not confuse**

 **Fact**

 **Film**

 **Note**

AVANT-PROPOS

Burning Issues est une version condensée de *The Big Picture, vocabulaire de l'actualité en anglais*, paru dans la même collection. Son objectif et sa méthode sont pour l'essentiel identiques mais il s'en distingue à plusieurs égards.

En effet, il s'adresse aux étudiants des premières années de l'enseignement supérieur, mais aussi aux élèves du second cycle du lycée qui souhaitent préparer leur entrée à l'université, dans les IEP ou en classes préparatoires.

Comme *The Big Picture*, le présent ouvrage propose au lecteur non seulement la liste des mots et expressions qu'il faut connaître pour aborder les grands thèmes de l'actualité mais aussi des éléments de réflexion sur ce thème sous forme de notes, d'informations et de citations pour la plupart tirées de la presse anglophone contemporaine. Ces brefs textes ont pour but non seulement de présenter les mots en contexte, mais aussi d'informer le lecteur et de stimuler son intérêt, ce qui facilitera son effort de mémorisation.

Chaque chapitre comporte en outre une partie intitulée *Language Practice* qui se compose d'exercices et de phrases à traduire : c'est l'occasion pour le lecteur de vérifier ses acquis et d'affiner ses moyens d'expression en anglais. On trouvera à la fin de cette partie plusieurs questions pouvant faire l'objet d'un « essay » sur le thème du chapitre.

Enfin, une aide à la rédaction en anglais intitulée *Writing Tip*, complète le chapitre. Ces conseils méthodologiques, qui sont destinés aux étudiants ayant à expliquer ou commenter un texte, ou bien devant rédiger un « essay », peuvent être lus indépendamment du chapitre.

Tous les corrigés des exercices de vocabulaire et de traduction sont donnés en fin de volume.

On trouvera en annexe une aide à l'expression orale ainsi qu'une brève sélection de vocabulaire général destiné à la rédaction.

Je tiens à remercier chaleureusement Mary Chalot et C. Jon Delogu pour leurs précieuses suggestions.

TABLE DES MATIÈRES

1. HEALTH 9
eating disorders • epidemics • AIDS • food scares • health care

2. DRUGS 19
drug trafficking • prevention • second-hand smoking • alcohol abuse • DEA

3. SEX & LOVE 29
dating • STDs • sex industry • same-sex marriage • intercourse

4. WOMEN 39
gender gap • abortion • glass ceiling • domestic violence • suffragettes

5. BIOETHICS 49
cloning • IVF • stem-cell research • euthanasia • surrogacy

6. ENGLISH 59
English-speaking world • RP • pidgin • standard English • Spanglish

7. GLOBALIZATION 69
BRICS • free trade • cultural exception • outsourcing • WTO

8. THE ECONOMIC CRISIS 79
bonuses • labour • slump • credit bubble • working poor

9. INEQUALITIES 89
NGOs • welfare state • philanthropy • social divide • pension system

10. SOCIAL ILLS 99
consumer society • teenage violence • couch potatoes • truancy • advertising

11. CULTURAL DIVERSITY 109
immigration policy • racial profiling • salad bowl • multiculturalism • PC

12. DEMOCRACY 119
free speech • surveillance • dictatorship • human rights • uprisings

13. CRIME 129
death penalty • on parole • justice system • serial killers • gun control

14. TERRORISM 139
hijacking • 9/11 • CIA • suicide bombers • fanaticism

15. INTERNATIONAL RELATIONS 149
armed forces • WMDs • nuclear deterrent • diplomacy • United Nations

16. ENVIRONMENTAL ISSUES 159
endangered species • natural disasters • deforestation • drought • overfishing

17. POLLUTION 169
asbestos • oil slicks • ozone layer • waste disposal • recycling

18. CLIMATE CHANGE & ENERGY 179
greenhouse gases • CO_2 • renewables • fossil fuels • nuclear

19. SCIENCE 189
creationism • NASA • technophobia • physics • guinea pigs

20. INFORMATION TECHNOLOGY 199
computers • video games • ISPs • digital piracy • social networks

CORRIGÉS 209

ANNEXES 251

1. ORAL PRESENTATIONS 253
2. ALL-PURPOSE VOCABULARY 261

1. HEALTH

9/11 • abortion • advertising • alcohol abuse • armed forces • asbestos • bonuses • BRICS • CIA • cloning • CO_2 • computers • consumer society • couch potatoes • creationism • credit bubble • cultural exception • dating • DEA • **AIDS** death penalty • deforestation • dictatorship • digital piracy • diplomacy • domestic violence • drought • drug trafficking • endangered species • English-speaking world • euthanasia • fanaticism • fossil fuels • free speech • free trade • gender gap • glass ceiling • greenhouse gases • guinea pigs • gun control • hijacking • human rights • immigration policy • intercourse • ISPs • IVF • justice **eating disorders** system • labour • multiculturalism • NASA • natural disasters • NGOs • nuclear • nuclear deterrent • oil slicks • on parole • outsourcing • overfishing • ozone layer • PC • pension system • philanthropy • physics • pidgin **food scares** • prevention • racial profiling • recycling • renewables • RP • salad bowl • same-sex marriage • second-hand smoking • serial killers • sex industry • slump • social divide • social networks • Spanglish **epidemics** • standard English • STDs • stem-cell research • suffragettes • suicide bombers • surrogacy • surveillance • technophobia **health care** • teenage violence • truancy • United Nations • uprisings • video games • waste disposal • welfare state • WMDs • working poor • WTO

a **disease** [dɪ'zi:z], an illness	une maladie
to catch a disease	attraper une maladie
to suffer from a disease	souffrir d'une maladie
to die of, to die from cancer	mourir du cancer
to eradicate a disease	éradiquer une maladie
lung / breast / skin cancer	cancer du poumon / du sein / de la peau
carcinogenic [ˌkɑ:sɪnə'dʒenɪk]	cancérigène
Severe Acute Respiratory Syndrome (SARS) [sa:s]	syndrome respiratoire aigu sévère (SRAS)
a sexually-transmitted disease (STD)	une maladie sexuellement transmissible (MST)

The World Health Organization (WHO [ˌdʌblju: eɪtʃ 'əʊ]) is a specialized agency of the United Nations that coordinates international efforts to control outbreaks of infectious disease, such as SARS, malaria, Tuberculosis (TB), swine flu, and AIDS. It supports the development and distribution of safe and effective vaccines and drugs. For instance, after over two decades of fighting smallpox (*variole*), the disease was eradicated in 1980 — the first disease in history to be eliminated by human effort. In addition, the WHO carries out various health-related campaigns — for example, to boost (*encourager*) the consumption of fruits and vegetables worldwide and to discourage tobacco use.

a **virus** (pl: viruses) ['vaɪərəs, 'vaɪərəsɪz]	un virus
bacteria [bæk'tɪərɪə]	des bactéries
a germ [dʒɜ:m]	un microbe, un germe
contagious [kən'teɪdʒəs], catching, infectious	contagieux, infectieux
to contaminate	contaminer
to go down with the flu	attraper la grippe
to be infected with a virus, by a virus	être contaminé par un virus
to carry a virus	être porteur d'un virus
a symptom	un symptôme
to cough [kɒf]	tousser
to have a temperature ['temprətʃəʳ]	avoir de la température
to have a fever, to run a fever	avoir de la fièvre

The French verb "*guérir*" is not always translated by the same English verb. For instance, you say that a doctor **cures** a patient or that a a disease can **be cured** (e.g. In the Middle Ages they did not know how to cure diabetes). But a patient **gets better** or **recovers**. Eventually he will **be cured** — hopefully. On the other hand a wound (*une blessure*) will **heal** after a while.

an epidemic [ˌepɪ'demɪk]	une épidemie
to check an epidemic	enrayer une épidémie
a pandemic	une pandémie
to break out	éclater, se déclarer
to spread	se propager

the spread of a virus	la propagation d'un virus
to affect a country	affecter, toucher un pays
the scope, extent	l'ampleur, l'étendue
flu [fluː], influenza [ˌɪnflu'enzə]	la grippe
swine flu / bird flu	la grippe porcine / la grippe aviaire

Contagion is a thriller directed by Steven Soderbergh (2011). It documents the spread of a deadly virus which brings about mass panic and the collapse of social order. Attempts by researchers and public health officials to contain the epidemic lead to the development (*mise au point*) of a vaccine. The film, which was inspired by the 2003 SARS epidemic and the 2009 flu pandemic, explores the various aspects of the tragedy using several interacting plot lines. It has been praised by scientists for its accurate description of medical and scientific practices.

AIDS, acquired immune deficiency syndrome	SIDA, syndrome d'immunodéficience acquise
to develop AIDS	contracter le SIDA
an AIDS sufferer, an AIDS patient	un malade du SIDA
HIV-positive [ˌeɪtʃaɪ'viː]	séropositif
a screening test	un test de dépistage
to screen sb for AIDS	faire passer un test de dépistage du SIDA à qn
to have unprotected sex	avoir des rapports non protégés
a needle	une aiguille
antiretroviral drugs	anti-rétroviraux

South Africa has witnessed an "unparalleled" five-year increase in life expectancy since 2005 thanks to the world's biggest programme of HIV/Aids drug treatment. The trend marks a spectacular reversal from when former president Thabo Mbeki was branded (*était catalogué*) an "Aids denialist" whose dogma was blamed for 330,000 deaths. Professor Salim Abdool Karim, president of the South African Medical Research Council, said the rise in life expectancy — from 54 years in 2005 to 60 in 2011 — was of the order usually only seen after a major societal shift (*mutation*), such as the abolition of slavery. In this case, the catalyst was the industrial scale distribution of antiretroviral (ARV) drugs by the public health sector, greatly reducing deaths among people in their 30s. In 2005, under Mbeki and health minister Manto Tshabalala Msimang — who promoted a "treatment" of beets (*betterave*) and garlic (*ail*) — only 133,000 patients were on ARVs. Now the total stands at 1.9m, the biggest programme on the planet.
The Guardian, Monday 3 December 2012

medical treatment	un traitement médical
health care	les soins médicaux OU les services de santé
the health system	le système de santé

to prescribe	prescrire
a prescription	une ordonnance
a general practitioner, a GP [dʒiː'piː]	un médecin généraliste
a surgeon ['sɜːdʒən]	un chirurgien
to have surgery, have an operation	se faire opérer
to diagnose ['daɪəgnəʊz]	diagnostiquer
a diagnosis [ˌdaɪəg'nəʊsɪs]	un diagnostic
to cure a patient	guérir un patient
a remedy, a cure	un remède
to recover	se rétablir, guérir
recovery	guérison, rétablissement

Medicare is a US social insurance program providing coverage to people who are over 65 while **Medicaid** does the same for low-income families.

a drug, a medicine	un médicament
a painkiller	un antalgique, analgésique
a side effect	un effet secondaire
an injection, a shot	une piqûre
a vaccine ['væksiːn]	un vaccin
to vaccinate	vacciner
a vaccination campaign	une campagne de vaccination

The **Food and Drug Administration** (FDA) is a US federal agency that was created in 1906 to protect and promote public health.

One of the obvious and measurable effects of noise pollution is hearing loss. However, a more difficult to measure, but increasingly significant, health hazard is the stress and agitation that may occur from exposure to loud noise. Persistent noise can increase stress levels, which in turn, can result in high blood pressure (*hypertension*), an important health concern. Known as the "silent killer" because there are few obvious symptoms, it can result in serious health problems requiring medical assessment and intervention. Sleep disruption (*troubles du sommeil*) is another common effect of loud and/or persistent noise...The social consequences include poor familial and social relationships, and poor work performance.

food scare	alerte à l'intoxication alimentaire
health scare	péril sanitaire, alerte aux risques sanitaires
bovine spongiform encephalopathy, BSE	ESB, encéphalopathie bovine spongiforme
mad cow disease	la maladie de la vache folle
dioxin [daɪ'ɒksɪn]	dioxine
traceability	la traçabilité

BSE, bovine spongiform encephalopathy, informally known as **mad cow disease**, is a brain disease affecting cattle. Its human form, **CJD** or Creuzfeldt-Jacob disease, is an incurable degenerative neurological disorder.

eating patterns, eating habits	les habitudes alimentaires
food	la nourriture
foodstuffs	denrées alimentaires, aliments
to cook	cuisiner
vegetables	légumes
fruit	fruits
green vegetables, greens	légumes verts

The **National Health Service** (NHS) is the British equivalent of the French *Sécurité sociale*. It was set up in 1945 and constitutes the mainstay (*principal pilier*) of the welfare state.

The world's **infant mortality rate** has been reduced from 13.4 % in 1970 to about 8.8% in 1990 and 5.7% in 2010.

weight	le poids
to weigh [weɪ] oneself	se peser
to put on weight	prendre du poids
to be overweight	être trop gros, en surpoids
fat	gros, gras
obese [əʊ'biːs]	obèse
bulimia [bə'lɪmɪə]	la boulimie
binge eating	les excès de nourriture
anorexia [ænə'reksɪə]	l'anorexie
to be underweight	être trop maigre, ne pas peser assez
thin	maigre
slim	mince

A **binge** is an informal word that is used to refer to a short period when you do too much of something, in particular eating or drinking but also shopping. Thus you may **binge on** chocolate, for instance, but you can also **go on a shopping binge**.

a fast food restaurant	un fast food
to eat junk food	manger des cochonneries
processed foods	des aliments préparés
fatty foods	aliments riches en graisses
sodas, fizzy drinks	boissons gazeuses
a chocolate bar	une barre chocolatée

a diet	un régime
to go on / be on a diet ['daɪət]	commencer / faire un régime
balanced / unbalanced diet	une alimentation équilibrée / mal équilibrée
diet foods / health foods	aliments basses calories / aliments diététiques
organic food	nourriture biologique, aliments bio
vegetarian [ˌvedʒɪ'tɛərɪən]	végétarien

It is no longer just the inhabitants of the rich world whose waistlines (*tour de taille*) are spreading dangerously. Though 40% of its 50m people live off less than $2 a day, South Africa has become one of the world's fattest countries. A study by London's Imperial College found as many as three-quarters of South African women to be overweight, up from 57% in 1980; it classified 43% as obese, up from 24% in 1980. Men are only a shade trimmer (*plus mince*), with 62% reckoned overweight. As in the richer world, South Africa's accumulating kilos are the result of rapid urbanisation, less physically demanding work, the spread of television, and a shift in diet from home-cooking to processed foods rich in fats and sugar. The country's fast-food industry is booming. But whereas most Westerners seek to be thin, many black Africans still admire bulk (*corpulence*) in men and big contours in women.
The Economist, 17th December 2011

LANGUAGE PRACTICE

1. Find the appropriate suffix.

un chirurgien	a surgeon	surg _ _ _	*chirurgie*
contagion	contagion	contagi _ _ _	*contagieux*
cancer	cancer	carcino _ _ _ _ _	*cancérigène*
se rétablir	to recover	recov _ _ _	*guérison*
retrouver	to trace	trace _ _ _ _ _ _ _	*traçabilité*

2. Find the words corresponding to the following abbreviations.

The **NHS** is the N................. H................. S.................

The **WHO** is the W.................... H.................... O.................

STDs are s................. t................. d.................

A **GP** is a g................. p.................

AIDS means A................. I................. D................. S.................

3. Associate the following words so as to form compound nouns and translate them: binge / breast / foods / screening / drinking/ fatty / test / vaccination / cancer / campaign

....

....

....

....

....

4. Find the appropriate prepositions or adverbial particles.

Adrian's lost two kilos since he went .... a diet last month.

My wife came .... with the flu twice last winter.

His grandfather suffers .... Alzheimer's or Parkinson's disease, I can't remember which.

Vince has put .... a lot of weight since he got married.

In my company, new employees are always screened .... AIDS.

5. Translate into French

Anorexia is estimated to affect 1% of adolescent girls.

My uncle, a heavy smoker, was diagnosed with lung cancer last year.

Ivor will have to be operated on if his heath doesn't improve.

Sophie's husband is at least ten kilos overweight.

Some young people don't realize how dangerous unprotected sex is.

6. Translate into English

Les soins médicaux représentent une part énorme de notre budget.

L'épidémie s'est déclarée il y a trois jours et se propage rapidement.

Il faudra changer tes habitudes alimentaires si tu veux perdre du poids.

On ne sert pas d'aliments diététiques dans les fast foods.

Les effets secondaires de ce nouveau vaccin sont encore mal compris.

Questions

Is medical tourism unethical?

A healthy mind in a healthy body. Discuss.

Do you think students should be allowed or even encouraged to use brainpower-enhancing drugs?

WRITING TIP N° 1: Form vs content*

If you take a language exam in which you have to write in English, you must be aware that your mark* will depend to a large extent* on the quality of the language used: *how* you express yourself counts as much as *what* you say. In some cases, it may count even more.

Students sometimes believe that their "ideas" are all-important, and that the way they are expressed does not make any difference. But examiners read words, not minds. This is particularly true in the context of a language exam, where form matters more than in other exams or in "normal", everyday, communication.

This means in particular that it is vital for you to save some time at the end of the exam to re-read your text in order to eliminate blunders* — those silly mistakes you made simply because you were concentrating on *what* you wanted to explain, not the grammar. Pay special attention to the final -ed (simple past, or past participle) or the final-s (which may be a plural -s, a third-person -s, or a genitive -s). Before the exam, prepare a checklist of the mistakes you make most frequently and reserve a few minutes to go over* your essay, focusing on one specific problem at a time: for instance, preterite and present perfect, verb constructions, prepositions, articles, spelling... This is the surest way of making certain you do not overlook* anything.

You may also need to do some grammar exercises to improve your command of the language. You will not make yourself understood if you have no idea of when and how to use the appropriate pronouns, articles, prepositions or modal verbs such as "must, will..." etc.

To be able to pay close attention to the way you express yourself, the best strategy is probably to dissociate content from form as much as possible. First focus on the content. Think about the question *as if* you were going to write in French. Then, when you have a clear idea of what you want to say, you will be able to devote* your attention to the best way of expressing yourself, paying attention to grammatical correctness, choice of vocabulary, use of idiomatic phrases... In this way, you will be less likely* to make silly mistakes. Of course it is impossible to make a strict separation between content and form, but you should nevertheless try to focus on content first, as much as possible.

Beware*: this does not mean you should write your answer in French first. That would be a waste of time and besides, you would probably make mistakes, translating word for word from the French.

form vs content: *forme contre contenu* • **mark**: *note* • **to a large extent**: *dans une grande mesure* • **blunders**: *bourdes, bévues* • **go over**: *vérifier* • **overlook**: *laisser échapper* • **devote**: *consacrer* • **will be less likely**: *aurez moins de risques* • **beware**: *attention*

2. DRUGS

9/11 • abortion • advertising • AIDS • armed forces • asbestos • bonuses • BRICS • CIA • cloning • CO_2 • computers • consumer society • couch potatoes • creationism • credit bubble • cultural exception • dating • death penalty • deforestation • dictatorship • digital piracy • diplomacy • domestic violence • drought • eating disorders • endangered species • English-speaking world • epidemics • euthanasia • fanaticism • food scares • fossil fuels • free speech • free trade • gender gap • glass ceiling • greenhouse gases • guinea pigs • gun control • health care • hijacking • human rights • immigration policy • intercourse • ISPs • IVF • justice system • labour • multiculturalism • NASA • natural disasters • NGOs • nuclear • nuclear deterrent • oil slicks • on parole • outsourcing • overfishing • ozone layer • PC • pension system • philanthropy • physics • pidgin • racial profiling • recycling • renewables • RP • salad bowl • same-sex marriage • serial killers • sex industry • slump • social divide • social networks • Spanglish • standard English • STDs • stem-cell research • suffragettes • suicide bombers • surrogacy • surveillance • technophobia • teenage violence • truancy • United Nations • uprisings • video games • waste disposal • welfare state • WMDs • working poor • WTO

alcohol abuse

drug trafficking

DEA

prevention

second-hand smoking

drugs (plural)	la drogue
a soft / hard drug	une drogue douce / dure
cannabis ['kænəbɪs]	le cannabis
marijuana [mærɪ'hwɑːnə]	la marijuana
amphetamines	les amphétamines
heroin	l'héroïne
to sniff cocaine	inhaler, sniffer de la coke
a needle	une aiguille
a syringe [sɪ'rɪndʒ]	une seringue
a recreational drug	*une drogue à usage récréatif occasionnel*
a designer drug, a synthetic drug	une drogue de synthèse
a psychoactive, psychotropic substance	un psychotrope
to become commonplace	se banaliser
a plague, a curse, a scourge [skɜːdʒ]	un fléau

Drugs commonly taken for **recreational** use are drugs taken on an occasional basis for enjoyment, especially when socializing. They include alcohol, tobacco, caffeine, cannabis, ecstasy…

drug trafficking	le trafic de drogue
a drugtrafficker	un trafiquant de drogue, un narcotrafiquant
a drug ring, a drug cartel	un réseau de trafiquants
a drug baron, a drug lord, a drug kingpin	un baron de la drogue
a mule [mjuːl]	un passeur, une mule
a drug pusher, a drug peddler, a drug dealer	un revendeur de drogues
drug-related crime	la criminalité due à la drogue

Requiem for a dream is a 2000 film drama film directed by Darren Aronofsky about addiction to various drugs such as heroin or amphetamines. The film was praised in particular for its clever depiction of the mental states of addicts thanks to the technique of "hip hop montage" (successions of extremely short cuts). It is a powerful description of the ravages caused by drugs, ranging from physical harm — the hero's arm has to be amputated following an infection — to hallucinations and psychosis.

In the US, the **Drug Enforcement Administration** (DEA) was created in 1973 to combat drug smuggling and use.

to use drugs, to take drugs	consommer, prendre de la drogue, se droguer
drug use	la consommation de drogue
drug abuse	la toxicomanie
a drug user	un usager de drogue

a casual / heavy user	un consommateur occasionnel / un gros consommateur
to experiment with heroin	essayer l'héroïne
a joint, a reefer	un joint
to be high, to be spaced out	planer, être défoncé

The distinction between **soft drugs** such as cannabis or ecstasy and **hard drugs** such as cocaine or heroin is controversial since it may imply (*laisser entendre*) that some of them are harmless (*inoffensif*) whereas in fact all drugs are dangerous, to various degrees. Moreover both soft and hard drugs are addictive, even if some are more so than others. It should also be pointed that alcohol and tobacco, although legal, are "harder", that is to say more addictive, than some illegal drugs. Finally, do not forget that the word **drug** is an ambiguous word because it can refer to a **narcotic** but also to a **medicine**. This other meaning is reflected in the American word **drugstore**, a place where you can buy medication and toiletries, but not marijuana or LSD.

substance abuse	la toxicomanie, la consommation de substances illégales
to be addicted to sth	être accro à qch
to be hooked on cocaine	être accro à la cocaïne
to crave sth [kreɪv]	avoir un besoin maladif de qch
addiction (to sth), dependency (on sth)	l'accoutumance (à qch), la dépendance
addictive	qui crée une accoutumance, addictogène
drug addiction	la toxicomanie
a drug addict, a drug abuser	un drogué, un toxicomane
a junkie, a druggie	un drogué, un camé, un toxico
to take an overdose, to OD [əʊ'diː]	faire une overdose, une surdose

> Though the Netherlands tolerates cannabis sales to locals in designated coffee shops and Portugal has decriminalised the consumption of all drugs, neither has legalised supply (*offre*), meaning that consumers' cash still goes to mobs (*gangs*) in Latin America. Last year George Papandreou, then prime minister of Greece, became the only sitting European leader to advocate legalising cannabis. Given the weight of opinion in rich countries such as America, caution (*prudence*) is understandable. "If someone wants to destroy their own neurones, that can be their own decision," says Mauricio López Bonilla, interior minister of Guatemala. But legalisation "is not politically backable (*défendable*)…it would have a political and economic cost for us."
> *The Economist*, January 21st 2012

prevention	la prévention
an awareness campaign, an awareness-raising campaign	une campagne de sensibilisation
to legalize cannabis use	légaliser la consommation de cannabis
to decriminalize	dépénaliser, décriminaliser

the pros and cons of legalization	les arguments pour et contre, les avantages et les inconvénients de la légalisation
treatment ['triːtmənt]	le traitement
to seek treatment	demander à être soigné
a rehabilitation center	un centre de désintoxication
to go into rehab	entreprendre une cure de désintoxication
to phase sth out	éliminer qch progressivement
to go cold turkey	arrêter la drogue d'un seul coup OU être en manque
withdrawal [wɪθ'drɔːəl] symptoms	les symptômes de (l'état de) manque
methadone	la méthadone

About half of all prisoners in US federal prisons are there for drug-related offences.

repression	la répression
to clamp down on, to crack down on drug abuse	réprimer la consommation de drogues
to impose penalties for drug possession	pénaliser la possession de drogues
a fine	une amende
to fine sb	condamner qn à une amende
the drug tsar [tsaʀ] (GB), the drug czar [dzaʀ] (US)	le responsable de la lutte contre la drogue

The phrase **drug czar** is an informal expression used to refer to the person in the US Administration in charge of the fight against drug abuse.

alcohol ['ælkəhɒl] **abuse**	l'abus d'alcool
alcoholism	l'alcoolisme
alcohol-related disease	une maladie liée à l'alcool
underage drinking	l'acoolisme des mineurs
the drinking age	l'âge auquel on a le droit d'acheter de l'alcool
to be a heavy drinker	boire beaucoup
binge drinking	les excès de boisson
a drinking binge	une saoûlerie
to get drunk	se saoûler
a drunk	un ivrogne
to drink and drive	conduire après avoir bu
to drive while intoxicated (US), drive under the influence (GB)	conduire en état d'ivresse
drunk(en) driving	la conduite en état d'ivresse

The sale and consumption of alcohol were banned in the US during **Prohibition**, starting in 1919. The result was that organized crime and corruption thrived as consumers bought their liquor illegally. Prohibition was eventually abolished in 1933.

> The original motive for banning the sale of alcohol in the United States was humanitarian. Evangelical Christians, and a growing number of female activists worried — quite rightly (*à juste titre*), it turns out — that many families were being driven into poverty as working-class men spent their weekly paychecks at the pub and left their families to starve. Ban alcohol, the Prohibitionists argued, and you eliminate most of America's social scourges. But when Prohibition ruled the land, from 1920 to 1933, it didn't stop people from drinking. It stopped them from drinking in public. Criminal syndicates smuggled alcohol into the country and sold it in speak-easy pubs, often under the winking eye of corrupt authorities... American folk musicians wrote countless songs to deride (*tourner en ridicule*) Prohibition, but it was probably the realization of lost tax revenues that eventually caused the US Congress to repeal (*abroger*) prohibition in 1933.
> Scott Baldauf, *Christian Science Monitor*, December 15, 2011

smoking	le tabagisme
tobacco	le tabac
a cigarette-manufacturer, a cigarette-maker	un fabricant de cigarettes, un cigarettier
a tobacconist	un marchand de tabac
a pack, a packet of cigarettes	un paquet de cigarettes
nicotine ['nɪkətiːn]	la nicotine
tar	le goudron
to light a cigarette, to light up	allumer une cigarette
a lighter	un briquet
to ask for a light	demander du feu
ash	la cendre
an ashtray	un cendrier
to put out a cigarette	éteindre une cigarette
a cigarette butt	un mégot
a heavy smoker	un gros fumeur
to cough [kɒf]	tousser

In Britain the legal drinking age is 18 and you may be asked to prove your age, for instance by showing your driving licence, when ordering alcoholic beverages in pubs or bars.

to give up smoking, to quit smoking	arrêter de fumer
to cut down on, to cut back on one's consumption	réduire sa consommation
a skinpatch, a nicotine patch	un patch
to resist temptation	résister à la tentation

a non-smoking area	une zone non-fumeurs
a smoke-filled room	une pièce enfumée
a smoking-related disease	une maladie provoquée par le tabac
the number of smoking-related deaths	le nombre de morts dus au tabac
lung / throat cancer	le cancer du poumon / de la gorge
passive smoking, second-hand smoking	le tabagisme passif
to inhale [ɪn'heɪl] smoke	respirer, avaler la fumée

Alcohol abuse and binge-drinking threaten to overburden (*surcharger*) the NHS, costing £2.9bn a year. So why do we still allow alcohol producers to sponsor our major UK sports? We have the "FA Carling Cup" for football, the "Guinness Premiership" for rugby and the "Stella Artois Tournament" for tennis. The list seems endless: anyone would think that beer and lager were performance-enhancing sports drinks. By associating alcohol with sports, brewing companies are creating a false association with fitness and health, at a time when rates of liver cirrhosis, stroke (*attque d'apoplexie*) and heart attacks from alcohol abuse are rising alarmingly.By contrast, cigarette smoking is in decline, driven partly by bans on advertising and sponsorship.
Dr Andrew M. Hill, London SW12, Letter to *The Independent*, Thursday, 7 January 2010

to prohibit, to ban smoking	interdire de fumer
in public places	dans les lieux publics
in the workplace	sur les lieux de travail
to deter, discourage people from smoking	dissuader les gens de fumer

LANGUAGE PRACTICE

1. Choose the appropriate word in the following pairs.

Their daughter smoked a few joints when she was a student but she's never dared (experiment / experience) with other psychoactive substances.

Sam got (drunken / drunk) every night and then went home to beat his wife.

Not least among the (pros / cons) of a less repressive policy is the fact it would help save a lot of money.

Some think that people who start smoking marijuana always move on to (soft / hard) drugs.

Phil became a (heavy / casual) cannabis user and after only six months, he was diagnosed with schizophrenia.

2. All the following compounds include the word "drug".

la toxicomanie ....

un toxicomane ....

une drogue de synthèse ....

un trafiquant de drogue ....

un réseau de trafiquants ....

3. Add the suitable prepositions or particles, or write ø where none is needed.

Most smokers find it very hard to cut down .... their consumption of cigarettes.

Adriana managed to phase .... her use of all mind-altering substances in record time after she met Tom.

Are price increases enough to deter people .... smoking?

He couldn't resist .... temptation and relapsed after a few weeks.

It is a well-known fact that you may become hooked .... crack cocaine very quickly.

4. Find the missing words in the following sentences.

Half the inmates in this prison have been convicted on drug-..................... charges.

You may be fined or even jailed if you are caught driving .... intoxicated.

People have only recently become aware of the damage caused by second-.................... smoking.

Working in a smoke-.................... environment may seriously damage your health.

He used heroin for a few months and then decided to quit cold ....

5. Translate into French

He was a chain-smoker and eventually died of throat cancer.

....

They used mules to smuggle LSD and amphetamines into the country.

....

You can become addicted even if you don't inhale the smoke.

....

Prohibition encouraged the spread of guns and crime.

....

Turning to crime may be the only solution some addicts have to pay for their daily dose.

....

6. Translate into English

Il faut aussi réduire la demande de drogue dans les pays riches.

....

Le tabac et l'alcool sont responsables de milliers de morts chaque année.

....

La cocaïne s'est beaucoup banalisée ces dernières années.

....

Il faut sensibiliser les jeunes aux dangers du cannabis.

....

Devrait-on dépénaliser les drogues douces ? Faut-il criminaliser l'abus d'alcool ?

....

Questions

Why is it that so many young people are attracted to drugs, whether legal or not?
Prevention or repression?
How far should the state regulate individual behaviour?

WRITING TIP N° 2: What to say

Students who do not specialize in English are usually required to do one (or both) of two things. Either they have to explain a text, part of a text and sometimes summarize it or else they must express their own views on a particular issue (the so-called* "essay" question). Let's tackle* the difficulties involved in these two assignments in succession.

• The important thing when you explain a text is to do so "in your own words": you must not just copy and paste* parts of the text into your answer. This implies that you must be able to do two things: first understand the words of the original text, and then convey* the same meaning in a different way. To do so, you must find synonyms for individual words and use different constructions*. For instance "a fifth of the voters" is exactly the same as "20% of the voters". When a jounalist writes about "tackling climate change", he is also "dealing with global warming".

Of course, if the question concerns, say, the rise in tuition fees* in Britain or Canada, you cannot help using* basic words like "student, university...", which are probably used in the text you are expected to explain. This is not a problem. What you must avoid copying are collocations (an adjective + a noun, a verb + a noun), metaphors, images, chunks* of text. The bottom line* is that you must not plagiarize instead of explaining.

This rephrasing* of the text necessarily implies a certain amount of interpretation, especially if you have to summarize a whole page in a paragraph or two, or present its main arguments in a few hundred words. However, you should remain as neutral as you can, avoid passing judgment on what is said in the passage or adding any information that is not included in it.

• In a way*, answering an essay question is exactly the opposite because it means you must take a stance* on a particular issue. For instance you may have to say whether or not you agree it would be a good idea to legalize cannabis, or to tax motorists driving into the centre of a city; you may have to explain what to do to put an end to racial profiling, or whether globalization has had a positive or a negative impact ...

The important thing in this type of question is that you should not shirk* the issue, but at the same time you must make sure you come to a balanced* conclusion. Most issues are complex and many-sided, not black and white. Start out by bringing together everything you know about the questions, remembering what you learned about it in your history or philosophy classes, adding facts and figures relating to it, considering the arguments in favour of a course of action as well as those opposing it etc. Avoid stereotypes: think outside the box*!

so-called: *ce que l'on appelle* • **tackle**: *aborder* • **copy and paste**: *copier-coller* • **convey**: *exprimer* • **whenever possible**: *chaque fois que c'est possible* • **tuition fees**: *droits d'inscription* • **you cannot help using**: *vous ne pouvez pas ne pas utiliser* • **chunks**: *morceaux* • **the bottom line**: *l'essentiel* • **rephrasing**: *reformulation, paraphrase* • **in a way**: *d'une certaine façon* • **take a stance**: *prendre position* • **shirk**: *éluder* • **balanced**: *équilibré* • **Think outside the box!**: *Sortez des sentiers battus !*

3. SEX & LOVE

9/11 • abortion • advertising • AIDS • alcohol abuse • armed forces • asbestos • bonuses • BRICS • CIA • cloning • CO_2 • computers **dating** • consumer society • couch potatoes • creationism • credit bubble • cultural exception • DEA • death penalty • deforestation • dictatorship • digital piracy • diplomacy • domestic violence • **intercourse** drought • drug trafficking • eating disorders • endangered species • English-speaking world • epidemics • euthanasia • fanaticism • food scares • fossil fuels • free speech • free trade • gender gap • glass ceiling • greenhouse gases • guinea pigs • gun control • health care • hijacking • human rights **sex industry** • immigration policy • ISPs • IVF • justice system • labour • multiculturalism • NASA • natural disasters • NGOs • nuclear • nuclear deterrent • oil slicks • on parole • outsourcing • overfishing • ozone layer • PC • pension system • philanthropy **same-sex marriage** • physics • pidgin • prevention • racial profiling • recycling • renewables • RP • salad bowl • second-hand smoking • serial killers • slump • social divide • social networks • Spanglish • standard English • stem-cell research • suffragettes • suicide bombers • surrogacy **STDs** • surveillance • technophobia • teenage violence • truancy • United Nations • uprisings • video games • waste disposal • welfare state • WMDs • working poor • WTO

to have sex, sexual intercourse with sb	avoir des rapports (sexuels) avec qn
a sex partner	un partenaire sexuel
desire	le désir
lust [lʌst]	le désir sexuel
eroticism [ɪ'rɒtɪsɪzəm]	l'érotisme
to be sexually aroused	être excité sexuellement
foreplay	les préliminaires amoureux
an orgasm	un orgasme
to come	jouir
anal sex, sodomy	la sodomie
oral sex	rapports bucco-génitaux
to be sex-starved	être frustré sexuellement

In a dark underground room in central London, a group of men scribble intently (*intensément*) in notebooks. They are in a class on "how to be funny" and they want to get it right. It has been a long day; they have already attended classes on teeth-whitening, self-esteem and personal finance as part of an intensive course on how to attract women. This evening they will put their work into practice as tutors assess (*évaluer*) their attempts to score dates in some of the city's leading clubs. The programme is run by Love Systems, an American firm that charges up to £3,000 ($5,000) for three-day boot camps (*stage d'entraînement*).
The Economist, November 5th 2009

sperm, semen ['siːmən]	le sperme
sperm count	le nombre de spermatozoïdes
a sexually transmitted disease (STD), a venereal [vɪ'nɪərɪəl] disease (VD)	une maladie sexuellement transmissible (MST), une maladie vénérienne
AIDS, acquired immune deficiency syndrome	le SIDA, syndrome d'immunodéficience acquise
a condom	un préservatif
safe sex, protected sex / unprotected sex	des rapports protégés / non protégés
chaste [tʃeɪst]	chaste
a virgin ['vɜːdʒɪn]	un(e) vierge
platonic love	l'amour platonique

Around 8% of Britons say they use dating websites, compared with 4%, on average, in the rest of Europe.

the sex industry	l'industrie du sexe
a brothel ['brɒθl]	une maison close, un bordel
a sex worker	un travailleur sexuel
sex tourism	le tourisme sexuel
a prostitute, a hustler	une prostituée
a rent boy (GB)	un prostitué

a procurer, a pimp	un proxénète, un souteneur, un maquereau
a gigolo, a toy boy (GB)	un gigolo
pornography [pɔː'nɒgrəfɪ]	la pornographie
a porn film, a blue movie	un film porno
sexual harassment ['hærəsmənt, hə'ræsmənt]	le harcèlement sexuel
to be sexually harassed by sb	être harcelé sexuellement par qn
a sex object	un objet sexuel
to rape [reɪp]	violer
a rapist	un violeur
domestic violence	violence conjugale, familiale
sexual abuse [ə'bjuːs]	les sévices sexuels, abus sexuel
to abuse sb sexually	faire subir des abus sexuels à qn
to be sexually assaulted	être violenté, agressé sexuellement

No animal spends more of its allotted time on Earth fussing (*se tracasser*) over sex than *Homo sapiens* — not even the famously libidinous bonobo [one of our closest primate relatives]. Although we and the bonobo both average well into the hundreds, if not thousands, of acts of intercourse per birth — way ahead of (*loin devant*) any other primate — their 'acts' are far briefer than ours. Pair-bonded 'monogamous' animals are almost always *hypo*sexual, having sex as the Vatican recommends: infrequently, quietly, and for reproduction only. Human beings, regardless of (*quelle que soit*) religion, are at the other end of the libidinal spectrum: *hyper*sexuality personified. Human beings and bonobos use eroticism for pleasure, for solidifying friendship, and for cementing a deal (recall that historically, marriage is more akin (*analogue*) to a corporate merger than a declaration of eternal love). For these two species (and apparently *only* these two species), nonreproductive sex is 'natural,' a defining characteristic.
Christopher Ryan and Cacilda Jetha, *Sex at Dawn: The Prehistoric Origins of Modern Sexuality*, Harper Collins, 2010

paedophilia (GB), pedophilia (US)	la pédophilie
a paedophile (GB), a pedophile (US) ['piːdəʊfaɪl]	un pédophile
a paedophile ring	un réseau pédophile
to interfere with a child	se livrer à des attouchements sur un enfant
a child molester	auteur de sévices sexuels sur enfant
child abuse [ə'bjuːs]	les sévices sexuels infligés à des enfants
an abuser [əb'juːzər]	un auteur de sévices
incest	l'inceste
an incestuous relationship	une relation incestueuse
a sex maniac	un obsédé sexuel
a nymphomaniac	une nymphomane
a sex offender	un délinquant sexuel
chemical castration	la castration chimique

A **metrosexual** is a young man with quite a lot of money to spend, living in large city (ie a metropolis, hence the element "metro"), who is interested in fashion and shopping, and generally pays a lot of attention to his physical appearance.

attractive	séduisant
to be attracted to sb	être attiré par qn
love at first sight	le coup de foudre
to woo [wuː] , to court sb	faire la cour à qn
to flirt with sb	flirter avec qn
to try and pick up sb, to chat sb up	draguer qn
to make a pass at sb	faire des avances à qn
a boyfriend / a girlfriend	un petit ami / une petite amie
a date	un rendez-vous avec un amoureux OU un(e) petit(e) amie(e)
to date sb	sortir avec qn
a dating site	un site de rencontres
to fall in love with sb, to fall for sb	tomber amoureux de qn
to be in love with sb	être amoureux de qn
to have a crush on sb	avoir le béguin pour qn
to be deeply in love	vivre un grand amour
to have an affair with sb	avoir une aventure avec qn
a one-night stand	une liaison sans lendemain

Through the centuries, English has borrowed many words from French to refer to love, especially illicit love —it has long been known that exoticism enhances eroticism. Thus in the eyes of an English speaker, a **billet doux** ['bɪleɪ duː] is more exciting than a love letter and **lingerie** more arousing than plain underwear (*sous-vêtements*), which is also why lingerie shops sell **négligés** or **deshabillés**. If a joke is **risqué**, it is slightly shocking probably because of its sexual content or innuendoes (*allusion*). A **rendezvous** ['rɒndɪvuː, 'rɒndeɪvuː] is often a secret meeting between two lovers who may give each other a **French kiss** (*un baiser avec la langue*) while a **voyeur** (also called a peeping Tom) watches them from a distance.

to marry sb, to get married to sb	se marier avec qn
a wedding	(cérémonie du) mariage
marriage ['mærɪdʒ]	le mariage (institution)
to propose (marriage) to sb	demander qn en mariage
to be in a relationship	avoir qn dans sa vie
to move in with sb, to set up house with sb	se mettre en ménage avec qn
to live together	vivre en concubinage
a partner	un compagnon OU une compagne
a live-in boyfriend	un petit ami avec lequel on vit
fidelity	la fidélité

The proportion of children born outside marriage rose from 18% to 41% between 1980 and 2007 in the United States, and from 11% to 50% in France over the same period.

The French word "*mariage*" corresponds to several words in English. To refer to the ceremony, you must use **wedding** (e.g. My sister's wedding will take place in August), but to refer to the institution, the correct translation is **marriage** or, more formally, **matrimony** (e.g. Marriage is out of fashion these days). Furthermore "*un mariage d'amour*" is called a **love match** while "*un mariage d'argent*" is a **money match**. When an unmarried couple have a baby, the child is said to have been born **out of wedlock** — that is to say, outside marriage. Finally, when two companies "marry", they merge and their union is called a **merger**.

extramarital sex	les relations sexuelles hors mariage
to cheat on sb, to be unfaithful to sb	être infidèle à qn
adultery [ə'dʌltəri]	l'adultère
a womanizer, a philanderer	un coureur de jupons
to fall out of love	cesser d'aimer qn
to split up with sb, break up with sb	rompre avec qn
to separate from sb	se séparer de qn
to get divorced from sb, to divorce sb	divorcer de qn

The Decline of the American Empire (*Le Déclin de l'empire américain*) is a French Quebecquois film directed by Denys Arcand and released in 1986. It is the story of eight intellectuals, all working in the History department of a Canadian university who are about to meet again. While preparing to have dinner together, they talk endlessly about their sex lives. But as they tell funny anecdotes, describe their particular tastes or explain how they have have cheated on a partner, for instance, the film turns out to be not just about sex as such (*en tant que tel*), but about its meaning in modern society.

homosexuality	l'homosexualité
homosexual	homosexuel
sexual orientation	l'orientation sexuelle
the age of consent	la majorité sexuelle
a lesbian	une lesbienne
bisexual ['baɪ'seksjuəl]	bisexuel
a transexual	un(e) transsexuel(le)
a transvestite [trænz'vestaɪt]	un travesti
transgender [trænz'dʒendə]	transgenre, transsexuel
to come out (of the closet)	se déclarer ouvertement homosexuel
to out sb	révéler l'homosexualité de qn (sans son consentement)
gay-friendly	favorable aux homosexuels

Many Nigerians strongly disapprove of homosexuality. The dominant role of religion is widely seen as the root of the country's homophobic culture. Punishing gays is one of the few common themes that politicians can promote with equal zest (*enthousiasme*) in the mainly Christian south and the largely Muslim north. Under federal law sodomy is punishable by (*passible* de) a 14-year jail sentence. An even more stringent (*sévère*) bill to ban gay-rights groups and homosexual displays of affection is also under consideration. It is a similar story in many other parts of Africa. Uganda, influenced by evangelical Christianity, has provoked an international outcry (*tollé*) over a still harsher bill that advocates the death penalty in certain cases of gay sex, for instance when one partner is HIV-positive.
The Economist , February 11th 2010

same-sex marriage	le mariage homosexuel
a civil partnership, a civil union	un PACS, une union civile
same-sex parents, LGBT parents	une famille homoparentale
same-sex parenting	l'homoparentalité
a homophobe	un homophobe
homophobia [ˌhəʊməʊˈfəʊbiə]	l'homophobie
homophobic [ˌhɒməʊˈfəʊbɪk]	homophobe

Gay marriage was first legalized in the Netherlands in 2001, then in Belgium (2003), Spain and Canada (2005), South Africa (2006), Norway and Sweden (2009), Argentina, Iceland and Portugal (2010). Civil partnerships were introduced in France in 1999.

LANGUAGE PRACTICE

1. Find the appropriate suffix to form the missing words.

érotique	erotic	....	*l'érotisme*
sexuel	sexual	to be ... aroused	*être excité sexuellement*
compagnon	partner	civil	*PACS*
homophobe (n)	homophobe (n)	....	*homophobe (adj)*

2. Find the words needed to complete the following sentences.

To Veronica it was just a one-night .... but Jim saw it as the beginning of a romance.

Many of those who approve of gay marriage think that ....-sex parenting should not be tolerated.

I haven't had sex for months, I am abolutely sex..................... .

Like so many others today, Adam and Eve decided not to bother with marriage and to set up .... at once.

3. These words are spelled nearly the same as their French translations.

nymphomane (adj, n)	....
homophobie	....
fidélité	....
mariage	....

4. Find synonyms for the following verbs.

to be unfaithful to sb	....
to fall for sb	....
to court sb	....
to get married to sb	....

5. Form four noun groups with the following nouns and translate them.

dating, count, offender, pedophile, site, sperm, sex, ring

....
....
....
....

6. Translate into French.

The most common age of consent worldwide is 16.

....

Hard-line Catholics have always taken a tough line on gay marriage.

....

Copenhagen is described as the world's most gay-friendly city.

....

Anthony made a pass at the waitress, but she did not respond.

....

They were deeply in love and decided to tie the knot straightaway.

....

7. Translate into English

Cela fait plusieurs années qu'il n'a pas eu quelqu'un dans sa vie.

....

Il faut avoir des rapports protégés pour éviter d'attraper la syphilis.

....

Elle a été agressée sexuellement à deux reprises par son employeur.

....

Aux États-Unis, un homme politique n'est pas censé avoir des aventures.

....

Les opposants au mariage homosexuel voudraient qu'il soit interdit pour toujours.

....

Questions

Should pre-marital sex be discouraged?
Marriage, a dying institution?
For or against same-sex parenting.

WRITING TIP N° 3: Opinions

If you are asked a question starting with: "Do you think that...?" or "According to you...?", you are expected to give your view on a particular issue. Beware: some students think so hard about the details of the problems raised by the question that they sometimes forget to answer it. You must make sure that you state* your opinion at least once, usually in the conclusion or towards the end of your introduction.

Remember that "I think that ..." is not the only way of introducing an opinion. You can also use adverbial phrases like "In my opinion", "In my view", "To my mind", "As far as I am concerned". But do not write: "In my view, I think that...", which is redundant. Remember that you use "according to" when you introduce someone else's opinion, but not your own — in other words, "according to" cannot be followed by "me".

You are entitled to* hold just about any opinion you like. Even so*, you should not start every sentence in your essay with: "I think that...". In fact, even if you must take sides* (for example, say whether or not you are in favour of a particular policy), what matters most is not your opinion itself, but the way you substantiate* it. Most of your essay should therefore be devoted to arguments and examples showing how you have come to have that opinion, or why you disagree with those holding other views. Otherwise you run the risk of sounding dogmatic.

Also, remember that opinions worth listening to are views based on reasons and evidence, not mere* impressions or feelings. No one really cares if *in your opinion* the Beatles were a better group than the Rolling Stones; however if you can *demonstrate* that George Harrison was a better guitarist than Keith Richards (or vice versa), that might be a view your reader is willing to consider.

What is more, you can write a very good essay even if you do not have an opinion at all to start with. It may well be that you will be asked a question about a topic to which you have never given serious thought. Do not panic: start by trying to find relevant* examples, explain, try to imagine the arguments of those favouring or opposing a particular policy... you will come to a conclusion later on.

Finally, even if you must answer the question at some point, it is often advisable* to remain cautious* in the way you express your sentiment; that is why rather than say "I think that..." it is often preferable to use expressions such as "it seems to me that..." or "I would say that..." to qualify* your claims. Otherwise you may sound too categorical. A balanced conclusion will probably be perceived as the sign that you have thought carefully about the issue and that you are aware of its complexity, not as a mark of indecision.

state: *exprimer* • **make it clear**: *préciser* • **you are entitled to**: *vous avez droit à* • **even so**: *cependant* • **take sides**: *prendre parti* • **substantiate**: *argumenter, justifier* • **mere**: *simple* • **relevant**: *pertinent* • **advisable**: *conseillé* • **cautious**: *prudent* • **qualify**: *nuancer*

4. WOMEN

9/11 • advertising • AIDS • alcohol abuse • armed forces • asbestos • bonuses • BRICS • CIA • cloning • CO_2 • computers • consumer society • couch potatoes • creationism • credit bubble • cultural exception • dating • DEA • death penalty • deforestation • dictatorship • digital piracy • diplomacy • drought • drug trafficking • eating disorders • endangered species • English-speaking world • epidemics • euthanasia • fanaticism • food scares • fossil fuels • free speech • free trade • greenhouse gases • guinea pigs • gun control • health care • hijacking • human rights • immigration policy • intercourse • ISPs • IVF • justice system • labour • multiculturalism • NASA • natural disasters • NGOs • nuclear • nuclear deterrent • oil slicks • on parole • outsourcing • overfishing • ozone layer • PC • pension system • philanthropy • physics • pidgin • prevention • racial profiling • recycling • renewables • RP • salad bowl • same-sex marriage • second-hand smoking • serial killers • sex industry • slump • social divide • social networks • Spanglish • standard English • STDs • stem-cell research • suicide bombers • surrogacy • surveillance • technophobia • teenage violence • truancy • United Nations • uprisings • video games • waste disposal • welfare state • WMDs • working poor • WTO

abortion

domestic violence

gender gap

glass ceiling

suffragettes

gender imbalance	le déséquilibre entre les sexes
women's status ['steɪtəs] in society	le statut, la position, la place des femmes dans la société
gender inequalities	les inégalités entre les hommes et les femmes
gender war	la guerre entre les sexes
a male chauvinist ['ʃəʊvɪnɪst]	un phallocrate, un machiste
machismo	le machisme
misogyny [mɪ'sɒdʒɪnɪ]	misogynie
a misogynist	un misogyne
sexism	sexisme

The English adjective **feminine** is partly a faux-ami because it is used to describe something that is considered to be typical of women, in particular gentle, delicate, and pretty (e.g. "She always wears very feminine clothes"). To translate the more neutral meaning of the French adjective "*féminin*", you must use **female** (e.g. "female labour" → "*la main d'œuvre féminine*"; "female voters" → "*les électrices*"). You can also use **womanly** to describe a woman's figure (*silhouette*), for example. The adjective **womanish**, on the other hand, is a pejorative adjective that is used to describe men who look or behave like women.

feminism	le féminisme
the women's rights movement	le mouvement des femmes, le mouvement pour les droits de la femme
to be disenfranchised	être privé du droit de vote
the right to vote	le droit de vote
to discriminate against sb	introduire une discrimination contre qn
to be discriminated against	être victime de discrimination
parity	la parité
to introduce quotas ['kwəʊtəz]	instaurer des quotas
equal opportunity	l'égalité des chances
egalitarian	égalitaire

Someone who is **disenfranchised** does not have any rights, in particular the right to vote, and therefore feels excluded from mainstream society. Women were first granted the **right to vote** in 1893 in New Zealand, in 1917 in Canada, in 1918 in the UK, in 1920 in the US, in 1944 in France, in 1971 in Switzerland.

domestic violence	la violence conjugale
a battered woman, a battered wife	une femme battue
rape [reɪp]	le viol
a forced marriage / an arranged marriage	un mariage forcé / arrangé
a sham [ʃæm] marriage, a marriage of convenience	un mariage blanc
a dowry ['daʊri]	une dot
polygamy [pɒ'lɪgəmɪ]	la polygamie

polygamous	polygame
female circumcision, female genital mutilation	l'excision
sexual harassment	le harcèlement sexuel

While about 1/3 of American mothers with young children held jobs in 1975, the ratio had risen to 2/3 at the beginning of the 21st century.

a housewife	une femme au foyer, une ménagère
to do the housework	faire le ménage
to do the cooking / washing / washing-up / shopping	faire la cuisine / la lessive / la vaisselle / les courses
to do the vacuuming / to vacuum ['vækjʊm]	passer l'aspirateur
domestic appliances [ə'plaɪəntsiz]	les appareils ménagers
household chores [tʃɔːrz]	les tâches ménagères

Has liberation made women happier? After a century of fitful (*intermittent*) change in the developed world, the question is still being asked... Belief that the lot (*sort*) of women has improved, at least over the past two generations, is near-universal. 93% [of respondents in a recent poll] said that they are in a better position than were their grandmothers. Only in Mexico and South Africa did many women express doubts about that belief. Yet, at the same time, a majority of all the women asked said that they believed themselves to be no happier than their grandmothers were. How much equality do women think they have achieved? Only 8% of the sample (*échantillon*) thought that they had all the same rights as men. A further 31% thought that they had almost all. Against this, a hefty 37% grumbled that they had only some of them.
The Economist, Oct 9th 1999

female labour ['leɪbər]	la main d'œuvre féminine
female employment	l'emploi des femmes
to have a career	faire carrière
to be a working woman	être une femme qui travaille
a career woman	une femme qui fait carrière
to work part time	travailler à temps partiel OU à mi-temps
to work full time	travailler à plein temps

North Country (2005) is a movie starring Charlize Theron which tells the story of a woman employed in a mine in Minnesota, in the north of the United States. After she is verbally and physically abused by her male co-workers who wrongly accuse her of being promiscuous, she decides to quit and file a lawsuit (*intenter un procès*) against her employer. She is unsuccessful at first but then eventually manages to enlist the support of other women who have suffered similar treatment. She goes on to win the first class action for male harassment and obtains substantial financial compensation. The film is based on the true story of Lois Jenson.

equal ['iːkwəl] **pay**	l'égalité des salaires
the gender pay gap, gender wage gap	le différentiel de salaire entre les sexes
to appoint sb to a post	nommer qn à un poste
a responsible job	un poste à responsabilités
a top job	un poste de haut niveau
a menial job	un emploi subalterne
a male preserve [prɪ'zɜːv]	une chasse gardée pour les hommes

In the US, the **Equal Pay Act** making it illegal to pay men and women different wage rates for jobs that require (*nécessitent*) equal skill and responsibility was adopted in 1963. A similar act was passed Great Britain in 1970. However, in most western countries, the typical full-time female worker earns only between 80 and 85% as much as the typical male doing the same job.

Most jobs are still man-shaped (*adapté aux hommes*): long hours, full-time, intensive, making demands that can only be met by someone without imperative outside commitments. While the women who would like them to be shaped differently still get sacked when they get pregnant, change will only come slowly. Meanwhile, the home is still woman-shaped. Four-fifths of mothers work, but they still do two-thirds of the chores and most of the parenting. Maybe that is why the growing concern is more marked among men (no clean socks in the drawer) than women. Meanwhile, the state still hesitates about engaging fully in providing the support that families most need. But in the end, equality needs more than government policy to make it happen. It starts at the kitchen sink (*évier*).
The Guardian, Monday August 18, 2008

to become **pregnant,** to fall pregnant	tomber enceinte
to be 6 weeks pregnant	être enceinte de six semaines
pregnancy	la grossesse
teenage pregnancy	les adolescentes enceintes
a pregnancy test	un test de grossesse
to have an ultrasound (scan)	passer, faire une échographie
the womb [wuːm]	l'utérus
an embryo ['embriəʊ]	un embryon

a fœtus ['fiːtəs] (US fetus)	un fœtus
a maternity hospital	une maternité
a gynecologist, a gynaecologist [gaɪnə'kɒlədʒɪst]	un gynécologue
a midwife	une sage-femme
to go on maternity leave	partir en congé maternité
parental leave, career break	congé parental
motherhood	la maternité
women's reproductive rights	droits des femmes en matière de reproduction

The phrase **glass ceiling,** which is sometimes literally translated as *plafond de verre*, refers to the obstacles faced by women who try to reach positions of power and responsibility. In modern democracies, there are no explicit rules actually forbidding them from becoming ministers, generals or CEOs — hence the reference to "glass", which is transparent — but the fact is that, proportionally, very few of them occupy such posts.

a birth	une naissance
the birth rate	le taux de natalité
to give birth to a girl / a boy	accoucher d'une fille / d'un garçon
to look after one's children	s'occuper de ses enfants
to bring up, to raise a child	élever un enfant
the upbringing of children, child rearing, parenting	l'éducation des enfants
school-age children	des enfants d'âge scolaire
a nursery, a day-care centre (GB), a child-care center	une crèche, une garderie
a nanny	une nounou, une nourrice
a childminder ['tʃaɪldmaɪndər]	une assistante maternelle, une nourrice
to balance, combine work and family	trouver un équilibre entre travail et famille
to juggle ['dʒʌgl] a career and a family	jongler pour concilier carrière et famille
to reconcile ['rekənsaɪl]	concilier

Abortion became legal in Russia in1920, in the United Kingdom in 1967, in the US in 1973, in France in 1975, and in Portugal in 2007.

a means of contraception	un moyen de contraception
birth control	le contrôle des naissances
family planning	le planning familial
a contraceptive	un contraceptif
a condom	un préservatif
a coil [kɔɪl], an intra-uterine device, an IUD	un stérilet
the (contraceptive) pill	la pilule (contraceptive)
to be on the pill ..... prendre la pilule	
the morning-after pill	la pilule du lendemain

> In 2011 India counted only 914 girls aged six and under for every 1,000 boys. Without intervention, just a few more boys would be born than girls. If you compare the number of girls actually born to the number that would have been born had a normal sex ratio prevailed, then 600,000 Indian girls go missing every year. India's sex ratio is widening, and has been for decades. Sex selection is now invading parts of the country that used not to practise it... Although parts of the country are poor, poverty alone does not explain India's preference for sons. The states with the worst sex ratios — Punjab, Haryana, Gujarat — are among the richest.
> *The Economist*, April 7th 2011

an **abortion**	un avortement
a termination (of pregnancy)	une interruption volontaire de grossesse, une IVG
to have an abortion	avorter, se faire avorter
to terminate a pregnancy	pratiquer une IVG OU se faire faire une IVG
to perform, to carry out abortions	pratiquer l'avortement
an abortion clinic	une clinique pratiquant l'avortement
to induce an abortion	provoquer un avortement
an abortionist	un avorteur, un faiseur d'anges
a backstreet abortion	un avortement clandestin
the pro-life lobby	le lobby des opposants à l'avortement
a pro-life campaigner, a pro-lifer	un militant contre l'avortement
a pro-choice campaigner, a pro-choice activist	un militant pour le droit à l'avortement

> The landmark case of Roe vs Wade legalised abortion across America in 1973. It remains one of the US Supreme Court's most controversial rulings. At the time, abortion had only been legal in restricted circumstances in 20 states. Under the pseudonym Jane Roe, Norma McCorvey claimed Texas abortion law was unconstitutional. She said she had become pregnant after she was raped, and was forced to give birth because abortions were only permitted if they saved a mother's life. The Texas Attorney General (*Procureur Général*), Henry Wade, defended the state's anti-abortion law, but the court ruled that governments did not have the power to ban the procedure, because a woman's right to an abortion was protected by the freedom of personal choice in family matters as enshrined in the 14th Amendment of the US Constitution.
> *The Independent*, 28 April 2012

LANGUAGE PRACTICE

1. Find the appropriate suffix to complete the following.

une mère	a mother	mother _ _ _ _	*maternité*
harceler	to harass	harass _ _ _ _	*harcèlement*
être enceinte	to be pregnant	pregn _ _ _ _	*grossesse*
contraception	contraception	a contracept _ _ _	*un contraceptif*
terminer	to terminate	a termina _ _ _ _	*une IVG*

2. Find the words corresponding to the following definitions.

A .... is money and / or property a wife or her family must pay to her husband when they get married.
A .... is someone, usually a woman, often a specially trained nurse, who helps women when they are giving birth.
A .... is someone whose job is to look after young children.
A .... is a small flat, round piece of medicine that you swallow without chewing it, for instance to avoid becoming pregnant.
A .... is a a piece of metal or plastic that is fitted inside a woman's uterus to prevent her becoming pregnant.

3. Associate the following adjectives and nouns to form compounds and translate.

circumcision, job, opportunity, leave, preserve

female	....	....
male	....	....
parental	....	....
equal	....	....
menial	....	....

4. Underline the appropriate word.

In 2009 a pro-(choice / life) activist shot and killed a doctor who performed abortions.
(Female / Feminine) employment has been rising in the West since the 1960s.
It has often been said that domestic (applications / appliances) such as the vacuum cleaner and the washing machine set women free.

Would you rather have a job or stay at home and do the (housework / homework)?

Even in a truly (equal / egalitarian) society, there might not be as many women as men in Parliament, for instance.

5. Translate into French

Women have always been discriminated against.

....

My daughter's been on the pill since she was 17.

....

Women now make up nearly half the workforce.

....

There are still many barriers to female advancement.

....

In the US, pro-life activists are a vocal minority.

....

6. Translate into English

Aux États-Unis, les femmes ont le droit de vote depuis près d'un siècle.

....

Serena a dû aller à la maternité à pied depuis chez elle.

....

Elle travaille à mi-temps pour pouvoir s'occuper de ses enfants.

....

La plupart d'entre elles ont du mal à trouver un équilibre entre travail et famille.

....

Elles sont encore loin d'avoir atteint l'égalité avec les hommes.

....

Questions

Is a quota policy the best way to improve the situation of women in the workplace?

In what ways has the pill changed the situation of women?

Has emancipation made women happier?

WRITING TIP N° 4: Structure

Whether you have to explain a text, comment on it, or express your views on a particular issue, it is essential that your answer should be logically organized. You should not start writing before you know more or less where you are heading*. To put it differently, you must have a sense of the whole before you write the first sentence, what conclusion you will come to and how you will progress towards that conclusion. Every word, clause* or sentence you write should be part of a demonstration leading up to that conclusion. In practice, you will probably find it useful to write a brief outline* with a few key words before writing your first draft*.

In most exams, you don't have much time, and your text must be short. It follows that your plan must not be too complex; two parts (possibly with two sub-parts* each), or three parts is usually the best solution.

You should also make this structure obvious to your reader by dividing your answer into several paragraphs (one for each part or sub-part), each of which should be devoted to one point. Your reader will thus see at a glance* how your text is structured and it will make your reasoning easier to follow.

Start with what is simple, obvious, what everyone knows and then move on to what is less well-known or more difficult to grasp*. Start with facts and then move on to what is controversial. In an essay, when you want to express your support for a particular opinion, start by explaining the arguments of those opposing it, and then say why you disagree.

Once you have identified a problem, it is often advisable* to examine first its causes, then its consequences, finally its possible solutions. Another option consists in examining the various dimensions (scientific, economic, political, social...) of the issue. In some cases, a chronological approach will be best. Keep in mind some elementary oppositions such as: time vs place / quantity vs quality / theory vs practice / the individual vs society / past vs present vs future. These general categories will help you come to terms with* your question.

As a rule*, in a brief essay, it is probably best to keep the most interesting idea, the most original insight*, the most subtle point for the end.

you are heading: *où vous vous dirigez* • **clause**: *proposition* • **outline**: *plan* • **first draft**: *premier jet, première version* • **sub-part**: *sous-partie* • **at a glance**: *du premier coup d'œil* • **grasp**: *saisir, comprendre* • **advisable**: *conseillé* • **come to terms with**: *traiter* • **as a rule**: *en règle générale* • **insight**: *idée, aperçu*

5. BIOETHICS

9/11 • abortion • advertising • AIDS • alcohol abuse • armed forces • asbestos • bonuses • BRICS • CIA • CO_2 • computers • consumer society • couch potatoes • creationism • credit bubble • cultural exception **cloning** • dating • DEA • death penalty • deforestation • dictatorship • **euthanasia** digital piracy • diplomacy • domestic violence • drought • drug trafficking • eating disorders • endangered species • English-speaking world • epidemics • fanaticism • food scares • fossil fuels • free speech • free trade • gender gap • glass ceiling • greenhouse gases • guinea pigs • gun control • health **IVF** care • hijacking • human rights • immigration policy • intercourse • ISPs • justice system • labour • multiculturalism • NASA • natural disasters • NGOs • nuclear • nuclear deterrent • oil slicks • on parole • **stem-cell research** outsourcing • overfishing • ozone layer • PC • pension system • philanthropy • physics • pidgin • prevention • racial profiling • recycling • renewables • RP • salad bowl • same-sex marriage • second-hand smoking • serial killers • sex industry • slump • social divide • social networks • Spanglish • standard English • STDs • **surrogacy** suffragettes • suicide bombers • surveillance • technophobia • teenage violence • truancy • United Nations • uprisings • video games • waste disposal • welfare state • WMDs • working poor • WTO

an ethical issue	un problème éthique
unethical	moralement contestable, contraire à l'éthique
ethically	d'un point de vue éthique, sur le plan éthique
code of ethics, code of conduct	déontologie, code de conduite
the sacredness ['seɪkrɪdnəs] of life	le caractère sacré de la vie
human dignity	la dignité humaine
stem cells	les cellules-souches
stem-cell research	la recherche sur les cellules souches

Ethical essentially means the same as **moral. Ethical** behaviour or practices are **morally right** while **unethical** behaviour or practices are **morally wrong**. Meanwhile, **ethics** is the study of what is right or wrong, or the rules applying in a particular field such as medicine or business. Such rules may be codified in a **code of ethics** (or **code of conduct**). Doctors and lawyers, among others, have to comply with such a code.

assisted reproduction	l'aide à la procréation
infertile, sterile	stérile, infertile
infertility, sterility	la stérilité
fertility treatment	traitement pour la fertilité
to fertilize an egg	fertiliser un ovule
an oocyte ['əʊəʊsaɪt]	un ovocyte
sperm, semen ['siːmən]	le sperme
sperm count	nombre de spermatozoïdes
to donate an egg / sperm	faire don d'un ovule / de sperme
a semen donor	un donneur de sperme
an egg donor	une donneuse d'ovule
an embryo ['embrɪəʊ]	un embryon
to freeze sperm / an embryo	congeler du sperme / un embryon
a fœtus, fetus (US)	un fœtus

The first successful birth of a test tube baby, Louise Brown, occurred in 1978. Soon after the Pope voiced his concern that women might become "baby factories". In the UK, 12,174 babies were born following IVF in 2009.

in vitro fertilisation, IVF	la fécondation in vitro, FIV
artificial insemination	l'insémination artificielle
a test-tube baby	un bébé-éprouvette
womb [wuːm], uterus ['juːtərəs]	utérus
to implant an egg / an embryo	implanter un ovule / un embryon
a surrogate mother	une mère porteuse
surrogacy	gestation pour autrui, GPA, maternité de substitution

A **surrogate mother** is a woman who gives birth to a child that is not her own, with the intention of giving it up to the biological parents after the delivery.

organ donation	le don d'organe
an organ donor	un donneur d'organe
organ removal	le prélèvement d'organe
organ transplant	la greffe, la transplantation d'organe
a recipient [rɪ'sɪpɪənt]	un receveur, une receveuse
to implant an organ	implanter un organe
organ rejection	le rejet d'organe
body parts	les produits du corps humain
the sale of body parts	la marchandisation du corps humain
medical tourism	le tourisme médical

There are now up to 1,000 clinics, all entirely unregulated, in India, specialising in helping Britons become parents. Couples and single people are paying an average of £25,000 a time to have children, getting around (*contourner*) rules in the UK which make commercial surrogacy illegal. Indian authorities believe the industry is worth as much as £1.5 million each year. Doctors who spoke to this newspaper told of British women who have babies through surrogates to avoid being pregnant and childbirth, raising fears of a "wombs to rent" culture. Bankers, senior civil servants (*hauts fonctionnaires*), executives at multinational companies and even NHS doctors have become parents through surrogacy in India.
The Sunday Telegraph, Shekhar Bhatia in New Delhi, 26 May 2012

a clone [kləʊn]	un clone
cloning	le clonage
a cell	une cellule
a cloned egg	un œuf cloné
human cloning	le clonage des êtres humains
therapeutic / reproductive cloning	le clonage thérapeutique / reproductif
a saviour sibling ['seɪvjər 'sɪb.lɪŋ]	un bébé-médicament

A **saviour sibling** is a child who is born with particular genes that have been chosen in order to treat an older brother or sister who has a disease.

While **reproductive** cloning aims at creating new living beings, the aim of **therapeutic** cloning is to produce stem cells that can be used in regenerative medicine, to help people with serious diseases.

eugenics [juː'dʒenɪks]	l'eugénisme
a eugenicist	un eugéniste, un partisan de l'eugénisme

a designer baby	un bébé sur mesure
to tamper with nature	porter atteinte à la nature, toucher à la nature
to play God	jouer à l'apprenti sorcier

Eugenics is the belief that the human race can be improved by discouraging the reproduction of individuals thought to have undesirable hereditary characteristics and encouraging that of individuals possessing desirable ones. The term was coined at the end of the nineteenth century by Sir Francis Galton, a scientist and a polymath (*un esprit universel*) and was supported by many prominent figures such as Emile Zola, George Bernard Shaw, John Maynard Keynes and Winston Churchill. Eugenic policies were first implemented (*appliquées*) in the early 1900s in the United States. Later, in the 1920s and 30s, the eugenic policy of sterilizing certain mental patients was implemented in a variety of other countries such as Belgium, Brazil, Canada, and Sweden. Eugenics was discredited by the abuses committed by the Nazi regime during Word War II and has been abandoned since then.

euthanasia [ˌjuːθəˈneɪʒə], mercy killing	l'euthanasie
active / passive euthanasia	l'euthanasie active / passive
to commit suicide, to kill oneself	se suicider
to put an end to one's life	mettre un terme à sa vie
a suicide attempt	une tentative de suicide
assisted suicide	le suicide aidé
doctor-assisted suicide	le suicide médicalement assisté
to give one's consent	donner son consentement
to die peacefully	mourir paisiblement
to die with dignity	mourir dignement
to practise, carry out euthanasia	pratiquer l'euthanasie
to stop, to withhold, to withdraw medical treatment	arrêter les soins
to disconnect a feeding tube	débrancher un tube d'alimentation
to turn off life support	débrancher l'aide respiratoire
the cessation, the withdrawal of treatment	l'arrêt des soins
to shorten sb's life	abréger la vie de qn
to speed, to hasten [ˈheɪsən] sb's death	accélérer la mort de qn
to inject sb with a lethal substance	faire une piqûre mortelle à qn

A British doctor suffering from an incurable illness killed herself yesterday in Zurich with the help of Dignitas, the Swiss voluntary organisation. Dignitas was founded by a Swiss lawyer, Ludwig Minelli, in 1998. The Zurich-based charity's aim is to help people with chronic illnesses to die a quick and painless death. Its motto (*devise*) is "Live with dignity, die with dignity." Patients die by drinking a lethal dose of barbiturates that kills them in about five minutes. The suicide is recorded on video to prove it is voluntary and the tape is examined by police and a coroner. Although the law here prohibits assisted suicide, no one has yet been prosecuted (*poursuivi*) for travelling to Switzerland to help a relative die.
The Guardian, January 25, 2006

a terminal disease, an incurable disease	une maladie incurable
a degenerative disease	une maladie dégénérative
to be terminally ill	être en phase terminale
to be brain-damaged	être atteint de lésions cérébrales
irreversible brain damage	des lésions cérébrales irréversibles
to be in a coma ['kəʊmə]	être dans le coma
to be brain dead	être dans un coma dépassé
to be in a vegetative state	être dans un état végétatif
to be a burden for one's family	être un fardeau pour sa famille

You Don't Know Jack (2010) is a television film starring Al Pacino. It is the true story of Doctor Jack Kevorkian, who helped more than a hundred persons to commit suicide by assembling a device allowing them to initiate an intravenous drip (*perfusion*) containing a lethal mixture of three chemicals. However, there were suspicions that not all of these people were terminally ill and even that some did not complain of pain. Some may have suffered simply from depression or hypochondria. Kervokian was tried and acquitted several times but eventually he was found guilty and spent eight years in jail.

paralysis [pə'ræləsɪs]	la paralysie
to be paralyzed ['pærəlaɪzd] from the waist down, to be paraplegic	être paraplégique, avoir les jambes paralysées
to be paralyzed from the neck down, to be quadriplegic	être tétraplégique, être paralysé des quatre membres
paralyzed on one side	hémiplégique
to be bedridden	être grabataire
to be on life support, to be hooked up to a respirator	être sous assistance respiratoire
to be hooked up to feeding tubes	être nourri artificiellement

Euthanasia was legalised in the Netherlands in 2001, in Belgium in 2002, in Switzerland in 2003 and in Luxembourg in 2008. Passive euthanasia (understood as the withdrawal of life support to patients in a permanent vegetative state) has been legal in a few other countries and some states in the US.

suffering	la souffrance
pain	la douleur
unbearable	insupportable
agony	douleur atroce
painful / painless	douloureux / indolore
a painkiller	un analgésique, un antalgique
to be under sedation [sɪ'deɪʃn]	être sous sédatifs
to prescribe tranquilizers	prescrire des tranquilisants, des calmants
to alleviate [ə'liːvieɪt] pain, to relieve pain	soulager la douleur
relief	soulagement

Following the first successful cloning of a mammal (*mammifère*) from the cells of an adult, Dolly the sheep], many people argued that in the light of man's proven propensity to abuse powerful technologies, it would be folly to put this new one into the hands of future dictators who may harbour mad dreams of master races or custom-bred slaves (*esclaves produits sur commande*). But this argument is not only impractical (a tyrant would invent the technology if he wanted it); it is an argument against technology in general. The putative tyrant has no need of Dolly technology; he could already breed athletes as if they were racing horses, or pass a law forbidding short men to have babies. It is what people do that is good or bad, not what they can do. To put it another way (*en d'autres termes*), the fact that it would be wrong to force contraception on people is no argument against the continued existence of contraceptives.
The Economist, 1 March 1997

health care, medical care	les soins médicaux
palliative treatment, palliative care	les soins palliatifs
a care unit for the terminally ill	une unité de soins palliatifs
a doctor	un médecin
a nurse	une infirmière
to cure a patient	guérir un patient
to keep sb alive	maintenir qn en vie
to prolong [prə'lɒŋ] life	prolonger la vie
prolonging life through medical means	l'acharnement thérapeutique

LANGUAGE PRACTICE

1. All the words needed to complete these sentences are based on the same root.

All medical staff have to adhere to a code of ....

The use of animal in scientific experiments raises difficult .... questions.

Doctors felt .... obliged to continue the treatment.

Even if the nurse did nothing illegal, her practices were considered .... by most of her colleagues.

2. What is the correct translation of the following faux-amis?

a terminal disease	*une maladie* ....
an organ recipient	*un* .... *d'organe*
agony	....
to provide relief	*apporter* ....

3. Find the appropriate suffixes and prefix to complete.

a surrogate mother	surrog _ _ _	*gestation pour autrui, GPA*
to bear	_ _ bear _ _ _ _	*insupportable*
to donate	an egg don _ _	*un donneuse d'ovule*
sacred	the sacred _ _ _ _ of life	*le caractère sacré de la vie*

4. Replace the words that are underlined with synonyms.

Not everyone agrees that the identity of the men donating semen must remain secret.

The old man needed palliative treatment.

You cannot withdraw treatment without the consent of the patient's family.

An egg fertilised by her 51-year-old husband was implanted in the woman's womb.

5. The spelling of the following translations is almost the same as in French.

l'eugénisme ....
controversé ....
le clonage ....
la paralysie ....

6. Translate into French.

After the crash, my uncle remained paralyzed from the waist down.

....

The decision of the British Medical Association caused an uproar.

....

Therapeutic cloning consists in replacing damaged organs with genetically identical cells.

....

Scientists may be tempted to play God.

....

I agree that morally questionable practices should be outlawed.

....

7. Translate into English.

Les partisans de l'euthanasie voudraient qu'elle soit dépénalisée.

....

On a dû mettre le jeune garçon sous assistance respiratoire.

....

Ma voisine est dans le coma depuis qu'elle a tenté de se suicider.

....

La fécondation in vitro a permis à des milliers de parents d'avoir un enfant.

....

La plupart des infirmières sont-elles opposées au suicide médicalement assisté ?

....

Questions

The case for and the case against euthanasia.
What risks does human cloning pose?
How far should man be allowed to play God?

WRITING TIP N° 5: Introduction and conclusion

The length of your introduction and conclusion should be proportional to your text as a whole*. Thus, the introduction of a French *dissertation* may take up a whole page but in a 250-word essay, two or three sentences should be enough.

It is a good idea to start the ball rolling* with a quotation, the definition of a key term in the question, a relevant* statistic, a historical allusion or a concrete example. But there is no point in repeating the question word for word because when you do that, you don't prove you can express yourself, or even that you've understood the question. Rephrasing* the question might be an option but it can be dangerous since it may convey the impression that you have decided to answer not the given question but another one you have concocted for yourself.

It may be a good idea to explain briefly how you are going to approach* the issue at the end of your introduction. However, do make sure* that it will not be disproportionately long as a result.

In an essay, it may be a good idea to state your point*, your "thesis" in the introduction. But you can also decide to mention it only in the conclusion.

It is often best to write your introduction last*, or even better, to write it at the beginning and to rewrite it at the end, after you know exactly what is in the body of your answer. Be aware that the way you start off is very important because this will be the first impression the reader has of your proficiency*, and first impressions always matter disproportionately*.

Finally, it is necessary to round off* your text with a brief conclusion. In most cases, one sentence is enough. In an essay, state or re-state your opinion in your conclusion; if you have already given it, rephrase it.

However it may also be a good idea to use the conclusion to mention an aspect of the problem you have not dealt with, to raise* another, related, issue or touch upon* possible future developments. Avoid repeating what you have just explained.

For more impact, it may be a good idea to isolate this conclusion in a separate paragraph, even if it consists of just one sentence.

your text as a whole: *l'ensemble de votre texte* • **start the ball rolling**: *enclencher le débat* • **relevant**: *pertinent* • **rephrase**: *reformuler* • **tackle**: *aborder* • **do make sure that**: *veillez bien à ce que* • **your point**: *ce que vous voulez démontrer* • **last**: *en dernier* • **proficiency**: *compétence* • **disproportionately**: *de façon disproportionnée* • **round off**: *boucler* • **raise**: *soulever* • **touch upon**: *évoquer*

6. ENGLISH

9/11 • abortion • advertising • AIDS • alcohol abuse • armed forces • asbestos • bonuses • BRICS • CIA • cloning • CO_2 • computers • consumer society • couch potatoes • creationism • credit bubble • cultural exception • dating • DEA • death penalty • deforestation • dictatorship • digital piracy • diplomacy • domestic violence • drought • drug trafficking • eating disorders • endangered species • epidemics • euthanasia • fanaticism • food scares • fossil fuels • free speech • free trade • gender gap • glass ceiling • greenhouse gases • guinea pigs • gun control • health care • hijacking • human rights • immigration policy • intercourse • ISPs • IVF • justice system • labour • multiculturalism • NASA • natural disasters • NGOs • nuclear • nuclear deterrent • oil slicks • on parole • outsourcing • overfishing • ozone layer • PC • pension system • philanthropy • physics • prevention • racial profiling • recycling • renewables • salad bowl • same-sex marriage • second-hand smoking • serial killers • sex industry • slump • social divide • social networks • standard English • STDs • stem-cell research • suffragettes • suicide bombers • surrogacy • surveillance • technophobia • teenage violence • truancy • United Nations • uprisings • video games • waste disposal • welfare state • WMDs • working poor • WTO

English-speaking world

pidgin

RP

standard English

Spanglish

English, the English language	l'anglais, la langue anglaise
a mother tongue	une langue maternelle
a working language	une langue de travail
an English-speaking country	un pays anglophone
a native ['neɪtɪv] English speaker, an Anglophone	un anglophone
the spread of English	la progression de l'anglais
the hegemony of English	l'hégémonie de l'anglais

English is an official language in 54 countries and even if it has fewer native speakers than Mandarin Chinese or Spanish, it is the most commonly used second language in the world. All 53 members of **the Commonwealth** are English-speaking —to some extent at least— since they were part of the British Empire, except for two of them which were recently admitted: Mozambique and Rwanda.

register	le registre, le niveau de langue
formal language	la langue soignée, soutenue
informal, colloquial language	la langue familière
academic English	l'anglais académique
slang	l'argot
spoken / written English	l'anglais parlé / écrit
a phrase [freɪz], an expression	une expression
to phrase	exprimer, formuler
to rephrase, to reformulate	reformuler
a catch phrase	une formule, un slogan
a set phrase	une expression figée, toute faite

Spotted this morning on an advertising hoarding (*panneau publicitaire*) in the Paris metro: the most extravagant mix of phoneticised French and franglais I have yet come across. It was an ad for Keljob (*quel job*), a recruitment agency, promising "*le speed recrutement*" and "*des ateliers coaching*" ("*atelier*" meaning workshop in French). The intrusion of franglais into French advertising also continues apace (*rapidement*). Examples that spring to mind include Livret BforBank, Crédit Agricole's new online private bank, or Freebox, the digital television decoder from Free, a French telecoms firm. Many companies simply splash a slogan in English on their ads, and then translate it in small print on the bottom as is required by French law. What makes Keljob's ad stand out is the brazen (*éhonté*) mix of all of the above.
The Economist, September 22nd 2010

a buzz word	un mot à la mode
a cliché ['kliːʃeɪ]	un cliché
a saying	un dicton
a neologism [ni'ɒlədʒɪzəm]	un néologisme
to coin a word	inventer un mot
a pleonasm ['pliːənæzəm]	une pléonasme

Nearly a quarter of the world's population speaks some English. That includes around 400m who speak it as their mother tongue and about the same number who speak it fluently as their second language. English is the global language of academic research, and perhaps 1,500 master's degrees are taught in English in countries where the language has no official status. It provides the vocabulary for some specialised fields, such as air-traffic control. And it is the working language of a growing number of international companies—a big reason why so many of them choose London for their headquarters (*sièges*)... At first sight this means that things are about to get even cushier (*plus confortable*) for native English speakers; they needn't lift a finger to learn other people's subjunctives. But there are two catches (*inconvénients*). The first is that they will lose the competitive advantage that once came with being among the relatively few to speak the world's most useful language. More subtly, as native Anglophones are increasingly outnumbered by people who speak English as a second language, the future of their own language is passing from their hands.

The Economist, December 13th 2006

a quotation, a quote	une citation
to quote sb	citer qn
to spell a word	épeler un mot
spelling	l'orthographe
a metaphor	un métaphore
a figure of speech	une figure de style
an understatement	une litote
a euphemism ['juːfəmɪzəm]	un euphémisme

The French verb "*citer*" can be translated in several ways. When you **report** someone's words, you **quote** these words (and you quote the person who said them). Journalists often say that a personality "**is quoted as saying** that...", by which they mean these were the actual words uttered (*prononcés*) by this person. But when you think of an example in the course of a discussion, you may decide to **cite** or to **mention** it (e.g. Paula claims she is an expert on German fiction but she's incapable of citing the name of a single German writer). When you mention someone's name, or the title of a book, you **name** them.

to mean	vouloir dire, signifier
meaning	le sens
meaningless	dénué de sens
in other words	en d'autres termes
to put it differently	pour le dire autrement
that is to say	c'est-à-dire
to translate a text into Arabic	traduire un texte en arabe
to translate a text from Japanese	traduire un texte du japonais
to mistranslate sth	mal traduire qch

The **Anglosphere** (*le monde anglo-saxon*) is an expression used to refer to the English-speaking world, that is to say essentially the United Kingdom, Ireland, the United States, Canada, Australia and New Zealand. These countries do not only share a common language but also a cultural background, in particular liberal democracy. In a wider sense, the Anglosphere also includes former British colonies such as India, Pakistan, South Africa, Nigeria etc. where English is an official language and is widely spoken even if it is not the language of the majority.

to speak Spanish well, to speak good Spanish	parler bien l'espagnol
sb's fluency in Swedish	l'aisance de qn à s'exprimer en suédois
proficiency in English	compétence en anglais
a proficiency test	un test de compétence
TOEFL (Test of English as a Foreign Language)	le TOEFL
TOEIC (Test of English for International Communication)	le TOEIC
to speak poor Dutch	parler un mauvais hollandais
to speak broken Chinese	parler mal le chinois
to speak heavily accented Turkish	parler le turc avec un fort accent
to express oneself	s'exprimer
to make oneself understood	se faire comprendre
the language barrier ['bærɪər]	la barrière de la langue

The English that is taught as a foreign language is usually called **standard English** and is the form of English that is spoken by educated native speakers. However, non-native speakers should be aware that there are many varieties of English, depending on where it is spoken, the social class of the speaker and the context in which it is used. This situation is the result of the spread of English with colonization since the seventeenth century and the unequalled extent (*étendue sans pareille*) of the British Empire, which means there are probably more local versions of English than of any other language. These local versions have contributed to the evolution of standard English. In particular, many Americanisms have now been incorporated into the English spoken in the British Isles. This variability is reinforced by the fact that Britain has never had a linguistic governing body similar to the *Académie Française* (or the *Real Academia Española* in Spain) which sets down (*pose*) rules establishing authorized usage.

to make a mistake	faire une faute
grammatical correctness	la correction grammaticale
to be good / bad / hopeless at languages	être bon / mauvais / nul en langues
to brush up one's German	rafraîchir son allemand
to do an Italian course	suivre un cours d'italien

As in every other language, new words are constantly being coined in English. According to some counts, there are now over 1 million words in English, which means that there are ten times as many words in English as in French.

pronunciation	la prononciation
to pronounce	prononcer
RP, Received Pronunciation	prononciation standard
a diphthong [ˈdɪfθɒŋ, ˈdɪpθɒŋ]	une diphtongue
unpronounceable	imprononçable
to mispronounce a word	mal prononcer un mot
word stress / sentence stress	l'accent de mot / de phrase
to have a broad accent	avoir un accent marqué, prononcé

My Fair Lady is a 1964 musical film directed by George Cukor and starring Audrey Hepburn as Eliza Doolittle and Rex Harrison as Professor Higgins. The film is based on George Bernard Shaw's play *Pygmalion* (1912). Convinced that accents determine people's prospects (*perspectives*) in society, Henry Higgins, a linguist and a professor of elocution, sets out (entreprend) to turn a young flower seller with a strong working-class accent into a duchess by giving her speech lessons. Her success becomes obvious when, after a period of traning, she manages to pass herself off as an aristocrat at Ascot Racecourse, a very select venue (*lieu de rendez-vous*) frequented by the upper crust of British society. The film's emphasis on the role and importance of accents in Britain is a critique of its rigid class system.

punctuation	la ponctuation
a punctuation mark	un signe de ponctuation
a full stop (GB), a period (US)	un point
a comma	une virgule
a colon [ˈkəʊlən]	deux-points
a semi-colon	un point-virgule
a question mark	un point d'interrogation
an exclamation mark (GB), exclamation point (US)	un point d'exclamation
a dash	un tiret
a hyphen [ˈhaɪfn]	un trait d'union

As the commercial director of one of the country's largest book-wholesaling companies, Annette Burgess makes an unlikely Eliza Doolittle. Yet this successful bookseller shares one thing in common with the cockney flower-selling heroine of Pygmalion and My Fair Lady: she has taken up elocution lessons. "Communication is a very important part of my job and has always been something I felt could be improved upon," she says. "I was very interested in looking at some form of elocution lessons to help me with my presentation skills. But I also wanted lessons to help me do away with my Devonian accent. I originally come from Plymouth, so there is a Devon twang to some of my speech that I would like to lose. I felt it was holding me back in terms of forward progression within my career."
The Independent, Thursday 19, January 2012

pidgin ['pɪdʒɪn] English	anglais de cuisine, mauvais anglais, sabir
a dialect	un dialecte
cant	la langue de bois
waffle, twaddle	verbiage, blabla
gibberish ['dʒɪbərɪʃ], gobbledygook ['gɒbldiguːk]	le charabia
jargon, lingo	jargon, sabir
mumbo jumbo	charabia incompréhensible
globish	l'anglais approximatif parlé par les non-anglophones
computerese	le jargon des informaticiens
journalese	le jargon des journalistes
management-speak, managementese	le jargon des écoles de commerce

A **pidgin** is a mixture of two languages used by people who do not speak each other's languages. Thus **pidgin French** is French mixed with words and grammar of another language.

Cant is insincere talk about moral or religious issues but also the special vocabulary used by a particular group of people such as priests or thieves in order to keep something secret. By extension, cant is also the insincere talk of politicians.

80 percent of the world's electronically stored information is in English.

LANGUAGE PRACTICE

1. Find the missing words to complete the sentences.

A lot of Indians speak very good English, even if it is not their .... tongue.

John said he had dumped his girlfriend, in .... words, that he no longer wanted to see her.

Both my parents did some Spanish at school when they were kids, but not enough to express .... fluently.

An .... is a way of describing something that makes it seem less important, good, bad etc. than it really is.

2. Find the appropriate preposition or adverbial particle or write ø if nothing is needed.

William Tyndale was the first to translate the Bible .... English directly from Hebrew and Greek texts, in the early 16th century.

My Hungarian is a bit rusty, I need to brush it ....

Suki is a brilliant physicist but she's not very good .... languages.

His proficiency .... Italian improved a lot during his stay in Florence.

3. Translate the following words, which are both verbs and nouns.

	NOUN	VERB
spread	....	....
phrase	....	....
coin	....	....
quote	....	....

4. Find the correct form of the verbs between brackets.

After four years of Russian, Yanis still could not make himself .... (understand).

Do you know what the word "pidgin" .... (mean)?

I met some tourists who spoke .... (break) English and I could not make head or tail of it.

Djamel's .... (write) English is all right, but his accent is not very good.

5. Associate the following words to form compound nouns and translate.

buzz, jumbo, language, mumbo, native, speaker, word, working

....
....
....
....
....

6. Translate into French.

When I said your father was a coward it was only a figure of speech.

....

What's the English for "*boulot*"?

....

Rita is… how shall I put it?… not always easy-going.

....

In 1990 the Netherlands considered making English the sole language of university education.

....

Some think the days of English as the world's lingua franca may be numbered.

....

7. Translate into English.

Que veut dire l'expression « recreational drug » ?

....

Je ne sais pas vraiment ce que veut dire le mot « indigent ».

....

Ivor parle déjà couramment l'arabe et le japonais.

....

Vous aurez du mal à parler le mandarin sans accent.

....

Il faut être un homme politique chevronné pour manier la langue de bois avec autant de brio.

....

Questions

Why do so many people throughout the world want to learn English?
Is the rise of English as a global language a good thing?
Will English ever be replaced as the world's lingua franca?

WRITING TIP N° 6: Sentence structure

In the same way as a text must be well-thought-out*, each sentence it contains must be carefully constructed. Make sure that your sentences are not too simple — because then, you might give the impression that your command* of the language is limited— but not too complex either, because this can easily become confusing*.

• Some writers tend to string* one idea after another without connecting them. This creates the impression that they are improvising, or that they do not see how the ideas they mention follow on from each other. Here is a very basic example. If you write: "Mr Gaddafi was a dictator, he was responsible for many killings.", you simply juxtapose two independent clauses*. It would be much better to connect them with a relative pronoun: "Mr Gaddafi was a dictator who was responsible for many killings."

• Now read the following sentence: "There is no doubt that, even if the new measures were adopted straightaway, critics of the governement would not relent* because the electoral season is getting closer and to some, getting rid of what they consider as a clique of corrupt no-gooders* matters more than taking useful and efficient measures, no matter how necessary, and if you try to remonstrate with them, they will claim that ...." There is nothing grammatically or semantically wrong with this sentence, but it is far* too long and complex to be effective.

• Beware of journalese*: for instance, in French newspapers you often come across* sentences without verbs, or sentences made up of just one subordinate clause. These structures should be avoided in English, especially in the context of an exam paper*. Rather than: "Murder rates are on the rise. Even if more policemen have been recruited.", you should write: "Murder rates are on the rise, even if more policemen have been recruited." Instead of "Italy is a member of the EU. Germany too.", write: "Italy is a member of the EU and so is Germany."

The underlying* principle is that a good writer pays close attention to the connections within and between sentences.

well-thought-out: *bien conçu* • **command**: *maîtrise* • **confusing**: *déroutant* • **string**: *enfiler* • **clause**: *proposition* • **relent**: *relâcher la pression* • **no-gooders**: *bons à rien* • **far**: *beaucoup, bien* • **journalese**: *le jargon des journalistes* • **come across**: *tomber sur* • **exam paper**: *épreuve d'examen* • **underlying**: *sous-jacent*

7. GLOBALIZATION

9/11 • abortion • advertising • AIDS • alcohol abuse • armed forces • asbestos • bonuses • CIA • cloning • CO_2 • computers • consumer society • couch potatoes • creationism • credit bubble • dating • DEA • **BRICS** • death penalty • deforestation • dictatorship • digital piracy • **cultural exception** • diplomacy • domestic violence • drought • drug trafficking • eating disorders • endangered species • English-speaking world • epidemics • euthanasia • fanaticism • food scares • fossil fuels • free speech • gender gap • glass ceiling • greenhouse gases • guinea pigs • **free trade** • gun control • health care • hijacking • human rights • immigration policy • intercourse • ISPs • IVF • justice system • labour • multiculturalism • NASA • natural disasters • NGOs • nuclear • nuclear deterrent • oil slicks • on parole • overfishing • ozone layer • PC • pension system • philanthropy • **outsourcing** • physics • pidgin • prevention • racial profiling • recycling • renewables • RP • salad bowl • same-sex marriage • second-hand smoking • serial killers • sex industry • slump • social divide • social networks • Spanglish • standard English • STDs • **WTO** • stem-cell research • suffragettes • suicide bombers • surrogacy • surveillance • technophobia • teenage violence • truancy • United Nations • uprisings • video games • waste disposal • welfare state • WMDs • working poor

The aim of the **World Trade Organization** (WTO, in French **OMC**), which replaced the GATT in 1995, is to liberalize international trade. Russia was the last big economy to join the organization in August 2012.

trade [treɪd]	le commerce, les échanges
overseas trade	le commerce extérieur
free trade	le libre-échange
a free trader	un partisan du libre-échange
a free trade area	une zone de libre-échange
a trading partner	un partenaire commercial
trade figures	les chiffres du commerce extérieur
the balance of trade	la balance commerciale
a trade surplus ['sɜːpləs] / deficit	un excédent / déficit commercial
fair trade	le commerce équitable
a border, a frontier	une frontière
a borderless world	un monde sans frontières
the global economy	l'économie mondiale

The five **BRICS** countries (Brazil, Russia, India, China and South Africa) are the five emerging economies with the most promising potential. They were identified as such by US investment bank Goldman Sachs in 2001 (except for South Africa, which joined the group in 2011). The **Next Eleven** (or **N-11**) is a group of eleven countries (Bangladesh, Egypt, Indonesia, Iran, Mexico, Nigeria, Pakistan, the Philippines, Turkey) which have been identified by the same bank as tomorrow's large economies.

the free-market system, liberalism,	le libéralisme (économique)
a free-marketeer [ˌmɑːkɪ'tɪə]	un partisan du libéralisme
the liberalisation of trade	la libéralisation des échanges
to deregulate	déréglementer
deregulation [ˌdiː'regjʊleɪʃən]	la déréglementation
the free flow of goods	la libre circulation des marchandises
capital flow	les flux de capitaux
flight of capital	la fuite de capitaux
a tax haven ['heɪvən]	un paradis fiscal
a tax dodger	un fraudeur
bank secrecy	le secret bancaire

As nations become more integrated into the world economy, they tend to maintain fewer barriers to trade and the movement of money. They are less likely to impose punishing corporate taxes and onerous regulations. Their technology policies are more favorable to innovation. Nations more open to the world economy score above the less globalized countries with respect to (*en ce qui concerne*) the rule of law and protection of property rights. More globalized countries also offer greater political stability… Globalization's critics argue that a more open world economy sets off a race to the bottom by encouraging countries to jettison (*abandonner*) protections for consumers, workers and the environment. In reality, the opposite is true: globalization prompts a race to the top by pushing countries to abandon policies that burden their economies in favor of those that fuel growth and economic opportunity. Richard W. Fisher and W. Michael Cox, *The New York Times*, April 10, 2006

to develop [dɪ'veləp]	se développer
to industrialize	s'industrialiser
economic [iːkə'nɒmɪk] growth	la croissance économique
the rich world	les pays riches
developed countries	les pays du Nord, les pays développés
developing countries	les pays du Sud, les pays en voie de développement
the Third World	le Tiers-Monde
an emerging country, an emerging economy	un pays émergent
LDCs, least developed countries	les PMA, les pays les moins avancés

The documentary film **Mondovino** (2004) by film maker Jonathan Nossiter deals with the impact of globalization on wine-producing regions in seven different countries. According to film critic Peter DeBruge, the film is an "attempt to rescue winemaking from the hands of profit-mongering capitalists. It suggests the world has lost the art of appreciating fine wines, as a result of the proliferation of a popular American style in which the flavor imparted by new wood barrels overpowers *(l'emporte sur*) the individual terroir, or region-specific quality, that gives each wine its personality."

an exporter / an importer	un exportateur / un importateur
an oil-exporting country	un pays exportateur de pétrole
protectionism	le protectionnisme
protectionist measures / policies	mesures / politiques protectionistes
a subsidy ['sʌbsɪdi]	une subvention
to subsidize ['sʌbsɪdaɪz]	subventionner
tariffs ['tærɪfs]	les tarifs douaniers, les droits de douanes
customs duties	les droits de douane
tariff barriers / non-tariff barriers	les barrières tarifaires / non-tarifaires
to lower / remove trade barriers	abaisser / supprimer les barrières douanières
the exchange rate	le taux de change

While **exportation** is defined as the process of sending goods to another country for sale, the word **export** is used to refer to those goods themselves. Thus to translate "*la valeur de nos exportations vers l'Asie*" you must use "export", not "exportation": the value of our exports to Asia. The same distinction exists between **importation** (bringing goods into one country) and **imports** (the said goods).

a multinational (company)	une multinationale
to break into a market	pénétrer sur un marché
to corner, capture a market	s'emparer d'un marché
offshoring, outsourcing, relocating	les délocalisations
to outsource, to relocate	délocaliser, externaliser
to set up a factory	implanter une usine
to settle abroad	s'implanter à l'étranger
a supplier [sə'plaɪər]	un fournisseur
economies of scale	économies d'échelle
a call center	une centre d'appels
manufacturing [ˌmænju'fæktʃərɪŋ]	le (secteur) secondaire, l'industrie
the service industries, the service sector	le (secteur) tertiaire, les services
de-industrialization	la désindustrialisation

The word **outsourcing** is a possible translation for *la délocalisation* or *les délocalisations*. However, it should be noted that strictly speaking, outsourcing occurs whenever a company pays to have part of its work done by another, and that therefore it does not always imply that the work should be done in another country. Thus the verb "to outsource" can also be transalted as *externaliser*. Another possible English translation of *délocalisation* is **relocating**, which means moving to another place —again, not necessarily to another country. The word **offshoring** is defined as "the practice of a company in one country arranging for people in another country to do work for it". Please note that, unlike *délocalisation*, the words outsourcing, relocating and offshoring are used exclusively in the singular.

France welcomes more tourists than any other country in the world (77 million in 2010), followed by the US (60 million) and China (55 million).

labour	la main d'œuvre
child labour [tʃaɪld 'leɪbər]	le travail des enfants
working conditions	les conditions de travail
labour / environmental standards	les normes en matière d'emploi / d'environnement
production / wage costs	les coûts de production / salariaux

> Who can doubt the appeal of American popular culture? If it dominates much of the world, it is because much of the world consumes it with relish (*délectation*). Indeed, while rejecting U.S. foreign policy, people in many countries happily embrace its movies, television programs and pop music. Iranians even lap up (*se délecter*) "Baywatch" via satellite. This also represents good business. Only last week at the Paris-based United Nations Educational, Scientific and Cultural Organization (UNESCO), Washington was almost alone in opposing a new convention on cultural diversity designed to promote alternatives to American-style cultural globalization. The convention was of course adopted anyway, but it poses no real threat to Hollywood and the like.
> Alan Riding, *The International Herald Tribune*, October 27, 2005

competition	la concurrence
unfair competition	concurrence déloyale
to trade at a loss	vendre à perte
dumping	le dumping
social dumping	le dumping social
a competitor	un concurrent
competitive	compétitif
competitiveness	la compétitivité
to compete with sb, to be in competition with sb	être en concurrence avec qn

Fair Trade involves the following principles:

* Producers receive a fair price.
* Forced labor and child labor are not allowed.
* Buyers and producers trade under direct long-term relationships.
* Producers have access to financial and technical assistance.
* Sustainable production techniques are encouraged.
* Working conditions are healthy and safe.
* Equal employment opportunities are provided for all.
* All aspects of trade and production are open to public accountability.

alter-globalization	l'altermondialisme
an antiglobalization activist, protester, an antiglobalist	un militant anti-mondialiste
Americanization	l'américanisation
Westernization	l'occidentalisation
standardization	l'uniformisation
cultural exception, cultural exemption	l'exception culturelle
deglobalization	la démondialisation

Alter-globalization (from the French "*altermondialisme*") is a social movement that supports global cooperation and interaction, but opposes the negative effects of economic globalization on environmental protection, economic justice, labour protection, indigenous cultures and human rights. Most members of this movement shun (*rejettent*) the label "anti-globalization" since they do not oppose economic globalization as such (*en tant que tel*). The **World Social Forum** is an annual meeting held by members of the alter-globalization movement. It is usually organized in January at the same time as its capitalist rival, the **World Economic Forum** in Davos, Switzerland, so that the answers to global economic problems it proposes get better coverage in the media.

LANGUAGE PRACTICE

1. Underline the appropriate word.

(Fair / Free) trade makes it possible to pay coffee growers a few cents per pound above the market price.

China's (economic / economical) growth in recent years has been spectacular.

A tax (heaven / haven) is a shelter used by wealthy people to hide their fortunes from their governments.

It is vital to put in place safeguards to prevent the endemic corruption and (flow/flight) of capital that plague so many poor countries.

Canada's trade (surplus / deficit) has been driven down as the recession swept through the US, its main customer.

2. The spelling of the following words poses a problem.

un pays émergent	an .... country
un pays développé	a .... country
déréglementer	to ....
tarifs douaniers	....
un exportateur	an ....

3. Find the nouns corresponding to the following definitions.

.... occurs when manufacturers sell at a price below the market price to force other producers out of a market.

.... occurs when a company decides to transfer its production to a country where labour is cheaper.

.... is the ability of a company, a country or a product to compete with its rivals.

.... is producing goods in factories, usually in large quantities.

.... consists in removing controls or rules from a business or industry.

4. Find the appropriate suffixes to complete these words.

être en concurrence	to compete	a compet _ _ _ _	*un concurrent*
norme	standard	standard _ _ _ _ _ _ _ _	*uniformisation*
marché	market	a free-market _ _ _	*partisan du libéralisme*
frontière	border	border _ _ _ _	*sans frontières*
subvention	subsidy	to subsid _ _ _	*subventionner*

5. Translate into French.

Some claim globalization dates back to the days of Christopher Columbus.

....

NAFTA is a free trade area between Canada, Mexico and the US.

....

Third-World countries need trade barriers to protect their nascent industries.

....

Higher taxation of company profits could lead to more outsourcing.

....

What measure of protectionism is desirable in the face of unfair trading practices?

....

6. Translate into English.

Les échanges de la Chine ont explosé depuis son admission à l'OMC.

....

Leur but est de profiter la main d'œuvre bon marché au Vietnam.

....

La baisse du taux de change du dollar est favorable aux importateurs.

....

Les altermondialistes ne tiennent pas compte des bienfaits du commerce mondial.

....

Plus la concurrence devient déloyale, plus on est tenté de rétablir des droits de douane.

....

Questions

How is globalization perceived in your country?
Is standardization the inevitable consequence of globalization?
Globalization and inequalities.

WRITING TIP N° 7: Punctuation

Punctuation is much more important than is generally believed. Indeed, putting punctuation marks in the wrong place can alter* your meaning completely, as shown by the following anecdote. A teacher once wrote a sequence of words on the blackboard: "Woman without her man is nothing". She then asked her students to add the punctuation. Some of them, mostly boys, wrote: "Woman, without her man, is nothing." Others: "Woman! without her, man is nothing." Or consider this advertising slogan published by the newspaper *The Sun*, on the occasion of the 2012 Olympics in London: "Let's make it great, Britain."

Punctuation marks* are not used in quite the same way in English and in French. For instance there are statistically more commas in French than in English. For example, adverbs or adverbial phrases placed at the beginning of a sentence are typically* followed by a comma in French. This is not the case in English (e.g. "On December 7 Japanese airplanes attacked Pearl Harbour).

In a sentence starting with "and, but, yet..." you do not add a comma after the adverb. The same goes for "That is why", which is not an adverb. (e.g. It was raining. That is why I took the subway.)

Do not add a comma when translating French constructions such as "*Le problème, c'est que...*" or "*L'important, c'est que...*". Since in the English construction, there is no "it", there can't be a comma either. "The problem is that...", "The important thing is that...", not "... , it is that...".

However a comma is necessary before the relative pronoun "which" when the clause it introduces is not just the preceding noun, but the whole clause (e.g. "At the last election the Greens won ten seats, which took everyone by surprise."). Commas are also indispensable before and after descriptive relative clauses, that is to say clauses which provide additional information but are not necessary to identify the antecedent (e.g. Mrs Thatcher, who was Prime Minister from 1979 to 1990, became Baroness Thatcher in 1992.)

To avoid using commas too often, remember to use colons* (or dashes*) to introduce an example or to clarify, justify or illustrate what you have just written (e.g. "America has one of the greatest assets a nation can have: people yearn* to live there"). Use colons also to introduce a quotation.

Use semi-colons* instead of full stops* before you mention something that is closely related to what you have just written, or to enumerate. (e.g. "In 1924 female players in the Olympics topped 100; they crossed the 1,000 mark in Munich in 1972.")

Avoid using brackets to mention an example in passing. Instead, use "like" or "such as": (e.g. "Several European countries, like the Netherlands or Portugal, have now decriminalized some forms of drug use").

alter: *modifier* • **punctuation marks**: *signes de ponctuation* • **typically**: *généralement* • **colon**: *deux-points* • **dashes**: *tirets* • **yearn**: *aspirer* • **semi-colon**: *point-virgule* • **full stop**: *point*

8. THE ECONOMIC CRISIS

9/11 • abortion • advertising • AIDS • alcohol abuse • armed forces • asbestos • BRICS • CIA • cloning • CO_2 • computers • consumer society • couch potatoes • creationism • cultural exception • dating • DEA • death penalty • deforestation • dictatorship • digital piracy • diplomacy • domestic violence • drought • drug trafficking • eating disorders • endangered species • English-speaking world • epidemics • euthanasia • fanaticism • food scares • fossil fuels • free speech • free trade • gender gap • glass ceiling • greenhouse gases • guinea pigs • gun control • health care • hijacking • human rights • immigration policy • intercourse • ISPs • IVF • justice system • multiculturalism • NASA • natural disasters • NGOs • nuclear • nuclear deterrent • oil slicks • on parole • outsourcing • overfishing • ozone layer • PC • pension system • philanthropy • physics • pidgin • prevention • racial profiling • recycling • renewables • RP • salad bowl • same-sex marriage • second-hand smoking • serial killers • sex industry • social divide • social networks • Spanglish • standard English • STDs • stem-cell research • suffragettes • suicide bombers • surrogacy • surveillance • technophobia • teenage violence • truancy • United Nations • uprisings • video games • waste disposal • welfare state • WMDs • WTO

bonuses **credit bubble** **labour** **slump** **working poor**

a recession, a slump [slʌmp]	une récession
a slowdown	un ralentissement
the global economic meltdown	l'effondrement de l'économie mondiale
inflation rate / unemployment rate	le taux d'inflation / de chômage
the credit bubble	la bulle du crédit
the credit crunch	la crise du crédit
the housing bubble / crisis	la bulle / crise immobilière
an investment bank	une banque d'affaires
a pension fund	un fonds de pension

A **credit-rating agency** (*agence de notation*) is a company (such as Fitch, Standard & Poor's, Moody's) which provides investors with assessments (*évaluation*) of an investment's risk. The higher a country's rating is, the less risk it involves for lenders, and therefore the lower the interest rate that country will have to pay to borrow on international markets.

the stock exchange, the stockmarket	la bourse (des valeurs)
shares, stock(s)	des actions
a shareholder	un actionnaire
to save	épargner
savings	économies
small savers	les petits épargnants
a bond	une obligation
a junk bond	une obligation pourrie
an investor	un investisseur
a speculator	un spéculateur
a hedge fund	un fonds spéculatif
a bonus (pl: bonuses) ['bəʊnəs, 'bəʊnəsiz]	une prime
insider dealing, insider trading	le délit d'initiés
a fat cat	un gros richard, un gros capitaliste

The "Occupy Wall Street" movement and its various offshoots complain that a malign 1%, many of them bankers, are ripping off (*exploiter*) the virtuous 99%. Hollywood has vilified financiers in "Wall Street", "Wall Street 2", "Too Big to Fail" and "Margin Call". Mountains of books make the same point without using Michael Douglas. Anger is understandable. The financial crisis of 2007-08 has produced the deepest recession since the 1930s. Most of the financiers at the heart of it have got off scot-free (*s'en tirer à bon compte*). The biggest banks are bigger than ever. Bonuses are flowing once again. The old saw (*rengaine*) about bankers—that they believe in capitalism when it comes to pocketing the profits and socialism when it comes to paying for the losses—is too true for comfort. But is the backlash in danger of going too far?
The Economist, January 7th 2012

economic policy	la politique économique
austerity measures	mesures d'austérité, politique de rigueur

a stimulus plan, a stimulus package	un plan de relance
a rescue plan	un plan de sauvetage
to bail out a company	renflouer une entreprise
bailout	renflouement, sauvetage
public spending	les dépenses publiques
to balance a budget	équilibrer un budget
budget cuts	réductions budgétaires
a budget deficit	un déficit budgétaire
a tax rise	une augmentation des impôts
a taxpayer	un contribuable

In most contexts, the equivalent of the French adjective "*économique*" is **economic**, which means "connected to the trade, industry etc. of a country" (e.g. **economic growth, economic policy**). Meanwhile **economical** means "advantageous, cheap". It is used in particular to refer to something that helps you save money, such as a car which does not use much petrol.

a bankruptcy ['bæŋkrʌptsi]	une faillite
to go bankrupt / to be bankrupt	faire faillite / être en faillite
debt [det]	une dette
to streamline	rationaliser
to downsize	dégraisser ses effectifs
restructuring	restructuration
to reduce wage / production costs	réduire les coûts salariaux / de production
to cut jobs	supprimer des emplois
to lay off workers, to make workers redundant	licencier des salariés
a redundancy [rɪ'dʌndənsɪ]	un licenciement (économique)
a voluntary redundancy	un départ volontaire
a redundancy plan	un plan social
redundancy payment, severance pay	indemnité de licenciement
a golden parachute, a golden handshake	un parachute doré
to recover	se redresser, se rétablir
recovery	la reprise

A **golden parachute** (or a **golden handshake**) is a large amount of money given to someone who holds an important position in a company when they are forced to leave their job.

a job	un travail, un emploi
a career [kə'rɪəʳ]	une carrière
the world of work	le monde du travail
the workplace	le lieu de travail
to work part time	travailler à temps partiel OU à mi-temps
to work full time	travailler à plein temps
the working population	la population active
working conditions	les conditions de travail

a workshop	un atelier
a factory, a plant	une usine

Capitalism: A Love Story is a 2009 documentary film directed by Michael Moore —who also directed *Bowling for Columbine* (2002) and *Sicko* (2007). His analysis of the 2008 financial crisis is an indictment of Wall Street's "casino mentality" and greed. Among other things he explains the mechanism of "derivatives", financial instruments that are so complex even their creators barely understand them: they are essentially bets on people's ability to pay back their mortgages, which means that financiers are little more than gamblers using other people's money. According to Moore, two-thirds of American personal bankruptcies are caused by the cost of health care.

unemployment, joblessness	le chômage
to be unemployed, jobless, out of work	être au chômage
unemployment rate, jobless rate	taux de chômage
the unemployed, the jobless	les chômeurs
long-term unemployment	le chômage de longue durée
youth unemployment	le chômage des jeunes
job market, labour market	le marché du travail, de l'emploi
a fixed-term contract	un contrat à durée déterminée, CDD
an open-ended contract	un contrat à durée indéterminée, CDI
job flexibility	la flexibilité de l'emploi
job security / insecurity	la sécurité / la précarité de l'emploi
the working poor	les travailleurs pauvres

NEETs is an acronym which is used mostly in Great Britain but also in some other countries to refer to the young people who are **n**ot in **e**ducation, **e**mployment or **t**raining.

to employ	employer
an employer	un employeur
an employee	un employé
to hire ['haɪəʳ] , to take on a worker	embaucher un travailleur
to recruit [rɪ'kruːt]	recruter
a trial period	une période d'essai
a job seeker	un demandeur d'emploi
to apply for a job	être candidat à un emploi, faire une demande d'emploi
an applicant	un candidat à un poste
a job applicatiion	une demande d'emploi
a job interview	un entretien d'embauche
a job offer, a job vacancy, a job opportunity	une offre d'emploi
labour ['leɪbəʳ]	travail OU main d'œuvre
labour standards	les normes en matière d'emploi
manpower, workforce	la main d'œuvre

a skilled / low-skilled / an unskilled worker	un travailleur qualifié / peu qualifié / non qualifié
a state employee, a civil servant	un fonctionnaire
to earn a living, to earn one's living, to make a living	gagner sa vie
a wage earner	un salarié
a perk [pɜːk], a fringe benefit	avantage (en nature), avantage annexe
reduction of working hours	réduction du temps de travail, RTT
the 35-hour working week	les 35 heures, la semaine de 35 heures

Labour means the same as 'work' (hence '**manual labour**' (*travail manuel*) or '**labourer**', another word for 'manual worker' (*travailleur manuel, manœuvre*). The British labour movement gave birth to the **Labour Party** (*parti travailliste*) in 1906. After its new leader, Tony Blair, moved it to the centre of the political stage, it became New Labour in the early 1990s. T. Blair went on to win three successive general elections and remained in power from 1997 to 2007. **Labor Day**, a bank holiday in the US and Canada, is observed on the first Monday in September. In the US, it traditionally marks the beginning of the official campaign for the presidential election which takes place approximately two months later, in early November.

an industrial dispute [dɪs'pjuːt]	un conflit social
to go on strike / be on strike	se mettre / être en grève
a shop steward ['stjuːəd]	un délégué syndical
a (trade) union	un syndicat
a claim	une revendication
wage claims, wage demands	des revendications salariales
a payrise (GB), a payraise (US)	une augmentation de salaire
to resume [rɪ'zjuːm] work	reprendre le travail

In the US, when a business or corporation becomes unable to pay its creditors, it can file with a federal bankruptcy court for protection (*demander la protection*) under **Chapter 11** of the Bankruptcy Code. It may thus remain in control of operations even it is subject to the oversight (*surveillance*) of the court.

retirement	la retraite
to retire [rɪ'taɪəʳ]	prendre sa retraite
a pensioner, an old age pensioner	un retraité
to take early retirement	partir en pré-retraite
retirement age	l'âge de la retraite

I have a solution for the problem of bankers who take risks that threaten the general public: eliminate bonuses. Critics like the Occupy Wall Street demonstrators decry (*dénigrer*) the bonus system for its lack of fairness and its contribution to widening inequality. But the greater problem is that it provides an incentive to take risks. The asymmetric nature of the bonus (an incentive for success without a corresponding disincentive for failure) causes hidden risks to accumulate in the financial system and become a catalyst for disaster. This violates the fundamental rules of capitalism; Adam Smith himself was wary of (*se méfier de*) the effect of limiting liability (*responsabilité*), a bedrock principle of the modern corporation.

Nassim Nicholas Taleb, *The New York Times*, November 7, 2011

LANGUAGE PRACTICE

1. All the missing words are based on the same root word.

It is much easier for skilled .... to find jobs than for unskilled ones.

Smoking in the .... has now been banned in several countries.

The .... population includes those actively employed but also those who are seeking employment and therefore do not have jobs.

Thailand's .... may be cheap but it is not highly skilled.

2. The following words are both verbs and nouns. Translate.

	VERB	NOUN
collapse	....	....
claim	....	....
share	....	....
recruit	....	....

3. Use the words "benefit", "fund", "insider", "shop" to form the compounds corresponding to these definitions.

A .... is a worker who is elected by members of a trade union to represent them in dealing with managers.

A .... is a financial service where money is invested so as to make big profits but which has a big risk.

.... are extra things an employer gives you as well as your wages.

.... is the crime of buying or selling shares in a company with the help of information known only by those connected with the business, before this information is available to everybody else.

4. What is the correct translation of the following faux-amis?

to retire	....
to resume work	.... *le travail*
to save money	.... *de l'argent*
to recover	....

5. All the following compound nouns include the word "job"

offre d'emploi ....
marché de l'emploi ....
demandeur d'emploi ....
sécurité de l'emploi ....

6. Translate into French.

The British economy went through a very bad patch in the 1970s.

....

There were too many people on the payroll of state-owned companies.

....

The financialization of the economy is said to be responsible for the global meltdown of 2007.

....

Portugal's economy was in the doldrums as a result of drastic budget cuts.

....

Public-sector employees account for a huge share of the French working population.

....

7. Translate into English.

Et ta femme, elle fait quoi, dans la vie ?

....

L'Administration Obama a été obligée de prendre des mesures d'urgence dès 2009.

....

Les petits épargnants ont beaucoup plus perdu que les gros investisseurs.

....

Le chômage des jeunes atteint plus de 50% dans plusieurs pays européens.

....

Faut-il supprimer les agences de notation ?

....

Questions

What are the pros and cons of the minimum wage?
Is a wealth tax a good idea?
Does the current financial crisis spell the end of capitalism?

WRITING TIP N° 8: Link-words

Link-words are used to signal logical transitions. But often these transitions are obvious and don't need to be highlighted*. French students sometimes seem to believe that writing good English amounts to* embellishing their texts with strategically placed link-words. But native English speakers tend to use comparatively fewer of them than do French speakers. So, while you should know them to be able to identify them to make sense of* a text you are reading, you should use them sparingly* in your own writing.

What is more, even sophisticated writers often prefer simple words such as "and, but, yet..." to more refined* phrases such as "in so far as*, be that as it may*". It's probably better to say "since" instead of "in so far as" or "however" instead of "be that as it may", which sounds rather stilted* today. The shorter linking words are also preferable in an exam when you have limited space.

Make sure you do not confuse link-words that are used to connect sentences with those connecting clauses* within* a sentence or with those connecting groups of words within a clause. For instance "contrary to" is a preposition which links a noun group with the rest of a sentence (e.g. "Contrary to popular belief, sport is not always good for your health"). But "on the contrary" is used to connect distinct sentences. (e.g. "Tocqueville is not a forgotten dead white male. On the contrary, he is cited in the press almost daily.").

Another common* confusion is between "despite", which is a preposition, and "although", which is a subordinating conjunction. This means that "despite" must be followed by a noun or noun group, and that "although" introduces a clause (e.g. "I found the answer despite the difficulty of the question", "I found the answer although the question was difficult.")

For more examples of useful link-words, read these writing tips again and highlight the ones you think will be useful to you later.

You will also find many of them in the section entitled "all-purpose vocabulary" at the end of this book.

highlight: *souligner, mettre en valeur* • **amount to**: *revenir à* • **make sense of**: *arriver à comprendre* • **sparingly**: *avec parcimonie* • **refined**: *raffiné* • **in so far as**: *dans la mesure où* • **be that as it may**: *quoi qu'il en soit* • **stilted**: *guindé* • **drawback**: *inconvénient* • **clause**: *proposition* • **within**: *à l'intérieur* • **common**: *fréquent*

9. INEQUALITIES

9/11 • abortion • advertising • AIDS • alcohol abuse • armed forces • asbestos • bonuses • BRICS • CIA • cloning • CO_2 • computers • **NGOs** consumer society • couch potatoes • creationism **pension system** • credit bubble • cultural exception • dating • DEA • death penalty • deforestation • dictatorship • digital piracy • diplomacy • domestic violence • drought • drug trafficking • eating disorders • endangered species • English-speaking world • epidemics • euthanasia • **philanthropy** fanaticism • food scares • fossil fuels • free speech • free trade • gender gap • glass ceiling • greenhouse gases • guinea pigs • gun control • health care • hijacking • human rights • immigration policy • intercourse • ISPs • IVF • justice system • labour • **social divide** multiculturalism • NASA • natural disasters • nuclear • nuclear deterrent • oil slicks • on parole • outsourcing • overfishing • ozone layer • PC • physics • pidgin • prevention • racial profiling • recycling • renewables • RP • salad bowl • same-sex marriage • second-hand smoking • serial killers • sex industry • slump • social networks • Spanglish • standard English • STDs • **welfare state** stem-cell research • suffragettes • suicide bombers • surrogacy • surveillance • technophobia • teenage violence • truancy • United Nations • uprisings • video games • waste disposal • WMDs • working poor • WTO

standard of living, living standards	le niveau de vie
GDP [dʒiːdiː'piː] per capita, per head	le PIB par tête, par habitant
lifestyle, way of life	mode de vie
purchasing power ['pɜːtʃɪsɪŋ paʊə], buying power	le pouvoir d'achat
income	le revenu
income tax	l'impôt sur le revenu
high-income / low-income families	familles à hauts / bas revenus
a taxpayer	un contribuable
unequal ['ʌn'iːkwəl], uneven	inégal
to share	partager
to share out	répartir
the distribution of wealth	la répartition de la richesse
a two-tier society [tɪəʳ]	une société à deux vitesses
the social fabric	le tissu social

The **Human Development Index** (HDI, in French *IDH*) is a measure of a country's well-being which is based not only on economic development and living standards but also on life expectancy and education. It was developed in the 1990s by a group of economists who were convinced that development should not be assessed solely by economic advances but also on improvements in well-being.

wealth	la richesse
rich, wealthy	riche
well-off, well-to-do	aisé
to be affluent	être nanti, vivre dans l'aisance
affluence	la richesse, l'abondance
the affluent society ['æflʊənt sə'saɪətɪ]	la société d'abondance
rich people, the rich	les riches
riches [rɪtʃɪz]	des richesses
a millionaire [ˌmɪljə'nɛəʳ]	un millionnaire
a billionaire	un milliardaire

The Remains of the Day (1983). Director: James Ivory. Adapted from Kazuo Ishiguro's eponymous novel. Set in Darlington Hall, a stately home (*manoir*) in England, in the 1930s, it tells the story of an aborted love affair between Stevens, the head butler (*majordome*), played by Anthony Hopkins, and Miss Kenton, the housekeeper (*gouvernante*), played by Emma Thompson. It is a detailed description of the chasm (*gouffre*) between the world of servants and that of the aristocracy they serve. An earlier movie, **The Servant**, directed in 1963 by Joseph Losey, also explores the gap between social classes in Britain.

poverty	la pauvreté
poor people, the poor	les pauvres
the working poor	les travailleurs pauvres
extreme poverty, dire ['daɪəʳ] poverty	la misère
destitution [ˌdestɪ'tjuːʃən]	le dénuement, la misère noire
the most destitute	les plus démunis

the have-nots	les démunis, les déshérités
to sink into poverty	sombrer dans la pauvreté
below / above the poverty line	en-dessous / au-dessus du seuil de pauvreté
deprived [dɪ'praɪvd], disadvantaged, underprivileged	défavorisé
to make ends meet	joindre les deux bouts
to struggle to get by, struggle by	peiner à s'en sortir
to scrape [skreɪp] by	vivoter
homeless ['həʊmlɪs]	sans abri
a soup kitchen, a breadline (US)	une soupe populaire
the underclass	le quart-monde

In 2012, 46 million Americans, that is to say 16% of the US population, lived below the **poverty line**. The poverty rate stood at 12.2% in 2000.

The most common measure of inequality is the Gini coefficient. A score of zero means perfect equality: everyone earns the same. A score of one means that one person gets everything. America's Gini coefficient has risen from 0.34 in the 1980s to 0.38 in the mid-2000s. Germany's has risen from 0.26 to 0.3 and China's has jumped from 0.28 to 0.4. In only one large country, Brazil, has the coefficient come down, from 0.59 to 0.55. Surprisingly, over the same period global inequality has fallen, from 0.66 in the mid-1980s to 0.61 in the mid-2000s. This is because poorer countries, such as China, have grown faster than richer countries.
The Economist, January 20th 2011

welfare ['welfɛər]	l'aide sociale, les assurances sociales, les prestations sociales OU le bien-être
the welfare state	l'État-providence
to contribute	cotiser
social contributions	les cotisations sociales
redistribution	la redistribution
social insurance, social protection	la protection sociale
welfare rights, welfare entitlements, welfare payments	les allocations sociales
a welfare worker, a social worker	une assistante sociale
social security cover, coverage	lacouverture sociale

An **NGO** (a non-governmental organization) is an organization that is not controlled by a government even if it may be partly or wholly funded by one. Its aim is not to make profits (like a company) or to seize political power (like a political party) but to further (*faire* avancer) a cause such as the fight against poverty or discriminations. Its action may therefore have economic or political implications.

a benefit, an allowance [ə'laʊəns]	une allocation, une prestation sociale
unemployment / child / housing benefit	allocation chômage / familiale / logement
a means-tested benefit	a allocation soumise à des conditions de revenu
to claim benefits	demander des prestations sociales
to be entitled [ɪn'taɪtld] to sth	avoir droit à qch
people living on state handouts	les assistés
welfare dependency	l'assistanat
a welfare scrounger ['skraʊndʒəʳ]	un parasite, un profiteur
to cheat	frauder
a benefit cheat [tʃiːt]	un fraudeur abusant du système d'allocations
benefit fraud	la fraude aux allocations
a freeloader	un profiteur, un parasite
freeloading	le parasitisme

The **United Nations Development Programme** (UNDP, in French *PNUD*) promotes development and contributes to the achievement of the **Millenium Development Goals** which were defined in the year 2000, that is to say the reduction of poverty and infant mortality, the improvement of health care, the promotion of democractic governance, human rights and the empowerment of women.

the pension system	le système de retraites
a pension	une (pension de) retraite
to receive a pension	toucher une retraite
a pensioner, an old age pensioner, a retiree (US), an OAP	un retraité
a pension fund	un fonds de pension
to retire [rɪ'taɪər]	prendre sa retraite
retirement	la retraite
retirement age	l'âge de la retraite

The first system of compulsory (*obligatoire*) state health insurance and old age pensions was introduced in Germany in 1880. Britain followed the German example when the Liberal Chancellor of the Exchequer David Lloyd George introduced a state pension for those over 70 in 1908. But the birth of the **welfare state** — that is to say the notion that the government should provide money, free medical care etc for people who are unemployed, ill, or too old to work, "from the cradle to the grave" ("*du berceau à la tombe*") — dates back to 1945, when the recently elected Labour government set up (*a créé*) the **National Health Service** (NHS), a publicly-funded health care organization. **National Insurance** is the system of contributions paid by both workers and employers to cover the costs of state benefits. Critics of the system, who believe that the state should not intervene too much in the lives of its citizens, call the welfare state **the nanny state** (a "nanny" is a woman whose job is to look after children).

the health care system	le système de santé
health care, medical treatment	les soins, les traitements médicaux
health coverage, medical coverage	la couverture médicale
universal health coverage	la CMU
health spending	les dépenses de santé
life expectancy	l'espérance de vie

The international target to halve the number of people who do not have access to safe drinking water has been met, five years before the 2015 deadline. According to the World Health Organization (WHO), between 1990 and 2010 more than 2 billion people gained access to improved drinking water sources, such as piped supplies and protected wells. Using data from household surveys and censuses (*recensements*), the WHO said that at the end of 2010, 89% of the population — 6.1 billion people — used improved drinking water sources, 1% more than the 88% target contained in millennium development goal (MDG) number seven, set in 2000.
The Guardian, Tuesday 6 March 2012

charity	la charité OU les œuvres caritatives
a charity, a charitable organization	une organisation caritative, une œuvre de charité
a non-profit making organization, a not-for-profit organization (US)	une organisation à but non lucratif
a volunteer [ˌvɒlən'tɪəʳ], a voluntary worker	un bénévole
volunteering, voluntary work	le bénévolat
an NGO [ˌendʒiː'əʊ], a non-governmental organization	une ONG, une organisation non-gouvernementale
humanitarian aid, assistance	l'aide, l'assistance humanitaire
emergency aid, emergency assistance	les secours d'urgence
development aid	l'aide au développement
a relief [rɪ'liːf] agency, a relief organization	une organisation humanitaire
debt relief	l'allègement de la dette
to cancel debts, to write off debts	effacer, annuler des dettes
debt-rescheduling	le ré-échelonnement de la dette

When your sister has her birthday, you may give her a **present** or a **gift**. But when you give to charity, you make a **donation**, or you **donate** money, and thus you become a **donor**. In other contexts, you can also **donate** blood or a body organ.

a philanthropist	un philanthrope
to give away, to donate money	donner de l'argent, faire un don
a donor ['dəʊnəʳ]	un donateur
a benefactor	un bienfaiteur
a recipient [rɪ'sɪpɪənt]	un bénéficiaire
to pledge, to promise to give money	promettre de donner de l'argent

to fund [fʌnd] a project	financer un projet
to support, to back an initiative	soutenir une initiative

An economist and former executive at the World Bank, David Beckmann believes it is possible to end world hunger and poverty through good politics and policies. As a Lutheran minister and president of Bread for the World, a nonprofit (*organisation à but non-lucratif*) aimed at turning decision makers' attention to those the Bible calls "the least of these," he believes a Christian has no other option. "If you want to get close to God, you've got to do right by the poor," he said last month at the National Press Club. Though Beckmann has rubbed elbows with (*côtoyer*) Bono and Angelina Jolie on the aid-to-Africa circuit, and though he continues to speak at the United Nations and to Congress on behalf of (*au nom de*) the world's poorest people—in Mozambique, for example, and Bangladesh—his recent mission has been to illuminate the plight (*triste sort*) of the domestic poor.
Newsweek, October 2, 2010

a sponsor	un parrain, un mécène, un sponsor
to sponsor	sponsoriser, parrainer
corporate sponsorship	le mécénat d'entreprise
corporate social responsibility, CSR	la responsabilité sociale de l'entreprise
social entrepreneurship	entreprenariat social
a tax break	une réduction d'impôts

Corporate social responsibility (CSR) is the notion that a company must take account of the interests not just of its shareholders —who own it— but of all its **stakeholders**, that is to say all the people who may be affected by its activities. Stakeholders include the company's shareholders but also its employees, its customers and the communities where it operates because these activities may have an impact on their environment. The proponents of CSR see it as a way of improving long-term profitability but its critics think its distracts (détourner) companies from their real economic role.

LANGUAGE PRACTICE

1. Find the correct translations of the following faux-amis.

Students can claim housing benefit.

Anyone can support a charitable cause by making a small donation.

As a volunteer working for a human rights NGO, Samantha does not get paid.

Many in this neighbourhood live in destitution, unable even to feed their children.

Oxfam is one of the best-known British charities.

2. Find synonyms for the following words.

lifestyle	....
a not-for profit organization	a .... organization
dire poverty	.... poverty
underprivileged	....
to pledge $1 million in aid	to .... $1 million in aid

3. Find the prepositions or adverbial particles needed to fill in the blanks.

As an unemployed single mother, you are probably entitled .... legal aid.

With the rescue plan, part of the Irish debt was quite simply written ....

During the Depression, millions lost their jobs and soon sank .... poverty.

The problem is not that our country is poor, but that its wealth is not shared .... satisfactorily.

With £300 a month, the family could barely scrape ....

4. Form five noun groups with the following nouns and translate them.

break, coverage, expectancy, health, kitchen, life, soup, state, tax, welfare

....

....

....

....

....

5. Translate into French.

Homelessness has been on the rise over the past few years.

....

Without work, you may have to live on state handouts.

....

Even today, more than one American in six lives below the poverty line.

....

Even bright students have difficulty moving up the social ladder.

....

My ex-wife will spend €500 on a handbag but won't make a €10 donation.

....

6. Translate into English.

Le fossé entre les pauvres et les riches ne cesse de se creuser.

....

De plus en plus de personnes ont du mal à joindre les deux bouts.

....

Vous ne toucherez votre retraite qu'après avoir travaillé 42 ans.

....

C'est un philanthrope qui a fondé une organisation humanitaire.

....

Pourquoi la répartition de la richesse ne pourrait-elle pas être plus juste ?

....

Questions

Is affirmative action the best way to reduce inequalities?
Foreign aid.
Have the elites lost touch with ordinary people?

WRITING TIP N° 9: Examples

One of the recurrent flaws in French students' essays (one that is often mentioned in examiners' reports) is that they are too abstract and too vague. This may be partly because the English language tends to be more concrete than French. For example, English speakers use verbs describing actions which are easier to visualize whereas French people tend to go for* abstract nouns.

It is true that the questions you have to answer are often very broad* — you are expected to solve the major challenges faced by humanity in half an hour! By their very nature, these questions therefore prompt* you to generalize excessively.

Do bear in mind that instead of philosophizing, it is often preferable to think of particular examples because concrete cases are more easily grasped* than hazy* conjectures. Mentioning an example can also be a good way of catching your reader's attention in an introduction.

When you think of an example, do not just mention it. Do not simply write "Chernobyl showed that nuclear is dangerous". Describe it in some detail: "The explosion at Chernobyl nuclear plant in April 1986 and the resulting radioactive contamination showed that..." and then explain why it is relevant* to the point you have been discussing. Do not take it for granted* that your reader knows everything about it. Be as precise as you can (within the limits set by the exam), mention dates, figures or statistics if they help shed light* on the problem. Moreover, remember that examples concerning the English-speaking world are always preferable in an English paper because it is also your knowledge of the English-speaking world that is assessed.

To be able to do this, you have to keep abreast of* recent developments in current affairs* or whatever topics you will have to write about. Naturally, reading the press assiduously will also enable you to learn useful vocabulary and familiarize yourself with common idiomatic constructions, so you will kill two birds with one stone*. The extracts from newspapers in this book have been selected because they show you how vocabulary is used but also because you will learn some useful facts concerning the issue.

go for: *avoir tendance à préférer* • **broad**: *large* • **prompt**: *inciter* • **grasp**: *saisir, comprendre* • **hazy**: *flou, vague* • **relevant**: *pertinent* • **take it for granted**: *considérer comme allant de soi* • **shed light**: *éclairer* • **keep abreast of**: *se tenir au courant de* • **current affairs**: *actualité* • **kill two birds with one stone**: *faire d'une pierre deux coups*

10. SOCIAL ILLS

9/11 • abortion • advertising • AIDS • alcohol abuse • armed forces • asbestos • bonuses • BRICS • CIA • cloning • CO_2 • computers • consumer society • couch potatoes • creationism • credit bubble • cultural exception • dating • DEA • death penalty • deforestation • dictatorship • digital piracy • diplomacy • domestic violence • drought • drug trafficking • eating disorders • endangered species • English-speaking world • epidemics • euthanasia • fanaticism • food scares • fossil fuels • free speech • free trade • gender gap • glass ceiling • greenhouse gases • guinea pigs • gun control • health care • hijacking • human rights • immigration policy • intercourse • ISPs • IVF • justice system • labour • multiculturalism • NASA • natural disasters • NGOs • nuclear • nuclear deterrent • oil slicks • on parole • outsourcing • overfishing • ozone layer • PC • pension system • philanthropy • physics • pidgin • prevention • racial profiling • recycling • renewables • RP • salad bowl • same-sex marriage • second-hand smoking • serial killers • sex industry • slump • social divide • social networks • Spanglish • standard English • STDs • stem-cell research • suffragettes • suicide bombers • surrogacy • surveillance • technophobia • teenage violence • truancy • United Nations • uprisings • video games • waste disposal • welfare state • WMDs • working poor • WTO

advertising

consumer society

couch potatoes

teenage violence

truancy

to consume	consommer
a consumer	un consommateur
consumption [kən'sʌmpʃən]	consommation
consumer goods	les biens de consommation
consumer society	la société de consommation
consumerism	le consumérisme
to meet a need	satisfaire un besoin
needless, unnecessary, superfluous	inutile, superflu

Affluenza is a portmanteau word composed of "affluence" (which is synonymous with "wealth") and "influenza" (*grippe*) and refers to the condition of people, mostly in rich Western countries, who feel unfulfilled (*insatisfaits, frustrés*) and dissatisfied in spite of their growing wealth. There is evidence showing that levels of happiness have not increased over the past fifty years even though material well-being (*bien-être*) has soared as a result of economic growth.

materialism	le matérialisme
materialistic	matérialiste (adj)
material goods	les biens matériels
greed [gri:d]	avidité, cupidité
greedy	avide
acquisitiveness	instinct de possession, goût de la propriété
the rat race	la compétition acharnée de la vie moderne
careerism	carriérisme
social status ['steɪtəs]	le statut social
status symbol	signe extérieur de réussite

In our society, you don't have to be wealthy to suffer from affluenza. Its symptoms — "debt, overwork, waste, and harm to the environment, leading to psychological disorders, alienation, and distress," in adults; "lack of motivation, apathy, laziness, or failure to commit to and achieve goals, overindulgence and attitudes of entitlement" in children, according to the New York University Child Study Center, are pervasive (*omniprésent*) — and no one is immune. If affluenza, in greater or lesser form, has infected wide swaths of the population at large, one group — the children of the rich — appears to be particularly susceptible to its ravages: teen suicide, pregnancy, substance use and violence.
The New York Times, 31 July 2008

advertising ['ædvətaɪzɪŋ]	la publicité
an advertisement [əd'vɜ:tɪsmənt], an advert, an ad	une publicité
advertising campaign [kæm'peɪn]	campagne de publicité
to advertise ['ædvətaɪz] a product	faire de la publicité pour un produit
an adman	un publicitaire
an advertiser	un annonceur

a commercial	une publicité (à la télévision ou à la radio)
a commercial break	une pause publicitaire, une page de publicité (TV)
a hoarding) ['hɔːdɪŋ] (GB), a billboard (US)	un panneau publicitaire
media hype	matraquage publicitaire
to deceive [dɪ'siːv] sb into a buying a product	tromper qn pour qu'il achète un produit
deceptive, misleading	trompeur, mensonger
to brainwash sb	faire un lavage de cerveau à qn
a brand (name)	une marque
brand image	image de marque
brand awareness	notoriété de la marque
brand loyalty	fidélité à la marque

Surplus: Terrorized into Being Consumers is a 2003 documentary film on consumerism and globalization. It attempts to demonstrate that the claim that capitalism leads to greater efficiency and therefore less work does not hold water (*ne tient pas debout*). The film includes interviews of John Zerzan, an American anarcho-primitivist associated with the anti-WTO protests in Seattle in 1999.

TV, television	la télévision
a programme (GB), a program (US), a show	une émission
reality television	la téléréalité
a TV channel, a TV station	une chaîne de télévision
a pay channel, a toll [təʊl] channel	une chaîne payante
audience ratings, audience figures	l'audimat
a subscription	un abonnement
a subscriber	un abonné
a TV viewer	un téléspectacteur
to watch the news	regarder les informations, les actualités
to watch sth live [laɪv]	regarder qch en direct
current affairs programme	une émission d'actualités
to switch channels	zapper
to be glued to the box	être collé à l'écran
a couch potato	quelqu'un qui passe son temps devant la télé

> When you think about it, it's one of the great ironies of our time: we now inhabit a modernized, industrialized, high-tech world that presents us with fewer and fewer legitimate threats to our survival, yet we appear to find more and more things to be anxious about with each passing year. Between our sustenance-packed superstores, our state-of-the-art hospitals, our quadruple-crash-tested cars, our historically low crime rates, and our squadrons of consumer-protection watchdogs (*organismes de surveillance*), Americans are safer and more secure today than at any other point in human history. But just try telling that to our brains, because they seem to believe that precisely the opposite is true. America now ranks as the most anxious nation on the planet, with more than 18 percent of adults suffering from a full-blown anxiety disorder in any given year, according to the National Institute of Mental Health. (On the other hand, in Mexico — a place where one assumes there's plenty to fret about — only 6.6 percent of adults have ever met the criteria for significant anxiety issues).
> Taylor Clark, *Nerve: Poise Under Pressure, Serenity Under Stress, and the Brave New Science of Fear and Cool*, 2011

a single-parent family	une famille monoparentale
a single mother	une mère célibataire
to be born out of wedlock ['wedlɒk]	naître hors mariage
family allowance, child benefit	allocations familiales
to get divorced, to get a divorce	divorcer
to divorce sb, to get divorced from sb	divorcer de qn
to have custody ['kʌstədɪ]	avoir la garde (des enfants)
alimony ['ælɪmənɪ]	pension alimentaire
to raise a child single-handed	élever un enfant seul, sans aide
a blended family	une famille recomposée
stepfather / stepmother	beau-père / belle-mère (conjoint(e) de la mère / du père biologique)
stepfamily	belle-famille
child poverty	la pauvreté des enfants
child abuse	la maltraitance des enfants
teenage pregnancy	les adolescentes enceintes
childhood obesity [əʊ'biːsɪtɪ]	l'obésité chez les enfants
teenage suicide	le suicide des jeunes
generation gap	le fossé entre les générations
truancy ['trʊənsɪ]	l'absentéisme scolaire
to play truant	faire l'école buissonnière
to skip a class	sécher un cours
to bully sb	malmener, brutaliser, intimider qn
bullying	harcèlement (à l'école)
a grant, a scholarship	une bourse
academic failure	l'échec scolaire
to drop out of school	abandonner ses études
a dropout	un étudiant qui a abandonné ses études
illiteracy	anaphalbétisme, illéttrisme

With youth unemployment set to nudge past the million marker, it's worth reflecting on what being out of work means for the 18-to 24-year-olds who have failed to find employment since the crash of 2008. Bright young people who left school or university with high hopes have had their ambitions dashed, finding only temporary, part-time work outside their chosen field, if they have found work at all. Many are left with a sense of growing up in a world that doesn't want them. They find themselves frantically competing for jobs and training courses as public sector work is being cut, and the private sector is failing to make up the difference. University fees are soaring as the worth of a degree in the labour market plummets (*dégringoler*). Housing is cramped and expensive. What work there is is temporary, badly paid or unpaid, and the best jobs go not to those who are best qualified or who have worked the hardest, but to those who have family connections or who can afford to slog their way through unpaid internships (*stages*).
The Independent, Laurie Penny, Tuesday, 11 October 2011

meritocracy	méritocratie
social mobility	mobilité sociale
the social ladder	l'ascenseur social
to move up the social ladder	monter dans l'échelle sociale
to start from scratch	partir de rien
equal opportunity, equality of opportunity	l'égalité des chances
egalitarian [iˌgælɪ'teəriən]	égalitaire
egalitarianism	l'égalitarisme
youth unemployment	le chômage des jeunes

Whereas in France, underprivileged neighbourhoods are usually located in the suburbs or the outskirts (*périphérie*) of towns, the English word **suburb** calls to mind (*évoque*) large houses and gardens — **leafy suburb** (*banlieue verte*) is a common collocation. Sociologically speaking, suburbs in America are associated with the middle-class. Indeed, the word **suburbia** is a slightly disapproving way of referring to the way of living and the rather conventional values of the middle-class people who live in the suburbs. By contrast, **inner-cities** or **inner-city areas** in the English-speaking world often face the problems of poverty, unemployment, bad housing conditions, ethnic tensions etc. that plague some French "*banlieues*".

teenage violence	la violence chez les jeunes
juvenile delinquency ['dʒuːvənaɪl dɪ'lɪŋkwənsɪ]	la déliquance juvénile
a juvenile delinquent, a young offender	un délinquant juvénile
a thug [θʌg], a yob	un voyou, un loubard
verbal abuse	violences verbales
to assault sb, to mug sb	agresser qn (physiquement)
a mugger	un agresseur
aggressiveness	agressivité

antisocial behavior	comportement anti-social
petty crime	petite délinquance
disorderly conduct, disruptive behaviour	incivilités
shoplifting	vol à l'étalage
a rough neighbourhood	un quartier difficile, chaud
council housing (GB), public housing (US)	HLM
a housing estate (GB), a project (US)	une cité
a suburb ['sʌbɜːb]	une banlieue
an inner-city area	un quartier déshérité du centre-ville
deprived [dɪ'praɪvd], disadvantaged, underprivileged	défavorisé
unrest	l'agitation
a no-go zone	une zone de non-droit

In Great Britain, an **anti-social behaviour order** (ASBO) is an official order that a person must behave in a particular way, for instance that they must not go to a particular place, must not speak to particular people, etc. If they do obey the order, they are given a stronger punishment.

LANGUAGE PRACTICE

1. Find the words corresponding to the following definitions.

.... is the right to take care of a child, given to one of the parents after they have divorced.

A .... is an amount of money given to a student to pay for their education.

.... is stealing things from shops.

A .... is a large board on the outside of a building or at the side of the road, used for putting advertisements on.

2. Find the appropriate prefix or suffixes to complete these words.

matériel	material	material _ _ _ _ _	*matérialiste (adj)*
agressif	aggressive	aggressive _ _ _ _	*agressivité*
tromper	to deceive	dece _ _ _ _ _	*trompeur*
ordre	order	_ _ _ order _ _ conduct	*incivilités*

3. Find the missing words.

The two boys were cited for many instances of .... social behaviour such as spitting at boaters from London's bridges and smashing windows.

They .... truant many times last year and were finally expelled from school.

More than half of children are now born out of ....

Crime rates at the time were unacceptably high and downtown Johannesburg was a no- .... zone for tourists.

4. Form four noun groups with the following nouns and translate them.

blended, obesity, television, young, reality, offender, childhood, family

....

....

....

....

5. Choose the appropriate word.

Our (consumption / consumer) society is producing far too much waste.

(Young / Youth) unemployment needs to be tackled urgently.

I would like to go into (advertising / advertisement) after my MBA.

In some areas, two thirds of marriages end in divorce creating whole neighbourhoods of (single / unique) parent families.

6. Translate into French

Money can't buy happiness… or can it?

……………………………………………………………………………………

Many dropouts come from broken homes.

……………………………………………………………………………………

The integration of young people into the world of work is a major issue of the campaign.

……………………………………………………………………………………

Consumers are brainwashed into buying gadgets they don't need.

……………………………………………………………………………………

She was a successful executive but she grew tired of the rat race.

……………………………………………………………………………………

7. Translate into English

Le problème de beaucoup de jeunes, c'est qu'ils n'ont pas de repères.

……………………………………………………………………………………

Ils ignorent tout des valeurs familiales traditionnelles.

……………………………………………………………………………………

La télé-réalité fait croire à certains qu'il suffit d'être jeune et beau pour devenir riche.

……………………………………………………………………………………

La méritocratie récompense les gens en fonction de leurs performances.

……………………………………………………………………………………

L'ascenseur social est-il en panne dans les quartiers défavorisés ?

……………………………………………………………………………………

Questions

Is it fair that footballers and bankers earn more money than they know what to do with while ordinary people struggle to pay the rent?
Can money buy happiness?
Is the hedonic treadmill driving us all mad?

WRITING TIP N° 10: Concision

Every word you write should lead your reader forward*. This is especially true in very short texts like those you are usually required to write in a language exam.

To start with, avoid lengthy introductions containing bland* general declarations such as: "This article deals with an important issue" because your reader will not learn anything from such a statement*. Remember that you are not writing a five- or ten-page long French-style *dissertation*: go straight to the point*. Avoid the expression "It is interesting to notice that more and more countries are becoming democracies"; simply write: "more and more countries are becoming democracies."

There is no point in* repeating the question word for word —you do not prove that you can express yourself if you do so. In your conclusion, do not repeat what you have just explained in the preceding paragraphs.

Naturally, it may be necessary for you to distinguish your opinions from those expressed in the text you are commenting on, but do not write "According to the writer" three times in a 200-word analysis.

In the following sentence: "In London there are a lot of video cameras so that people are spied on all the time in this city," you can leave out the last three words without losing any of the meaning. You can also cut out* the last four words in: "In the 80s, personal computers were more expensive than they are now." Talking about "predictions for the future" is redundant.

Avoid pleonasms such as: "In my opinion, I think that the Third Way was a failure.". Write: "In my opinion, the Third Way… " or "I think that the Third Way…" . Remember that "the phenomenon of globalization" is nothing more than "globalization".

Beware of exaggeration and bombast*. When you are tempted to write "the crisis is really serious" ask yourself if what you mean is not simply "the crisis is serious" (or perhaps "very serious"). Avoid sweeping generalizations*.

In some cases, it is possible to say one thing in several ways. If so, it is often best to opt for the shorter solution. For instance, "despite the fact that" (four words) means exactly the same as "although" (one word), "due to the fact that" (five words) the same as "since" (one word). Other examples include:

- "in the same way", which is synonymous with "similarly" or "likewise"
- "first of all" means "first"
- "in spite of" means "despite"
- "in any case" means "anyway"
- "more and more" means "increasingly"
- "little by little" means "gradually"
- "at that time" means "then".

As a rule, avoid "the fact that". In many cases the gerund is a better option: instead of "the fact that he was Irish", write "his being Irish".

lead your reader forward: *faire progresser le lecteur* • **lengthy**: *très long* • **bland**: *terne, fade* • **statement**: *affirmation* • **go straight to the point**: *aller droit au but* • **there is no point in**: *cela ne sert à rien de* • **cut out**: *éliminer* • **bombast**: *grandiloquence* • **sweeping generalizations**: *généralisations abusives*

11. CULTURAL DIVERSITY

9/11 • abortion • advertising • AIDS • alcohol abuse • armed forces • asbestos • bonuses • BRICS • CIA • cloning • CO_2 • computers • consumer society • couch potatoes • creationism • credit bubble • cultural exception • dating • DEA • death penalty • deforestation • dictatorship • digital piracy • diplomacy • domestic violence • drought • drug trafficking • eating disorders • endangered species • English-speaking world • epidemics • euthanasia • fanaticism • food scares • fossil fuels • free speech • free trade • gender gap • glass ceiling • greenhouse gases • guinea pigs • gun control • health care • hijacking • human rights • intercourse • ISPs • IVF • justice system • labour • NASA • natural disasters • NGOs • nuclear • nuclear deterrent • oil slicks • on parole • outsourcing • overfishing • ozone layer • pension system • philanthropy • physics • pidgin • prevention • recycling • renewables • RP • same-sex marriage • second-hand smoking • serial killers • sex industry • slump • social divide • social networks • Spanglish • standard English • STDs • stem-cell research • suffragettes • suicide bombers • surrogacy • surveillance • technophobia • teenage violence • truancy • United Nations • uprisings • video games • waste disposal • welfare state • WMDs • working poor • WTO

immigration policy **multiculturalism** **PC** **racial profiling** **salad bowl**

to emigrate to New Zealand	émigrer en Nouvelle-Zélande
to immigrate to France	immigrer en France
large-scale / mass immigration	immigration à grande échelle / de masse
illegal immigration	immigration clandestine, irrégulière
uncontrolled immigration	immigration sauvage
an illegal immigrant, an illegal alien ['eɪlɪən]	un immigrant clandestin
an undocumented alien	un sans-papiers
native ['neɪtɪv] country, home country	pays natal, pays d'origine
a host country	un pays d'accueil
to welcome	accueillir
a newcomer	un nouvel arrivant
a foreigner	un étranger

The word **stranger** is a faux-ami which is used to describe someone you do not know, not someone who has a different nationality. To refer to someone who comes from another country, you must say **foreigner** or, mostly in the US, **alien**. Aliens may also come from other planets.

a border, a frontier	une frontière
border controls	les contrôles aux frontières
identity checks	les contrôles d'identité
to turn sb back at the border	refouler qn à la frontière
a holding centre, a detention centre	un centre de rétention
a passport	un passeport
an identity card	une carte d'identité
a visa ['viːzə]	un visa

Immigrants benefit America because they study and work hard. That is the standard argument in favour of immigration, and it is correct. Leaving your homeland is a big deal. By definition, it takes get-up-and-go to get up and go, which is why immigrants are abnormally entrepreneurial. But there is another, less obvious benefit of immigration. Because they maintain links with the places they came from, immigrants help America plug into (*se brancher sur*) a vast web of global networks. Many people have observed how the networks of overseas Chinese and Indians benefit their respective motherlands. Diasporas speed the flow of information.
The Economist, April 22nd 2010

a refugee [ˌrefjʊ'dʒiː]	un réfugié
a displaced person	une personne déplacée
a stateless person	un apatride
to take refuge, take shelter	se réfugier
to seek political asylum [ə'saɪləm]	demander l'asile politique
an asylum-seeker	un demandeur d'asile
to flee persecution / destitution	fuir la persécution / la misère
human trafficking	le trafic des êtres humains

a smuggler	un contrebandier, un passeur
a smuggling ring	un réseau de passeurs

Arizona's Republican governor, Jan Brewer, signed into law a bill known as "SB 1070" on 23 April, giving police who merely (*simplement*) have "reasonable suspicion" the right to stop and demand identification from passers-by, who then face incarceration and a heavy fine if they fail to produce those all-important papers... If you're Latino, as 30 per cent of Arizona's population of 6.6 million are, you now face the prospect of constant harassment by the police if they have "reasonable suspicion" that you are "an alien who is unlawfully present in the US". To hell, then, with the Fourth Amendment of the US constitution, which is supposed to protect you from this kind of thing. "If you look or sound foreign, you are going to be subjected to never-ending requests [from] police to confirm your identity and to confirm your citizenship," says Alessandra Soler Meetze, executive director of the American Civil Liberties Union. President Felipe Calderón of Mexico, too, says that the new law "opens the door to intolerance, hate, discrimination and abuse in law enforcement".
The New Statesman, 29 April, 2010

immigration policy	la politique migratoire
selective immigration, controlled immigration	immigration choisie
to restrict / curb immigration	limiter / freiner l'immigration
to regularise the status of illegal immigrants	régulariser la situation des clandestins
regularisation	la régularisation
to escort sb back to the border	reconduire qn à la frontière
to deport sb	expulser qn
a migrant worker	un travailleur migrant
a work permit / a resident permit	un permis de travail / de séjour
brain drain / brain gain	fuite des cerveaux / afflux des cerveaux
family reunion [rɪ'juːnjən], reunification	le regroupement familial
a sham [ʃæm] marriage, a marriage of convenience	un mariage blanc

A **sham marriage** is a false or fake marriage for instance involving a foreign national who is not entitled to regularization and who wants to obtain citizenship. Such a marriage is often referred to as a **marriage of convenience** (*mariage de convenance*) although the latter expression does not always imply an intention to cheat.

racial bias ['baɪəs], racial prejudice	les préjugés raciaux
skin colour	la couleur de peau
racial discrimination	la discrimination raciale
a racist attack, a racially motivated attack	une agression à caractère racial
racial abuse [ə'bjuːs] , racist abuse	des insultes à caractère racial
hate speech	des propos racistes
the colour bar, the colour line	la discrimination raciale

Australian pride at having forged a successful, multicultural country sits oddly with (*détonner*) the country's constitution. Promulgated in 1901, when Australia's six states formed a federation, the document still contains clauses that constitutional legal experts say allow discrimination on racial grounds. The document thus reflected the attitudes of the white men who drafted it in the 1890s. A referendum in 1967 partly made amends. Australians voted overwhelmingly then to repeal a clause that had excluded aborigines from being counted in the census (*recensement*). But that left two jarring (*discordant*) constitutional clauses intact. One accepts that people of "any race" could be disqualified from voting in state elections at the whim of state governments. The other allows the federal parliament to make "special laws" for "any race" it liked.
The Economist, 14 January 2012

apartheid [ə'pɑːteɪt, ə'pɑːtaɪd]	l'apartheid
to propagate ['prɒpəgeɪt] hatred ['heɪtrɪd]	propager la haine
to foster hatred ['heɪtrɪd]	favoriser la haine
to fuel hatred	nourrir, alimenter, entretenir la haine
to incite religious racial / religious hatred	inciter à la haine raciale / religieuse
incitement to racial hatred	l'incitation à la haine raciale
to fuel [fjʊəl] tensions	alimenter, nourrir les tensions

Apartheid is a system of racial segregation which was enforced in South Africa between 1948 and 1994. The term is used more widely to describe strict segregation with strongly racist overtones.

The notion of the **melting pot** was first used in a play published in the US in 1908 and is a metaphor describing the way in which the ingredients in the pot (that is to say people of different cultures, races or religions) combine so as to create a diverse but essentially homogeneous society. The phrase **E pluribus Unum** (Latin for *Out of Many, One*) which was the motto (*devise*) of the United States until 1956, is another expression of the same conception. By contrast, the image of the **salad bowl** (or **cultural mosaic** in Canada), which became widespread in the late 20th century, suggests that the various cultures that make up a nation, like the ingredients in a salad, cohabit but do not "melt" or merge into a single homogeneous culture.

segregation	la ségrégation
a black neighbourhood	un quartier noir
a lily-white suburb	une banlieue entièrement blanche
a ghetto	un ghetto
ghettoization [ˌgetəʊaɪ'zeɪʃən]	la ghettoïsation
inner-city areas ['ɛərɪəz]	les quartiers déshérités des centre-villes américains
disadvantaged, underprivileged	défavorisé
second-class citizens	des citoyens de seconde zone
a two-tier [tɪəʳ] society	une société à deux vitesses

to exclude sb	exclure qn
to marginalize sb	marginaliser qn
racial profiling	délit de faciès
to be discriminated against	être victime de discrimination
to be victimized	être victime de brimades
to feel alienated, excluded	se sentir exclu

Slavery was abolished in Great Britain in 1807, in France by the Second Republic in 1848. In the USA, Lincoln pronounced Emancipation in 1863. This was ratified by Congress in the 13th Amendment after the end of the Civil War (*Guerre de Sécession*) two years later.

a multiracial society	une société multiraciale
multiculturalism	multiculturalisme
an ethnic minority	une minorité ethnique
to become integrated, assimilated	s'intégrer
a mixed marriage, a mixed-race marriage	un mariage mixte
to be mixed-race	être métis
a citizen	un citoyen
citizenship	la citoyenneté
second-generation immigrants	des immigrés de deuxième génération
to be dual heritage, to have dual heritage ['herɪtɪdʒ]	avoir une double culture
African-American, Afro-American	afro-américain
Asian-American	américain d'origine asiatique
a native ['neɪtɪv] of France	un Français de naissance
North Africa	le Maghreb
North Africans	les Maghrébins
Pakistani / Bangladeshi	pakistanais / du Bangladesh
Spanish-speaking / Hindi-speaking	hispanophone / parlant le Hindi

The expression **politically correct** became widely used in the 1990s in conservative circles to deride (*tourner en ridicule*) the attitude of those, usually on the left of the political spectrum, who think prejudices concerning race, gender, ethnicity, disability or sexual orientation are deeply embedded in our everyday language and that therefore, to change mentalities, it is necessary to avoid using some expressions such as "black American" or "Indian" and replace them with neutral phrases like "African American" or "native American".

incomprehension, lack of understanding	l'incompréhension
the language barrier ['bærɪəʳ]	la barrière de la langue
mainstream culture	la culture dominante, majoritaire
mistrust, distrust	méfiance
to reject Western values	rejeter les valeurs occidentales
the rejection of Western cultural standards	le rejet des normes culturelles occidentales
secular ['sekjʊləʳ]	laïc
secularism	laïcité
the separation of church and state	la séparation de l'Église et de l'État

Dirty Pretty Things is a thriller directed by Stephen Frears (2002) about two illegal immigrants, a Nigerian man and a Turkish woman, who work in a London hotel where the manager illegally tricks immigrants into swapping kidneys (*rein*) for forged passports. Senay (Audrey Tautou) has to quit her job at the hotel to work in a clothing sweatshop to hide from immigration police who want to deport her. She is forced to leave her job but finally manages to flee to New York City with the help of her Nigerian friend.

anti-Semitism	l'antisémitisme
Jewish	juif
a Jew [dʒuː]	un juif
to desecrate ['desɪkreɪt] a grave	profaner une tombe
revisionism	le négationnisme
a revisionist	un négationniste
to deny	nier
a scapegoat	un bouc émissaire

A **revisionist** is someone who challenges the main beliefs of a system. People who deny that concentration camps ever existed or, like the British historian David Irving, who claim that Hitler had no knowledge of the Holocaust, are also called **Holocaust deniers**.

affirmative action	la discrimination positive
colour-blind	sans discrimination raciale
desegregation	la déségrégation
to desegregate schools	supprimer la ségrégation raciale dans les écoles
equal opportunity	l'égalité des chances

In the United States, the **civil rights movement** was the fight to outlaw discrimination against African Americans between 1955, when Rosa Parks refused to give up her seat and make room for a white passenger on a bus, and 1968, when its most famous leader, Martin Luther King, was assassinated.

LANGUAGE PRACTICE

1. The spelling of the translations of the following words is very close to the French one.

un passeport	....
l'asile poltique	political ....
exclure	....
l'antisémitisme	....

2. All the missing words are based on the same root.

Samira had been born in France but she made up her mind to .... to Britain as soon as she was able to get a job there.

It seems that highly-qualified .... workers tend to prefer settling in North America rather than in the EU.

Those who .... into our country must abide by our laws, whatever their own beliefs or customs.

Canada's .... policy has not always been selective.

3. The following words are both verbs and nouns.

	VERB	NOUN
mistrust	....	....
fuel	....	....
shelter	....	....
abuse	....	....

4. What are the correct translations of the following faux-amis?

A 17-year-old black student was stabbed in the chest in an unprovoked racist attack.

Family reunion is a way for some newcomers to obtain regularization.

Living in a secular society like the French or the British ones implies certain obligations.

Authoritarian regimes do not hesitate to deport thousands of illegals at a time.

5. Find the appropriate prefix and suffixes to form the missing words.

citoyen	citizen	....	*citoyenneté*
inciter	to incite	.... to racial hatred	*incitation à la haine raciale*
contrôler	to control	.... immigration	*immigration sauvage*
profil	profile	racial	*délit de faciès*

6. Translate into French.

Most of my friends have at least one foreign-born grandparent.

....

He was turned away at the border because his papers were not in order.

....

It could take you years before you are granted British citizenship.

....

Every citizen regardless of race or ethnicity must have access to education.

....

There is no evidence that immigration hurts indigenous workers.

....

7. Translate into English

On quitte généralement son pays natal à la recherche de meilleures conditions de vie.

....

Si sa femme n'apprend pas la langue, elle risque d'être coupée du reste de la société.

....

Les partis d'extrême-droite distinguent les Français « de souche » des autres.

....

Plusieurs Musulmans d'origine pakistanaise ont été la cible d'insultes à caractère racial.

....

L'élection d'un président métis signifie-t-elle que la société américaine est devenue « post-raciale » ?

....

Questions

Selective immigration.
Why is the multicultural model under fire today?
Are people in Western Europe right to fret about illegal immigration?

WRITING TIP N° 11: Precision

As I have already explained, your text will be all the more convincing if it is based on concrete examples and precise arguments.

The way you express yourself should reflect this. In particular, try to avoid general, colourless words such as "people, good, bad etc." whenever you can. For example, to talk about "people", use the words "citizens, inhabitants, voters, taxpayers, human beings,...", depending on the context, or, collectively: "the electorate, public opinion...". Instead of repeating the verb "say" over and over again, think of using "point out, argue*, claim*, add*, suggest, imply*..." — each with its own nuances — see the appendix: all-purpose vocabulary at the end of the book. Instead of the adjective "good", employ "positive, beneficial, right, efficient, fair...". Of course, these words are not interchangeable and you must learn what adjectives can be associated with a given noun, the connotations of each verb etc.

Beware in particular of the adjective "important", which does not cover all the meanings of its French counterpart. For instance "*un nombre important*" is "a large number", "*une hausse importante*" is "a sharp increase", "*une somme importante*" is "a substantial sum", "*une part importante*" is "a significant part", "*un problème important*" is "a serious problem", "*un homme d'affaires important*" is "a prominent businessman".

The same goes for "*intéressant*", which is not always translated as "interesting"; when talking about "*des prix intéressants*", you have to say "attractive prices".

When you use precise words you help your reader have a clearer picture of what you mean. Naturally, the more words you know, the easier it will be for you to find the right one in a given context. Hence* the need to learn as many words as you can... and how they are used.

argue: *avancer, soutenir* • **claim**: prétendre • **add**: *ajouter, préciser* • **imply**: *laisser entendre, sous-entendre* • **hence**: *d'où*

12. DEMOCRACY

9/11 • abortion • advertising • AIDS • alcohol abuse • armed forces •
asbestos • bonuses • BRICS • CIA • cloning • CO_2 • computers • consumer
society • couch potatoes • creationism • credit
bubble • cultural exception • **dictatorship** dating • DEA •
death penalty • deforestation • digital piracy •
diplomacy • domestic violence • drought • drug trafficking • eating disorders
• endangered species • English-speaking world
• epidemics • euthanasia • fanaticism • **human rights** food
scares • fossil fuels • free trade • gender gap •
glass ceiling • greenhouse gases • guinea pigs • gun control • health care •
hijacking • immigration policy • intercourse • ISPs •
IVF • **free speech** justice system • labour • multiculturalism •
NASA • natural disasters • NGOs • nuclear • nuclear
deterrent • oil slicks • on parole • outsourcing • overfishing • ozone layer •
PC • pension system • philanthropy • physics • pidgin • prevention • racial
profiling • **surveillance** recycling • renewables • RP • salad bowl •
same-sex marriage • second-hand smoking • serial
killers • sex industry • slump • social divide • social networks • Spanglish
• standard English • STDs • stem-cell research •
suffragettes • suicide bombers • surrogacy • **uprisings** technophobia
• teenage violence • truancy • United Nations •
video games • waste disposal • welfare state • WMDs • working poor • WTO

a dictator [dɪk'teɪtəʳ]	un dictateur
dictatorship	la dictature
authoritarian [ˌɔːθɒrɪ'tɛərɪən]	autoritaire
authoritarianism	l'autoritarisme
totalitarian	totalitaire
totalitarianism	le totalitarisme
a military junta ['dʒʌntə]	une junte militaire

A **junta** (derived from the Spanish) is a military government which has taken power by force.

a coup [kuː], a coup d'état	un coup d'État
a regime [reɪ'ʒiːm]	un gouvernement autoritaire
corruption, sleaze [sliːz], bribery	la corruption
corrupt [kə'rʌpt]	corrompu
a bribe	un pot-de-vin
to bribe sb	acheter, soudoyer qn
a political system	un régime politique
to take, seize power	prendre le pouvoir, s'emparer du pouvoir
to come to power, to come into office	arriver au pouvoir
to be in power	être au pouvoir
the right to vote	le droit de vote
vote rigging, ballot rigging, electoral fraud	la fraude électorale

The words **elector** and **voter** both refer to someone who has the right to vote. But **voter** is much more common. The word **elector** is used mostly to refer to a member of an electoral college such as the one which elects the President of the United States. Suffrage is indirect, which means **voters** cast a vote not for a presidential candidate but for **electors** who have pledged (*s'engager à*) to support one of them.

a political opponent [ə'pəʊnənt]	un opposant politique
a dissident	un dissident
multi-party system	le multi-partisme
single-party system	un système de parti unique
free and fair elections	des élections libres et régulières
to declare a state of emergency	déclarer l'état d'urgence
human rights	les droits de l'homme
human rights abuses, violations	des atteintes aux droits de l'homme
a crime against humanity	un crime contre l'humanité
the duty to interfere	le devoir d'ingérence

The English **Bill of Rights** (1689), which resulted from the **Glorious Revolution**, is an Act which limits the powers of the monarch and sets out (*énoncer*) the rights of Parliament. In the US, the **Bill of Rights** is the name given to the first ten Amendments to the Constitution which were ratified in 1791, not long after the Constitution itself was adopted in 1787.

discontent	mécontentement, malaise
unrest	agitation, troubles
turmoil ['tɜːmɔɪl]	agitation, confusion
an upheaval [ʌp'hiːvəl]	un bouleversement
a demonstration, a protest march	une manifestation
a demonstrator, a protester	un manifestant
a riot ['raɪət]	une émeute
a rioter	un émeutier, un casseur
anti-riot police	les CRS
a petrol bomb, a Molotov cocktail	un cocktail Molotov
tear gas ['tɪə gæs]	du gaz lacrymogène
a clash	un heurt, un affrontement

India scarcely has a human rights record it can be proud of. Killings of human rights activists, intimidation and 'disappearance' of those who question the state's ways, widespread use of torture by law enforcement agencies underscore a disregard (*mépris*) for basic humanitarian laws. The recently-released Asian Center for Human Rights Report, 'Torture in India 2011' states that between 2001 and 2010, 14,231 persons — or more than four persons per day — died in police and judicial custody (*détention*) in India. According to the ACHR's director, Suhas Chakma, 99.99 percent of deaths in police custody can be ascribed to torture and occur within 48 hours of the victim being taken into custody.

Asia Sentinel, Friday, 25 November 2011

an uprising	un soulèvement
to revolt	se révolter
to rebel [rɪ'bel]	se rebeller
a rebel ['rebl]	un rebelle
a rebellion [rɪ'beljən]	une rébellion, une révolte
to overthrow, to topple a dictator	renverser un dictateur
to oust a dictator	évincer un dictateur
to hold a leader to account	tenir un dirigeant pour responsable
to collapse	s'effondrer
to restore democracy	restaurer la démocratie
to put down, to suppress a rebellion	réprimer une rébellion
to quell [kwel] the protests	réprimer, étouffer la contestation
crackdown, clampdown	des mesures de répression

The notion of **accountability** is essential to modern democracy: it is the principle that elected leaders are accountable to those who elected them (the electorate), in other words, that they must "account for" or justify the decisions they make, the policies they adopt because they are responsible for their consequences. The right of voters to hold their representatives to account means that they may be punished in case of misconduct (*mauvaise conduite, abus*). In parliamentary systems such as Britain's or France's, the leaders of the executive (the government) are accountable to the assemblies that brought them to power: they can vote a motion of no confidence (*motion de censure*) and thus remove them from power.

free speech, freedom of speech	la liberté d'expression, de parole
freedom of the press	la liberté de la presse
a free press	une presse libre
freedom of worship ['wɜːʃɪp]	la liberté de culte, la liberté religieuse
basic rights	les droits fondamentaux
basic / individual liberties	les libertés fondamentales / individuelles
to be enshrined in the constitution	être garanti par la constitution
civil liberties	les libertés civiques
to infringe (on) people's rights	empiéter sur les droits des gens
an infringement on sb's rights	une atteinte, une entorse aux droits de qn
to restrict free speech	restreindre, limiter la liberté d'expression
to encroach on basic liberties	empiéter sur les libertés fondamentales
an encroachment of the state	un empiètement de l'État
to detain a suspect without charge	détenir un suspect sans l'inculper
to remand sb in custody	placer qn en détention provisoire
to censor ['sensəʳ]	censurer
censorship	la censure
to block / restrict internet access	bloquer / restreindre l'accès à internet

"The British Constitution has always been puzzling and always will be," Queen Elizabeth II was once overheard saying. Until recently it was a puzzle that 99% of Britons would happily have left unsolved… Britain does have a written constitution, of course, but it is not written all in one place, with a catchy preamble to make clear its basic principles. Lacking a "constitutional moment"—a sharp and unreversed break in its history—Britain saw its constitution evolve through centuries of accumulated legislation and conventions. For the constitutional theorists of Victorian times, the guiding principle was simple: Parliament was sovereign (though, after the rise of party politics in the 19th century, the executive drawn from it called the shots) and its laws were unchallengeable throughout the land. The constitution was not a set of fundamental and broadly unalterable rules. It seemed to ensure both stability and freedom. It was envied abroad and taken for granted at home.
The Economist, 25 June 2009

surveillance [sɜː'veɪləns]	la surveillance
a surveillance society	une société surveillée
a police state	un État policier
to stop and search	interpeller et fouiller
to arrest sb	arrêter qn
privacy ['prɪvəsɪ, 'praɪvəsɪ]	(le droit à) la vie privée, l'intimité
sb's private life	la vie privée de qn
to breach [briːtʃ], to violate ['vaɪəleɪt] sb's privacy	violer la vie privée de qn
a breach of privacy, a privacy violation	une atteinte à, une violation de la vie privée
to intrude upon sb's privacy	porter atteinte à la vie privée de qn

Apart from being the dictator in the totalitarian state described by George Orwell in his novel "1984", **Big Brother** is also the title of the first major reality-TV show, which started in 1999.

Primary Colors is a 1998 movie directed by Mike Nichols in which John Travolta plays the role of a Southern governor, Jack Stanton —loosely (*librement*) based on Bill Clinton— who is trying to win the Democratic Party nomination as Presidential candidate. The story is seen through the eyes of a young political idealist, Henry Burton, who joins Stanton's team of advisers after impressing him with his enthusiasm. Even if Stanton is highly charismatic, his campaign is hampered (*entraver*) by allegations of past indiscretions (*écarts de conduite*). A woman from the candidate's home state claims to have had an affair with him and to have tapes to prove it. To defend himself, he decides to leak damaging information about his main rival to the press. In the end, Henry is deeply disillusioned with the whole political process.

video surveillance	la vidéosurveillance
CCTV, closed circuit television	télévision en circuit fermé
to record [rɪ'kɔːd]	enregistrer
to monitor sb's movements	suivre de près les mouvements de qn
to spy on sb, to snoop on qn	espionner qn
to track sb	suivre la trace de qn
to monitor a border / sb's mail	surveiller une frontière / le courrier de qn
to bug a room	placer des micros dans une pièce
to tap sb's phone	mettre qn sur écoute téléphonique
phone tapping, wiretapping	les écoutes téléphoniques

The **Watergate scandal** broke out in the early 1970s after a break-in (*effraction*) at the Watergate Building, which housed the headquarters of the Democratic Party in Washington. After President Nixon was found to be involved in the wiretapping (*mise sur écoute*) of his political opponents, he unsuccessfully tried to cover up the scandal. When it became clear that he had lied to Congress and faced certain impeachment (*destitution*), he resigned on 9 August, 1974, the only US President ever to have done so. Since then, the element -**gate** is used in portmanteau words to refer to political scandals (e.g. Contragate, Monicagate, Climategate, Irakgate).

personal data, personal details	des informations personnelles
biometric [ˌbaɪə'metrɪk] data	des données biométriques
a medical record / a school record	un dossier médical / scolaire
a criminal record	un casier judiciaire
a telephone bill	un relevé de téléphone
a bank statement	un relevé bancaire
to collect, gather data	recueillir, rassembler des informations
to store data	conserver, stocker des données
to retrieve data	rechercher et extraire des données
a database	une base de données
a DNA database [ˌdiːen'eɪ]	une base de données ADN

Theresa May, the Home Secretary, faced criticism from across the political spectrum and from civil liberties groups yesterday over her plans to give police and security services the power to monitor the email traffic and internet use of every person in Britain… Law enforcement agencies will gain extra powers to access information about contacts through Skype and social networking sites such as Facebook and Twitter. Internet companies will also reportedly be told to install hardware allowing GCHQ (*service gouvernemental d'interception des communications*) to examine "on demand" any phone call made, text message or email sent and website accessed, in "real time" and without a warrant (*mandat*). Similar proposals were abandoned in 2009 by the Labour government.
The Independent, 3 April 2012

LANGUAGE PRACTICE

1. **Choose the appropriate words to complete these sentences.**

Democracy may not be perfect, but it is probably the best political (system / regime).

Dissidents have called for an end to Vietnam's dictatorial (multi / single) party system.

After a government building was burned down by the rioters, the government declared (a / the) state of emergency.

The Conservative Party lost the election and Labour came into (office / power).

The authorities have taken steps to address racial profiling, notably in stop and (search / arrest) operations carried out by police.

2. **Use: "account", "charge", "circuit", "junta", "worship" to fill in the blanks.**

Closed .... TV has enabled the police to track a number of dangerous criminals.

Freedom of .... is enshrined in the First Amendment to the US Constitution.

After the coup, the military .... ruling the country banned all public meetings.

The right to detain a suspect without .... is a violation of the principle of habeas corpus.

Can a country whose leaders cannot be held to .... be described as democratic?

3. **Find synonyms for the following words.**

to overthrow a dictator	....
a protester	a ....
a crackdown	a ....
sleaze	....
a breach of privacy	a ....

4. **What are the prepositions that are needed to fill in the blanks?**

In his novel "1984", George Orwell described the archetypal police state, in which Big Brother is constantly snooping .... every citizen.

Some consider that restricting someone's internet access is an infringement .... their basic rights.

In those days, granting black people in the Deep South the right .... vote was unthinkable.

In 2003 Tony Blair had been .... power for six years.

Can slavery be considered as a crime .... humanity?

5. Translate into French.

In a parliamentary system, the prime minister is accountable to an elected assembly.

....

It became clear that the election had been rigged when the outgoing president was re-elected with 97.6% of the vote.

....

After the murder, several suspects were DNA-swabbed, to no avail.

....

It took the French Republic decades to admit the Vichy regime had deported Jews.

....

Which country has the worse human-rights record, North Korea or Iran?

....

6. Translate into English.

La plupart des pays d'Amérique Latine se sont démocratisés dans les années 70.

....

Les émeutes ont éclaté peu après la chute du gouvernement de gauche.

....

La police a le droit de ficher qui elle veut et de conserver ces informations durant des années.

....

Les dirigeants élus démocratiquement du Mali ont été renversés avant-hier.

....

Il aurait fallu surveiller les frontières de plus près.

....

Questions

Is the spread of democracy unstoppable?
The right to privacy.
Freedom vs security.

WRITING TIP N° 12: Register

You should be aware of the register of the words or constructions you make use of, that is to say, whether they are colloquial (= informal), vulgar, formal, literary, old-fashioned*, archaic, or just standard*. The register you should aim for in an examination is between "standard" and "formal*".

Keep in mind that slack* spoken English is not suitable in an exam paper, so abstain* from writing "gonna, wanna" instead of "going to, want to". Do not write "I sort of understood" to mean: "I more or less understood". Do not pepper your sentences with "like", "you know" the way some people do in conversation because this is usually considered as slipshod*. Some examiners may consider contractions such as "isn't don't, can't etc." as inappropriate: so it may be better for you to write "is not, cannot etc." to be on the safe side*.

At the other extreme, expressions such as "to be loath to do sth" *répugner à faire qch* or "the former, the latter" *les premiers, les derniers,* which are formal, are acceptable only if the rest of your text demonstrates the same level of sophistication. Even then, make sure you do not sound like a character in an Oscar Wilde play.

Another pitfall* students should avoid is using prefabricated phrases which are perfectly correct as such, but may sound artificial when they are not relevant* to the context in which they appear. For instance, writing:"There is no denying* that democracy has gained ground in the Arab world recently" is fine only if you actually mean that the progress of democracy in those countries is truly undeniable. If it is not the case, you should get rid of "There is no denying that...". You must not only say what you mean, but also mean what you say... and be able to back it up with reasons and evidence.

Some expressions (e.g. "first and foremost", "to put it in a nutshell") often sound academic* and should be replaced by "first" and "in short", respectively. When you enumerate arguments, make sure that the element following "last but not least" is indeed an important one, not just the last one you can think of. If not, use "Finally..."

Beware of buzz-words (words you can read in the media hundreds of times a day) because they may irritate your reader. You must also avoid English words that are used in French (so-called* Frenglish) because many of them do not have quite the same meaning in the two languages. Thus "*un dealer*" in French sells illegal drugs. But a British or American "dealer" may sell nearly anything, from art to second-hand cars.

Finally, beware of* Latinate words (words of Latin origin which sound more French than English), such as "initiate" (instead of "begin, launch") or "ameliorate" (instead of "improve") because they may seem snobbish to some readers.

old-fashioned: *désuet, dépassé* • **standard**: *normal* • **slack**: *négligé* • **formal**: *soutenu* • **abstain**: *s'abstenir* • **pepper**: *truffer* • **slipshod**: *négligé* • **to be on the safe side**: *par précaution* • **pitfall**: *piège* • **relevant**: *pertinent* • **there is no denying**: *on ne peut nier* • **to put it in a nutshell**: *en bref* • **academic**: *scolaire* • **so-called**: *ce que l'on appelle* • **beware of**: *méfiez-vous*

13. CRIME

9/11 • abortion • advertising • AIDS • alcohol abuse • armed forces •
asbestos • bonuses • BRICS • CIA • cloning •
CO_2 • **death penalty** computers • consumer society • couch
potatoes • creationism •
credit bubble • cultural exception • dating • DEA • **gun control**
deforestation • dictatorship • digital piracy • diplomacy
• domestic violence • drought • drug trafficking • eating disorders •
endangered species • English-speaking world • epidemics • euthanasia •
fanaticism • food scares • fossil fuels • free speech • free trade • gender gap
• glass ceiling • greenhouse gases • guinea pigs • health care • hijacking
• human rights • immigration policy •
intercourse • ISPs • IVF • labour **justice system** • multiculturalism
• NASA • natural disasters • NGOs • nuclear
• nuclear deterrent • oil slicks • outsourcing • overfishing • ozone layer • PC
• pension system • philanthropy • physics • pidgin •
prevention **on parole** • racial profiling • recycling • renewables •
RP • salad bowl • same-sex marriage • second-hand
smoking • sex industry • slump • social divide • social networks • Spanglish
• standard English • STDs • stem-cell **serial killers** research
• suffragettes • suicide bombers • surrogacy •
surveillance • technophobia • teenage violence • truancy • United Nations •
uprisings • video games • waste disposal • welfare state • WMDs • working
poor • WTO

crime, criminality	la criminalité
the crime rate	le taux de criminalité
organized crime	la criminalité organisée, le grand banditisme
white-collar crime	la criminalité en col blanc
petty crime	la petite délinquance
a crime, a felony	un crime
to commit a crime	commettre un crime
a criminal record	un casier judiciaire
an offense	un délit, une infraction

Whenever someone breaks the law, an **offence** (GB) or offense (US) is committed. Offences may be minor or serious. A minor offence is often called a **misdemeanour** (GB) or misdemeanor (US). A serious offence, for instance murder or rape, is a **crime** or a **felony**.

White-collar crime includes fraud, bribery, embezzlement, insider trading, money-laundering, copyright infringement and cybertheft. It does not involve violence and is usually committed by persons of high social status.

an offender	un délinquant, un contrevenant
a repeat offender, a recidivist	un récidiviste
murder	le meurtre
a murderer [ˈmɜːdərə(r)]	un meurtrier
manslaughter [ˈmænslɔːtə^{r}]	homicide
a serial killer	un tueur en série
rape [reɪp]	le viol
a rapist	un violeur
a sex offender	un délinquant sexuel
to mug sb, to attack sb	agresser qn

In Shiner, Texas, there's little doubt among residents that a 23-year-old man who reportedly killed a man he found molesting (*agresser sexuellement*) his 5-year-old daughter should be hailed as a hero, not denounced as a criminal. Yet some legal experts question why the father hasn't yet been arrested and charged with murder, saying vigilante justice, no matter how the circumstances come about, can't be tolerated in a civil society. A Texas grand jury will have to deal with those questions next week as it takes a deeper look at the circumstances of the killing, and whether the father was justified in hitting the man so hard with his fists (*poings*) that he died.
The Christian Science Monitor, 16 June 2012

theft	le vol
a thief, a robber	un voleur
a burglar	un cambrioleur
to steal a watch	voler une montre
to rob sb of sth	voler qch à qn

armed robbery	vol à main armée
money-laundering	le blanchiment d'argent
lawful / unlawful	légal / illégal
to break a law	enfreindre une loi
a lawbreaker	un délinquant, une personne qui enfreint la loi
to obey the law	obéir à la loi
to abide by the law [ə'baɪd]	respecter la loi

New York's police stopped nearly 700,000 people last year, according to a New York Civil Liberties Union report that uses police data. More than half of those were also frisked. A weapon was found in less than 2% of searches. More than half of all stops were of blacks and a third were of Latinos. Young black and Latino men make up less than 5% of the city's population, but more than 40% of those stopped. More young black males — 168,126 — were stopped by police last year than live in the city (158,406).
Police are allowed to stop anyone briefly, but only upon reasonable suspicion that they are about to commit or are committing a crime. Critics think that racial profiling is playing a part.
The Economist, 2 June 2012

the justice system	la justice, le système judiciaire
a court, a court of law	un tribunal
a judge [dʒʌdʒ]	un juge
a lawyer, a barrister (GB), an attorney (US)	un avocat
to prosecute sb	poursuivre qn (en justice)
the prosecutor	le procureur
to sue sb [suː]	intenter un procès à qn, engager des poursuites contre qn
to suspect sb of stealing sth	soupçonner qn d'avoir volé qch
to charge sb with murder	accuser, inculper qn de meurtre
a charge	une accusation, un chef d'inculpation
to confess to a crime	avouer un crime
confession	un aveu
a defendant	un accusé, un prévenu

The French verb "condamner" corresponds to several verbs in English. At the end of a trial, when a jury gives their verdict, the accused may be acquitted (if the evidence against him or her is not sufficient) or **convicted**, that is to say **found guilty**. If the defendant is convicted, the judge then **sentences** him or her to, say, 6 months' imprisonment or a £300 fine. The verb **condemn** can refer to the same notion (e.g. He was condemned to death for murder) but is mostly used in non-legal contexts in which it means expressing strong disapproval of something (e.g. Politicians of all stripes (*de tout bord*) condemned the bomb attack that took place last night).

a case [keɪs]	une affaire
a trial ['traɪəl]	un procès

to be tried, to stand trial	passer en jugement, être jugé
forensic evidence	preuves relevées lors d'une expertise médicolégale
a witness / an eye witness	un témoin / un témoin oculaire
a culprit ['kʌlprɪt]	un coupable
a conviction	une condamnation
to convict sb, to find sb guilty	condamner qn, reconnaître qn coupable
a fine	une amende
to fine sb	condamner qn à une amende
a life sentence	une condamnation à perpétuité
a suspended sentence	une condamnation avec sursis
to sentence sb to death	condamner qn à mort
to be sentenced to five years' imprisonment, five years in jail	être condamné à cinq ans de prison
to appeal against a decision	faire appel d'une décision
a miscarriage of justice	une erreur judiciaire
a wrongful conviction	une condamnation à tort
to quash, to overturn a decision	casser une décision (*de justice*)
to prove sb innocent, to exonerate sb	innocenter qn
DNA analysis, DNA testing	les tests ADN

LOUISIANA DEATH ROW INMATE FREED AFTER 15 YEARS – WITH A LITTLE HELP FROM DNA

Damon Thibodeaux has been proved innocent of a crime for which Louisiana has spent 15 years trying to kill him. He walked out of Angola jail in Louisiana as the 300th prisoner in the US to be freed as a result of DNA testing and one of 18 exonerated from death row. With the help of science, he has been proved innocent of a crime for which the state of Louisiana spent 15 years trying to kill him. For those years Thibodeaux was in a cell 1.8m x 3m for 23 hours a day. His only consolation was reading the Bible; his only exercise pacing up and down for an hour a day in a the "exercise yard" — a metal cage slightly larger than his cell. Like most death rows in the United States, the prisoners in Angola are treated as living dead things: they are going to be executed so why bother rehabilitating them?

The Guardian, Friday 7, December 2012

to jail sb, to incarcerate sb, to imprison sb	incarcérer qn
a prisoner, an inmate	un détenu, un prisonnier
a prison officer, a prison warder ['wɔːdəʳ] (GB)	un gardien de prison
prison overcrowding	la surpopulation carcérale
to free, to release a prisoner	libérer, relâcher un prisonnier
to parole sb [pə'rəʊl]	mettre qn en liberté conditionnelle
to be on parole	être en liberté conditionnelle
an electronic tag	un bracelet de surveillance électronique

With 730 people out of every 100,000 in jail, America now has the highest incarceration rate in the world. In the past thirty years, its prison population has grown from 300,000 inmates to 2.2 million. Moreover, it is worth noting that 70% of all convicts in US prisons are African Americans.

capital punishment, the death penalty	la peine de mort, la peine capitale
a death sentence	une condamnation à mort
to be on death row	être dans les couloirs de la mort
to commute a death sentence to life	commuer une condamnation à mort en réclusion à perpétuité
to grant a convict a stay of execution, a reprieve [rɪ'priːv]	surseoir à l'exécution d'un condamné
to pardon ['pɑːdən] a convict	grâcier un condamné

In the past, **capital punishment** was used in most countries, but it has now been abolished in many of them —for instance in Britain in 1969 and in France in 1981. Belarus (*la Biélorussie*) is the only European country that still uses it. Singapore, Japan and the U.S. are the only developed countries that have kept it and in the US, 14 of the 50 states have abolished it. China carries out several thousand executions every year, by far the largest number in the world. By comparison, in the early 2010s, about 40 people have been put to death every year in the United States.

to execute a convict	executer un condamné
to put sb to death	mettre qn à mort
a lethal injection	une piqûre mortelle
to inject sb with a lethal substance	faire une piqûre mortelle à qn
to hang sb	pendre qn
the electric chair	la chaise électrique
to stone sb to death	lapider qn, tuer qn à coups de pierre
to abolish, to do away with capital punishment	abolir la peine capitale
an abolitionist	un abolitionniste, un partisan de l'abolition de la peine de mort
to reinstate, to reintroduce the death penalty	rétablir la peine de mort

firearms	les armes à feu
a gun	une arme à feu
an assault [ə'sɔːlt] rifle	un fusil d'assaut
a bullet ['bʊlɪt]	une balle
to shoot	tirer
a shooting	des coups de feu, une fusillade
gunfire, gunfight	coups de feu, fusillade
a gunman	un homme armé

School massacres are quite frequent in the United States. Even if it was not the deadliest, the **Columbine High School massacre**, which took place in April 1999 and resulted in the deaths of 13 people (apart from the two murderers who committed suicide), is remembered by many as one of the most shocking because its perpetrators and most of their victims were teenagers. Another killing took place in December 2012, when a twenty-year old shot 26 people, including 20 children under seven, in the village of Sandy Hook, Connecticut.

a gun-owner	propriétaire d'armes à feu
to bear, to carry a gun	porter une arme
to register ['redʒɪstəʳ] a gun	déclarer une arme
a gun permit, a gun license	un permis de port d'arme
the gun lobby	le lobby des armes à feu
a gun maker, a gun manufacturer	un fabricant d'armes
to take the law into one's own hands	se faire justice
self-defence	la légitime défense
a vigilante [ˌvɪdʒɪ'læntɪ]	un membre d'un groupe d'autodéfense

The National Rifle Association of America, or NRA [ˌenɑːr'eɪ], an organization whose goal is the promotion of gun ownership in the US, has close links with the Republican Party. It boasts nearly four million members and is said to be the single most powerful lobbying organization in the US. The NRA is the main element of the gun lobby and is largely funded by gun-makers such as Smith and Wesson, the largest manufacturers of handguns in the US. It has used studies to argue that increasing gun ownership diminishes violent crime. On balance (*dans l'ensemble*), however, the evidence suggests the opposite: more guns mean more deaths.

a slaughter, a massacre ['mæsəkəʳ]	un massacre
to be trigger-happy	avoir la gâchette facile
to go on a killing spree, a shooting spree, a shooting rampage	être pris d'un accès de folie meurtrière
to injure sb, to wound sb [wuːnd]	blesser qn
a corpse [kɔːps]	un cadavre
gun control	la réglementation du port d'armes
to restrict access to guns	limiter l'accès aux armes

Director Gus Van Sant's **Elephant** (2003) is an exploration of the way violence can make its way into a typical American high school, partly based on the tragedy that occurred in Columbine High School, Colorado. It describes the lives of two adolescents living in a well-to-do suburb of Portland (Oregon). The two boys are fascinated by Nazi imagery, enjoy violent videogames and eventually buy rifles over the Internet to ambush their schoolmates. The film was awarded the Golden Palm at the 2003 Cannes Festival.

LANGUAGE PRACTICE

1. What is the correct translation of the following faux-amis?

to charge sb ....

to confess ....

to pardon sb ....

a corpse ....

2. Choose the appropriate word in the following contexts.

Someone in the metro tried to (rob / steal) my wallet.

In most countries, capital punishment has now been replaced by a (life / death) sentence.

Ms Mantel was accused of (murder / manslaughter) after it was established that she had killed her husband accidentally.

The parents of the dead boy decided to (sue / prosecute) the hospital for gross negligence.

3. Find the appropriate endings to form the missing words.

un voleur	a thief	....	*le vol*
une arme à feu	a gun	....	*un homme armé*
juger	to try	....	*un procès*
assassiner	to murder	....	*un assassin*

4. Find the nouns corresponding to these definitions.

A .... is the cruel killing of large numbers of people.

A .... is someone who tries to prevent crime or punish criminals, often because they think the police are not doing their job effectively.

A .... is a small piece of metal that is fired from a gun.

A .... in a court of law is the person who has been accused of doing something illegal.

5. All the following compound nouns include the word "crime"

la petite délinquance ....
la criminalité organisée ....
le taux de criminalité ....
la criminalité en col blanc ....

6. Translate into French.

In Antiquity, it was very common to demand an eye for an eye and a tooth for a tooth.

....

According to the Declaration of Human Rights, a defendant is innocent until proven guilty.

....

Many convicts on death row spend decades in jail.

....

If you own a gun, you may be tempted to take the law into your own hands.

....

Dozens of convicts have now been cleared by DNA analysis.

....

7. Translate into English.

Le comptable a avoué avoir détourné 40 000 euros l'an dernier.

....

C'est pourquoi il a été condamné à six mois de prison.

....

Proportionnellement, les États-Unis ont la population carcérale la plus importante du monde entier.

....

Eric agissait en état de légitime défense et il a donc plaidé non coupable.

....

La peine de mort a-t-elle vraiment un effet dissuasif ?

....

Questions

How can people be deterred from turning to crime?
How come a developed nation like the United States still retains the death penalty?
Should people be allowed to own firearms?

WRITING TIP N° 13: Authenticity

Writing authentic English does not mean embellishing one's prose by adding a metaphor, an idiomatic phrase or a link-word here and there: it means using the words and expressions that native English speakers use spontaneously. Authentic (or idiomatic) English is not just grammatically correct: it is also English that does not look or sound as if it has been translated from the French.

To do that, you need first to be aware of what characterizes English as opposed to French. Even when the literal translation of a French word, expression or structure is perfectly comprehensible, there may be another one which sounds more "natural" to the ear of a native English speaker.

This may concern the grammar. As you have already seen, you should use fewer link-words and punctuation marks than you would in French. The passive form is used much more often in English than in French (and is often the best equivalent of the French idiomatic pronoun "*on*", see WRITING TIP N° 17). You have probably been told about "used to + infinitive", a verb form which has no equivalent in French and is used to insist on the contrast between a past situation and the present. Another example is modal verbs such as "can, may, must, will etc." (see WRITING TIP N° 18), so that for instance, instead of systematically using the adverb "maybe", you should think of "may" (e.g. "He may have changed his mind" instead of "Maybe he changed his mind.")

But writing idiomatic English also means choosing words carefully, even simple ones. For instance, short words are often preferable to long ones: "to use" is much more common than "to utilise", which means the same; "about" is more widely* used, and hence more idiomatic than its synonym "approximately"; "oil*" is much more common than "petroleum*", a technical term; "phenomenon", originally a Greek word, is possible but when you refer to what the French call "un phénomène de société", the English word "trend" comes to mind; the same goes for "enough" which is preferable to "sufficient", the verb "to list" to "to enumerate", "huge" to "enormous", "tiny" to "minuscule" and so on…

As some of the above examples show, you should also prefer words of Anglo-Saxon origin to words originating in Latin, which look similar to their French translations. Thus "aware" can be said to be more idiomatic than its synonym "conscious"; "to inundate" means the same as "to flood" but is mostly used metaphorically (e.g. We've been inundated with offers of help) so when you mean the literal sense of "inonder", you must use "to flood"; likewise*, "pacific" is far less common than its synonym "peaceful".

For the same reason it is advisable* to use phrasal verbs (verbs combined with an adverb or a preposition or both). Thus instead of "to increase", think of "to go up"; instead of "to represent", use "account for" or "stand for" depending on the context; instead of "resist", use "stand up to"; instead of "eliminate", use "cut out" or "dispose of" depending on the context.

widely: *couramment* • **oil, petroleum**: *le pétrole* • **likewise**: *de la même façon* • **advisable**: *conseillé*

14. TERRORISM

abortion • advertising • AIDS • alcohol abuse • armed forces • asbestos • bonuses • BRICS • cloning • CO_2 • computers • consumer society • couch potatoes • **9/11** creationism • credit bubble • cultural exception • dating • DEA • death **fanaticism** penalty • deforestation • dictatorship • digital piracy • diplomacy • domestic violence • drought • drug trafficking • eating disorders • endangered species **CIA** • English-speaking world • epidemics • euthanasia • food scares • fossil fuels • free speech • free trade • gender gap • glass ceiling • greenhouse gases • guinea pigs • gun control • health care • human rights • immigration policy • intercourse • ISPs • IVF • justice system • labour • multiculturalism • NASA • natural disasters • NGOs • nuclear • nuclear deterrent • oil slicks • on parole • outsourcing • **hijacking** overfishing • ozone layer • PC • pension system • philanthropy • physics • pidgin • prevention • racial profiling • **suicide bombers** recycling • renewables • RP • salad bowl • same-sex marriage • second-hand smoking • serial killers • sex industry • slump • social divide • social networks • Spanglish • standard English • STDs • stem-cell research • suffragettes • surrogacy • surveillance • technophobia • teenage violence • truancy • United Nations • uprisings • video games • waste disposal • welfare state • WMDs • working poor • WTO

a terrorist	un terroriste
a terrorist attack	un attentat (terroriste)
a bomb [bɒm] attack, a bombing ['bɒmɪŋ]	un attentat à la bombe
an attempted bomb attack	une tentative d'attentat
a failed bomb attack	un attentat manqué
a terrorist plot	un complot terroriste
homegrown terrorism	le terrorisme « d'origine intérieure »
a plotter	un comploteur
a conspiracy [kən'spɪrəsɪ]	une conspiration, un complot
a target	une cible
to target an embassy	viser, avoir pour cible une ambassade

Homegrown terrrorism is the use of threats or violence by an individual born, raised or operating primarily within a country to intimidate or coerce (*contraindre*) his or her government for political ends.

a terrorist organization	une organisation terroriste
to resort to violence	avoir recours à la violence
to terrorize	terroriser
to scare, to frighten people	faire peur aux gens
scare tactics	terrorisme psychologique
blackmail	le chantage
to blackmail sb	faire chanter qn
to intimidate sb	intimider qn
indiscriminate violence	la violence aveugle
to sow [səʊ] fear	semer la terreur
obsessive fear	la psychose
panic	la panique
to panic	paniquer

Faisal Shahzad, a Pakistani-born American citizen, attempted to detonate an improvised bomb inside a car in the heart of Times Square on May 1st, 2010. Street vendors noticed the smoking SUV and alerted the authorities who quickly evacuated the area and defused the device. The alarming thing is that it was an inside job. Mr Shahzad seemed to be living the American dream. He came to America as a student, eventually earning his MBA. He married, had two children, worked as a financial analyst and owned a house in suburban Connecticut. Yet, according to the authorities, he recently received bomb-making training in Waziristan, probably from the Pakistani Taliban. Fortunately, he seems to have been a poor student in that subject.
The Economist, May 6th 2010, New York

a threat [θret]	une menace
to threaten	menacer
to give in to a threat, to yield to a threat	céder à une menace
to carry out a threat	exécuter une menace
a bomb threat	une menace d'attentat à la bombe
a bomb scare	une alerte à la bombe

a bomb hoax [həʊks] — une fausse alerte à la bombe
a vulnerable site — un site sensible

A **booby trap** is a bomb that is hidden inside something that looks safe and explodes when you touch it or something connected to it.

9/11 [naɪn ɪ'levn]	le 11 septembre
a suicide bomber ['sʊɪsaɪd 'bɒmər]	un kamikaze
to commit suicide, kill oneself	se suicider
to plant a bomb	poser un bombe
to detonate, to set off a bomb ['detəneɪt]	faire exploser une bombe
to go off, to explode	exploser
an explosive device [dɪ'vaɪs]	un engin explosif
an explosive [ɪk'spləʊsɪv]	un explosif
plastic explosive	le plastique
Semtex	le semtex
an explosive mixture	un mélange détonant, un mélange explosif
a time bomb	une bombe à retardement
a letter bomb	une lettre piégée
a booby trap	un objet piégé
a car bomb..... une voiture piégée	
to defuse [diː'fjuːz] a bomb	désarmorcer une bombe

9/11 (pronounced "nine-eleven", also called **the September 11 attacks**) were a series of coordinated suicide attacks on the United States that took place on September 11, 2001. The terrorists hijacked four airplanes and crashed them into the Twin Towers of the World Trade Center in New York City and into the Pentagon in Arlington, Virginia. They caused the deaths of 2,974 people. A similar shock was caused by the bombings that took place in Madrid on 11 March, 2004 and in London on July 7, 2005 (sometimes referred to as **the 7/7 bombings**), killing 56 people on three underground trains and on a bus. Mumbai had its own "9/11" on 26 November, 2008.

a casualty ['kæʒjʊltɪ], a victim	une victime
to be injured	être blessé
to be maimed [meɪmd]	être mutilé
the death toll	le nombre de victimes
a slaughter, a massacre ['mæsəkər]	un massacre
carnage ['kɑːnɪdʒ]	un carnage
bloodshed ['blʌdʃed]	une effusion de sang, un massacre

The verbs **injure** and **wound** both mean "to cause physical harm". But the latter is used specifically to harm caused by a weapon such as a gun or knife, and is therefore used mostly to describe what may happen to soldiers on the battlefield or to the victims of a gunman or a bomb attack (e.g. to be mortally wounded). When talking about people suffering physical harm as a consequence of an accident, earthquake etc., you should use **injure** or **hurt** (e.g. Fifty people died and hundreds were injured in the earthquake). You should use **damage** to refer to what happens to things (e.g. The house was damaged beyond repair).

the war on terror	la guerre contre le terrorisme
to tackle terrorism	s'attaquer au terrorisme
to combat, to fight terrorism	combattre, lutter contre le terrorisme
counterterrorism	le contre-terrorisme
the battle, the fight against terrorism	la lutte antiterroriste
to thwart [θwɔːt] a plot	faire échouer un complot
to foil [fɔɪl] a terrorist attack	déjouer, faire échouer un attentat
to dismantle a terrorist network	démanteler un réseau terroriste
to eradicate terrorism	éradiquer le terrorisme

After the 2005 bomb attacks on the London public transport system, New York began erecting a "ring of steel" in Lower Manhattan, outfitting (*équiper*) a 1.5-square-mile area with 3,000 surveillance cameras and radiation detectors. City and state officials are pushing Washington to provide an additional $24 million to expand the protective barrier to Midtown, which would include Times Square as well as Grand Central Terminal and Penn Station. But city leaders face the problem of how to further circle the wagons without turning New York into a U.S. version of the Green Zone, the fortified enclave in Baghdad. "There is a balance between being so safe you can't go out of your house, and enjoying freedom — freedom to come and go, and to talk and to be in charge of your own destiny," Bloomberg said.
Los Angeles Times, May 08, 2010, Tina Susman and Geraldine Baum

intelligence	le renseignement
an intelligence agency ['eɪdʒənsi]	un service de renseignement
security measures	mesures de sécurité
to tighten security	renforcer les mesures de sécurité
to intercept a message	intercepter un message
to monitor phone calls	surveiller les appels téléphoniques
extraordinary rendition	transfert illégal de détenus vers des prisons où ils peuvent être torturés
waterboarding	simulation de noyade

For most British journalists today, the idea of non-Muslim terrorism perpetrated by non-Irish white folk is inconceivable. Why? Because too many of them reflexively subscribe to the notion that maybe not all Muslims are terrorists, but certainly all terrorists are Muslims. Figures compiled by Europol, the European police agency, suggest that the threat of Islamist terrorism is minimal compared with "ethno-nationalist" and "separatist" terrorism — terrorism committed by white people, in other words. According to Europol, in 2006, one out of 498 documented terrorist attacks across Europe could be classed as "Islamist"; in 2007, the figure rose to just four out of 583 — that's less than 1 per cent of the total. By contrast, 517 attacks across the continent were claimed by or attributed to nationalist or separatist terrorist groups, such as ETA in Spain.
New Statesman, 9 July 2009

a fanatic, a zealot ['zelət]	un fanatique
fanaticism [fə'nætɪsɪzəm]	le fanatisme
a fundamentalist	un intégriste
fundamentalism	l'intégrisme
bigotry	le sectarisme
an extremist	un extrémiste
the Axis of Evil	l'axe du mal
a rogue [rəʊg] state	un État-voyou
to sponsor terrorism	soutenir le terrorisme
to harbour ['hɑːbəʳ] terrorists	héberger, abriter des terroristes
to foster violence	encourager la violence

My Name is Khan is a 2010 film which tells the story of an Indian Muslim, Rizwan Khan, who marries a Hindu woman after moving to San Francisco. After 9/11, they experience anti-Islam prejudice and their small son is killed in a racially motivated schoolyard fight. His shattered mother then accuses the boy's father of being responsible for his death because "his name is Khan" and tells him she no longer wants to live with him. He sets out on a journey across the United States and is mistakenly arrested as a terrorist suspect even if he has just reported to the FBI a Muslim cleric preaching racial hatred in a mosque. Khan is later able to prove his innocence with the help of a psychiatrist and two journalists who obtain his release from jail and he regains the love of his wife.

It may be worth noting that 14 of the 17 men involved in 9/11 came from wealthy Saudi Arabian families.

a hostage ['hɒstɪdʒ]	un otage
to take / hold sb hostage	prendre / retenir qn en otage
to be taken hostage	être pris en otage
to free, to release a hostage	libérer, relâcher un otage
to abduct sb, to kidnap sb	kidnapper, enlever qn

an abduction, a kidnapping	un enlèvement, un kidnapping, un rapt
a hostage-taker, an abductor, a kidnapper, a captor	un ravisseur, un preneur d'otage
a ransom ['rænsəm]	une rançon
to negotiate [nɪ'gəʊʃɪeɪt]	négocier
hijacking	détournement d'avion
to hijack ['haɪdʒæk] a plane	détourner un avion
a hijacker	un pirate de l'air

Hostages sometimes end up feeling sorry for their captors, sometimes to the point of defending them, despite the suffering they have to endure. This psychological phenomenon is known as **Stockholm syndrome**. According to the FBI, roughly 27% of hostages show evidence of Stockholm syndrome.

LANGUAGE PRACTICE

1. Find the verbs corresponding to the following definitions.

To .... a bomb is to remove the fuse to prevent it from exploding.

To .... a plane or a ship is to use violence to take control of it.

To .... someone is to force them to do something they don't want to do by threatening them.

To .... terrorism is to get rid of it completely and for ever.

2. The following words are both nouns and verbs. Translate.

	NOUN	VERB
plot	....	....
fear	....	....
harbour	....	....
target	....	....

3. The spelling of the following words is almost the same as in French.

une conspiration	....
le fanatisme	....
un otage	....
démanteler	....

4. Find the missing words in the following sentences.

The .... bomber was maimed when the explosive device he was carrying went off accidentally.

The phrase " .... state" is a controversial term used mostly by the US to describe dangerous authoritarian regimes such as Iran, North Korea or Sudan.

Someone called the police saying a device would explode at 4.30 pm, but nothing happened: it was a bomb ....

The death .... in the 1995 sarin gas attacks in the Tokyo subway system eventually rose to 13.

5. Find synonyms for the following verbs.

to foil a plot ....
to scare people ....
to combat terrorism ....
to yield to a threat ....

6. Translate into French.

No-one has claimed responsibility for last week's bomb attack yet.

....

A spate of bombings hit Paris in the late eighties.

....

A dozen people were killed in the attack which took place last night.

....

Many analysts think that terrorism is here to stay.

....

The hijackers attempted to blackmail the Israeli authorities into freeing some prisoners.

....

7. Translate into English.

Ils ne se rendent pas compte qu'en recourant à la violence, ils discréditent leur cause.

....

Un groupe d'extrême-droite a fait sauter plusieurs bâtiments officiels.

....

La CIA a pu démanteler plusieurs réseaux terroristes islamistes en 2010.

....

L'expression de l'Administration Bush, « la guerre contre la terreur », ne veut pas dire grand-chose.

....

Le terrorisme sera-t-il jamais éradiqué ?

....

Questions

When will terrorism be eradicated?
Terrorism and the media.
How should terrorist threats be dealt with?

WRITING TIP N° 14: Rhetorical questions and other attention-seeking devices*

In an essay, it is a good idea to ask rhetorical questions, i.e.* questions you do not expect your reader to answer (e.g. "Why do so many Americans oppose gun control?"). Asking a question is a way of attracting your reader's attention. It is also the construction that comes naturally to mind when you pose a problem. You may ask a rhetorical question in the introduction, but also at the beginning of a paragraph or as a conclusion.

When forming a question, do remember to introduce an auxiliary if necessary and to place it before the subject (e.g. Why do people distrust politicians?) if the question is in direct speech. But if the subject of the verb is the interrogative word or phrase at the beginning, no auxiliary is needed (e.g. Which country produces the largest number of cars in the world?")

It is possible to form many questions starting with "how" followed by an adjective or adverb. Many of these questions cannot be translated literally. (e.g. "How serious is the crisis?" → "*Quelle est la gravité de la crise ?*", "How likely are the Democrats to win the next election?" → "*Quelles sont les chances des Démocrates de gagner les prochaines élections ?*", "How far can it be said that...?" → "*Dans quelle mesure peut-on dire que... ?*").

You can also address your reader directly. "Would *you* agree to eat meat from a cloned animal? *I* certainly wouldn't", underlining the pronouns "you, I" to suggest the emphasis.

Another way of lifting your examiner out of the torpor which threatens anyone who spends hours marking papers is to use exclamations. (e.g. "What a shame!", "How interesting!"). Don't do it too often, though, as it may become irritating.

The imperative is yet another way of catching your reader's attention. Instead of writing "We can take the example of Poland*", a more dynamic approach would be to write: "Let us take the example of Poland" Here is another example: "Let's face it*: there is no easy way out* of the current crisis". The imperative in the second person is also possible: "Take the case of Poland". Here is another example: "Even if it claims to be a model democracy, the US sometimes seems to be living in the Middle Ages. Think of the death penalty".

attention-seeking devices: *procédés pour attirer l'attention* • **i.e.**: *c'est-à-dire* • **Poland**: *la Pologne* • **Let's face it**: *Regardons les choses en face* • **way out**: *issue*

15. INTERNATIONAL RELATIONS

9/11 • abortion • advertising • AIDS • alcohol abuse • asbestos • bonuses • BRICS • CIA • cloning • CO_2 • computers • consumer society • couch potatoes **armed forces** • creationism • credit bubble • cultural exception • dating • DEA • death penalty • deforestation • dictatorship • digital piracy • domestic violence • drought • drug **diplomacy** trafficking • eating disorders • endangered species • English-speaking world • epidemics • euthanasia • fanaticism • food scares • fossil fuels • free speech • free trade • gender gap • glass ceiling • greenhouse gases • guinea pigs • gun control • health care • hijacking • human rights • immigration **nuclear deterrent** policy • intercourse • ISPs • IVF • justice system • labour • multiculturalism • NASA • natural disasters • NGOs • nuclear • oil slicks • on parole • outsourcing • overfishing • ozone layer • PC • pension system • philanthropy • physics • pidgin • prevention • racial profiling • recycling • renewables • RP • salad bowl • same-sex marriage • second-hand smoking • serial killers • **United Nations** sex industry **WMDs** • slump • social divide • social networks • Spanglish • standard English • STDs • stem-cell research • suffragettes • suicide bombers • surrogacy • surveillance • technophobia • teenage violence • truancy • uprisings • video games • waste disposal • welfare state • working poor • WTO

the world stage, the international stage	la scène internationale
a sovereign ['sɒvrɪn] state	un État souverain
sovereignty	la souveraineté
international law	le droit international
foreign ['fɒrən] affairs	les affaires étrangères
foreign policy	la politique étrangère, extérieure

Jawaharlal Nehru's nonalignment policy continues to hover (*planer*) over India's foreign relations. Later this month, New Delhi will host its first BRICS summit, a gathering of authoritarian and democratic nations united only by regional heft (*poids*) and implicit opposition to the U.S.-led international order. Instead of using an ongoing two-year term (2011 to 2013) on the U.N. Security Council to underscore its democratic credentials, India has mostly sided with the Russians and the Chinese in their battles on behalf of Bashar al-Assad and the late (*feu*) Muammar al-Qaddafi. Does this really sound like the foreign policy of America's new strategic partner? India's behavior reflects an ongoing battle in New Delhi for the soul of Indian foreign policy. On one side you have those for whom a go-it-alone attitude is an end in itself. Arrayed against this view are those who say nonalignment has outlived its purpose, and seek to strengthen mutually beneficial ties with the West.
Sadanand Dhume, March 16, 2012, *Foreign Policy*

geopolitics	la géopolitique
a diplomat	un diplomate
diplomacy [dɪ'pləʊməsɪ]	diplomatie
to break off / resume diplomatic relations	rompre / reprendre les relations
a superpower / a hyperpower	une superpuissance / une hyperpuissance
hegemony [hɪ'dʒeməni, hɪ'geməni]	l'hégémonie
imperialistic (adj)	impérialiste
balance of power	l'équilibre des forces

In 1945 there were 53 sovereign states but in 2011, there were 193.

the UN system	le système onusien
a member state	un État-membre, un pays membre
to implement, enforce a resolution	appliquer une résolution
to impose sanctions on a country	imposer des sanctions à un pays
an embargo (pl: embargoes) [ɪm'bɑːgəʊ]	un embargo
to maintain peace	maintenir la paix
a peace-keeping operation	une opération de maintien de la paix
a blue helmet	un casque bleu
the duty to interfere, to intervene [ˌɪntə'viːn]	le devoir d'ingérence
the European Union, the EU	l'Union européenne, l'UE
to join the EU	adhérer à l'UE
to apply to join the EU, to apply for EU membership	demander son adhésion à l'UE

Britain has long had ambivalent feelings towards the European club it joined in 1973. Sceptical of grand projects like the single currency, it has directed its diplomatic efforts towards freeing up trade and expanding the membership of the European Union. But it has also sought to retain influence within the EU. That changed at a summit of European leaders on December 8th, when David Cameron, the British prime minister, refused to agree to a fiscal compact (*paquet fiscal*) designed to safeguard the euro's future. MPs from his largely Eurosceptic Conservative Party were delighted. Some now want Britain to leave the EU altogether and, like Norway or Switzerland, have a limited trading relationship with the club. Polls suggest that almost half of British voters agree. But opponents argue that a medium-sized power like Britain can only exert international influence through the EU.
The Economist, January 2012

to negotiate [nɪ'gəʊʃɪeɪt]	négocier
negotiations, talks	négociations, pourparlers, discussions
to make, issue a statement	faire une déclaration
a communiqué [kə'mjuːnɪkeɪ]	un communiqué
a summit (meeting)	une réunion au sommet, un sommet
a spokesman, spokeswoman, spokesperson	un porte-parole
a counterpart, an opposite number	un homologue
a stalemate, a deadlock, a stand-off	une impasse
to reach / break a stalemate	aboutir à une impasse / sortir d'une impasse
to broker ['brəʊkəʳ] an agreement	négocier un accord
a compromise ['kɒmprəmaɪz]	un compromis
to compromise	transiger
to sign / ratify a treaty	signer / ratifier un traité
to reach a settlement	conclure un accord
to veto ['viːtəʊ] a decision	mettre son véto à une décision
an NGO [ˌendʒiː'əʊ], a non-governmental organization	une ONG, une organisation non-gouvernementale
human rights	les droits de l'homme
human rights abuses, violations	les violations des droits de l'homme

In *Bound to Lead: The Changing Nature of American Power* (1990), Joseph S. Nye pioneered the theory of **soft power**, that is to say the ability for a country to influence the behaviour of other states through attraction and persuasion rather than force. Soft power is opposed to **hard power**, which involves the use of military forces and / or economic coercion. Soft power relies essentially on diplomatic and cultural ties between countries and aims at "winning people's hearts and minds", as the phrase goes. Governments may actively seek to expand their soft power, but a country's soft power may also be furthered or hindered by the action of its prominent citizens or the international image of its companies. For instance, the American film-making industry is thought to have popularized the American way of life throughout the world since WWII, thus indirectly contributing to the collapse of the Communist ideology.

an armed conflict	un conflit armé
military / civilian	militaire / civil
enemy ['enəmi]	ennemi
warmongering	la propagande belliciste
militaristic	militariste
to be at war / at peace	être en guerre / en paix
to declare war on a country	déclarer la guerre à un pays
to wage war on an enemy, against an enemy	faire la guerre à un ennemi
an ally ['ælaɪ]	un allié
to conquer ['kɒŋkə(r)]	conquérir
conquest	la conquête
to invade	envahir

The distinction between **patriotism** and **nationalism** is a subtle one and has evolved over time. To put it in a nutshell, patriots love their country and are willing to defend it if necessary, but nationalists think their nation is better than any other. Romain Gary, a French novelist, expressed this crucial nuance in a pithy (*concis*) phrase: whereas patriotism means loving one's country, he said, nationalism means hating all the others.

armed forces	les forces armées
troops	les troupes
a serviceman, a soldier	un militaire, un soldat
a professional soldier, a career soldier	un militaire de carrière
to join the Air Force, to enlist in the Air Force	s'engager, s'enrôler dans l'armée de l'air
to withdraw troops from a place	retirer des troupes d'un endroit
withdrawal [wɪθ'drɔːəl]	le retrait
a blockade [blɒ'keɪd]	un blocus
to defeat an adversary	vaincre un adversaire
to retaliate against sb	user de représailles envers qn
a prisoner of war, a POW	un prisonnier de guerre
NATO, the North Atlantic Treaty Organization	l'OTAN

NATO (that is to say the North Atlantic Treaty Organization) is a military alliance that was created in 1949 and has 28 members, including the US, most of Europe as well as Turkey.

The phrase **friendly fire** is used when people are injured or killed by bombs or weapons fired by their own side. This notion should not be confused with that of **collateral damage**, which is damage inflicted on civilians or ordinary buildings instead of military personnel or installations.

weapons, arms	des armes
weapons of mass destruction, WMDs [ˌdʌbljʊem'diːz]	des armes de destruction massive

a bomb [bɒm]	une bombe
to bomb	bombarder
a bombing, a bombardment	un bombardement
a bomber ['bɒməʳ]	un bombardier
smart weapons	des armes intelligentes
a surgical strike	une frappe chirurgicale

It is far cheaper to move electrons across the globe than to move large ships across long distances. The costs of deploying multiple carrier forces (*porte-avions*) and submarine fleets create enormous barriers to entry, enabling US naval dominance. Mountains and oceans are hard to move, but portions of cyberspace can be turned on and off by throwing a switch. The barriers of entry in the cyber domain are so low that non-state actors and small states can play a significant role at low cost.
Joseph Nye, *AlJazeera*, 21 April 2012

a stealth [stelθ] **bomber**	un bombardier furtif
an aircraft carrier	un porte-avions
a fighter (plane)	un avion de chasse, un chasseur
nuclear / biological / chemical warfare ['wɔːfeə]	la guerre nucléaire / biologique / chimique
the wounded	les blessés
the casualties ['kæʒjʊltɪz]	les morts et les blessés
intelligence	le renseignement
to spy on an enemy	espionner un ennemi

Syriana is a 2005 thriller directed by and starring George Clooney about the oil industry in several countries from Kazakhstan to the Persian Gulf to Texas to Switzerland and Lebanon. It involves oil traders but also arms dealers, Arab princes, Washington lobbyists, Hezbollah fanatics etc and uses multiple story lines that make the film nearly impossible to understand. The complexity of these interlocking plots (*intrigue*) and sub-plots is meant to give viewers and idea of the complexity of the politics of oil, which no-one, not even oil company executives or CIA spies totally understand.

a war crime [kraɪm]	un crime de guerre
a war criminal	un criminel de guerre
a crime against humanity	un crime contre l'humanité
a genocide ['dʒenəʊsaɪd]	un génocide
ethnic cleansing ['klenzɪŋ]	purification ethnique

Ethnic cleansing is the systematic attempt by a racial or political group to remove from a country or an area anyone belonging to another particular group. It is akin to (*apparenté* à) **genocide**.

peace talks	des pourparlers de paix
the peace process	le processus de paix
a peace agreement, a peace settlement	un accord de paix
a peace treaty	un traité de paix
the peace dividend	le dividende de la paix
disarmament	le désarmement
a veteran, a vet	un ancien combattant
Post Traumatic Stress Disorder, PTSD	névrose post-traumatique

The **International Criminal Court** (*Cour pénale internationale*) was set up in 2002 to investigate war crimes, genocide and crimes against humanity. Russia and the US have signed the treaty creating the ICC but not ratified it.

nuclear weapons, nuclear arms	les armes nucléaires
weapons of mass destruction, WMDs [ˌdʌbljʊem'diːz]	les armes de destruction massive
the arms race	la course aux armements
a nuclear umbrella	un parapluie nucléaire
nuclear capability [ˌkeɪpə'bɪlɪtɪ]	la capacité nucléaire
nuclear weapons facilities [fə'sɪlɪtɪz]	des installations de production d'armes nucléaires
the nuclear deterrent [dɪ'terənt]	la dissuasion nucléaire
nuclear testing	les essais nucléaires
a rogue state	un État-voyou
to conduct [kən'dʌkt] a test	réaliser un essai
nuclear fallout ['fɔːlaʊt]	les retombées d'une explosion nucléaire
a short-range / long-range missile	un missile courte / longue portée
an intercontinental ballistic missile, an ICBM	un missile balistique inter-continental
an anti-missile defence system	un bouclier anti-missile

Apart from the five permanent members of the UN Security Council (China, France, Russia, the United Kingdom and the United States), only four states have acquired nuclear weapons: Israel, India, Pakistan and North Korea. A fifth one, Iran, is in the process of doing so.

LANGUAGE PRACTICE

1. **What do the letters in these abbreviations stand for?**

NGO: n....................-g.................... o....................

POW: p................................ of w....................

WMD: w.................................. of m.................... d....................

PTSD: p.................... -t.................... s.................... d....................

ICBM: i.................... c.................... b.................... m....................

2. **Use "deterrent, facilities, fallout, testing, warfare" to complete these compounds.**

Nuclear .... is the dangerous radioactive dust which is left in the air after a nuclear explosion and slowly falls to earth.

On the whole, it may be argued that the nuclear .... has played its role satisfactorily since 1945.

The doctrine of MAD (Mutual Assured Destruction) is based on the assumption that adversaries will shrink from using nuclear weapons because nuclear .... would lead to the annihilation of the human race.

President Chirac banned any nuclear .... by the French military soon after coming to power in the mid-90s.

Israel is the only country that refuses to submit its nuclear .... to IAEA inspections.

3. **The following words are both nouns and verbs. Translate.**

	NOUN	VERB
bomb	....	....
spy	....	....
defeat	....	....
veto	....	....
compromise	....	....

4. **Find the appropriate prepositions to complete these sentences.**

Many of the coalition partners wanted to withdraw their troops .... Bosnia.

No country would dare wage a war .... such a formidable enemy.

A country has the right to retaliate .... any neighbour that threatens its borders.

The American-led intervention disrupted the balance .... power in the Middle East.

Economic sanctions may be imposed .... any member state which does not abide by the terms of the treaty.

5. Translate into French.

Russia did not hesitate to flex its muscles and issue threats.

....

Iran's new plutonium-processing facility is unlikely to make the world a safer place.

....

The liberation of the prisoners was indispensable to the resumption of talks.

....

Will the deployment of troops at the border deter the dictator from attacking?

....

A two-thirds majority is required before EU membership negotiations start.

....

6. Translate into English.

Les membres du Conseil de sécurité de l'ONU se sont engagés à aider le nouvel État.

....

La Pologne joue un rôle croissant sur la scène internationale.

....

En définitive, les États-Unis ont ramené Israël à la table des négociations.

....

La Grande-Bretagne a fait pression sur l'Afrique du Sud dès les années 1960.

....

Cela sert-il à quelque chose de voter des résolutions que l'on ne pourra pas faire respecter ?

....

Questions

What challenges is the European Union faced with?
Is today's world a safer place than it used to be?
Is there such a thing as a just war?

WRITING TIP N° 15: Word order

Here are the most common problems encountered by French-speaking students concerning word order.

• Remember that adjectives are always placed before the nouns they modify. This is also true when the superlative is used or when the adjective is itself modified by an adverb (e.g. "*des problèmes très graves*" "very serious problems"; "*l'aspect le plus important du problème*" "the most important aspect of the problem"; "*une théorie prouvée scientifiquement*" "a scientifically proven theory").

• In a question, the auxiliary comes before the subject unless the subject is the interrogative word itself (e.g. "What should the government do?" but "Who knows that Indonesia has the largest Muslim population in the world?"). But this is true only in direct speech. When you report the question in indirect speech, the auxiliary follows the subject as it does in an assertion (e.g. "I don't know what the government should do.")

• As a rule, you should not separate a verb from its direct object in English, while in French adverbs are often placed between them (e.g. "*Il parle bien anglais*" is "He speaks English well"; "*Les inondations ont détruit progressivement les digues*" is "The floods gradually destroyed the dykes.")

• Adverbs of frequency are placed before the verb they modify (e.g. "*Les hommes politiques tiennent rarement leurs promesses*" is "Politicians seldom keep their promises"). This does not hold* with the verb "be", however (e.g. "*Les élections sont parfois truquées*" is "Elections are sometimes rigged").

• Adverbs are usually placed as close as possible to the words they apply to. See for instance the difference between "I really don't think that..." → "*Je ne pense vraiment pas que...*" and "I don't really think that..." → "*Je ne pense pas vraiment que...*".

• Pay special attention to the place of adverbs such as "any more" or "yet", which come at the end of the clause* (e.g. "People do not buy newspapers any more."), as opposed to "no longer", which is placed before the verb (e.g. "People no longer buy newspapers").

• The French adverb "*aussi*" can usually be translated by "also", which comes before the verb, and by "too" or "as well", which are placed at the end of the clause or sentence (e.g. Immigration can also be regarded as an asset. Immigration can be regarded as an asset too.)

• Beware of* "not": with an infinitive, it is usually placed before "to" (e.g. "... *afin de ne pas perdre les élections*" is "...in order not to lose the election"). When translating "*Tout le monde n'est pas d'accord avec cette décision*", "not" should be placed before the word it modifies: "Not everyone agrees with this decision.")

this does not hold: *cela n'est pas vrai* • **clause**: *proposition* • **beware of**: *méfiez-vous*

16. ENVIRONMENTAL ISSUES

9/11 • abortion • advertising • AIDS • alcohol abuse • armed forces • asbestos • bonuses • BRICS • CIA • cloning • CO_2 • **deforestation** computers • consumer society • couch potatoes • creationism • credit bubble • cultural exception • dating • DEA • death penalty • dictatorship • digital piracy • diplomacy • domestic violence **drought** • drug trafficking • eating disorders • English-speaking world • epidemics • euthanasia • fanaticism • food scares • fossil fuels • free speech • free trade • gender gap • glass ceiling **endangered species** • greenhouse gases • guinea pigs • gun control • health care • hijacking • human rights • immigration policy • intercourse • ISPs • IVF • justice system • labour • multiculturalism • NASA • NGOs • nuclear • nuclear deterrent • oil slicks • on parole • outsourcing • ozone layer • PC • pension system • philanthropy • physics • pidgin • **natural disasters** prevention • racial profiling • recycling • renewables • RP • salad bowl • same-sex marriage • second-hand smoking • serial killers • sex industry • slump • social divide • social networks • Spanglish • standard English • STDs • stem-cell research • suffragettes • suicide bombers • **overfishing** surrogacy • surveillance • technophobia • teenage violence • truancy • United Nations • uprisings • video games • waste disposal • welfare state • WMDs • working poor • WTO

environmental [ɪnˌvaɪərən'mentl]	écologique, lié à l'environnement
an environmentally-friendly policy, an eco-friendly policy	une politique qui respecte l'environnement
to protect, to preserve the environment	protéger l'environnement
the preservation of the environment	la protection de l'environnement
nature ['neɪtʃəʳ]	la nature
wildlife	la faune et la flore
fauna / flora	la faune / la flore
an environmentalist, an ecologist	un écologiste
a green activist	un militant écologiste
a conservationist [ˌkɒnsə'veɪʃənɪst]	un défenseur de l'environnement
an awareness(-raising) campaign	une campagne de sensibilisation
a natural reserve, a national park	un parc naturel

There is no direct French translation for the term **wildlife**, which includes all the animal and plant species that live 'in the wild', i.e. that are non-domesticated. The natural home of an animal or a plant in the wild is its **habitat**.

damage ['dæmɪdʒ]	dégâts
to damage sth	endommager qch, porter atteinte à qch
to do damage, to cause damage	causer des dégâts
to harm the environment, to do harm to the environment	nuire à l'environnement
to jeopardize sth ['dʒepədaɪz], to endanger sth [ɪn'deɪndʒəʳ]	mettre en danger qch
to be at risk, to be in danger	être en danger
to declare a state of emergency	déclarer l'état d'urgence
a disaster victim	un sinistré

The word **damage** does not have the same meaning when it is used in the singular and in the plural. In the singular, it refers to the physical harm suffered by someone or something or to the harmful effects of something on someone or something. In this sense, it is uncountable: "*Les dégâts sont immenses.*" should therefore be translated as: 'The damage is huge'. In the pural, **damages** refers to the amount of money that a court decides should be paid to someone (like a disaster victim, for instance) whose property has been **damaged** (by flooding etc.).

sustainable development	le développement durable
scarcity ['skɛəsɪtɪ]	la rareté
an ecosystem	un écosystème
natural resources [rɪ'sɔːsɪz]	les ressources naturelles
the depletion [dɪ'pliːʃən] of resources	l'épuisement des ressources
raw materials	les matières premières
biodiversity [ˌbaɪəudaɪ'vɜːsətɪ]	la biodiversité
a species ['spiːʃiːz]	une espèce
an animal / plant species	une espèce animale / végétale
an endangered species	une espèce en voie de disparition

to be threatened with extinction	être menacé d'extinction
to become extinct	disparaître

Sustainable development is a pattern of development that seeks "to meet the needs of the present without compromising the ability of future generations to meet their own needs", according to the Brundtland Commission, which was established by the United Nations to investigate the deterioration of the environment and first defined the term in 1983.

The International Union for the Conservation of Nature assessed 63,837 animal or plant species and concluded 19,817 were threatened with extinction. At risk are 41% of amphibians, 33% of corals, 25% of mammals, 13% of birds and 30% of conifers.

a rainforest, a tropical forest	une forêt tropicale
to fell, cut down trees	abattre des arbres
deforestation	le déboisement, la déforestation
to reforest [riːˈfɒrɪst]	reboiser
reforestation	le reboisement
overfishing	la surpêche
bluefin tuna [ˈtjuːnə]	le thon rouge
a dolphin / a whale	un dauphin / une baleine
whaling	la pêche à la baleine

Decades of overfishing, much of it in seas far from Japan, are threatening tuna populations with extinction. Stocks of bluefin in the eastern Atlantic and the Mediterranean dropped 60 per cent in the decade after 1997. Apart from the impact on stocks of the fish, the tuna industry kills many other marine species including sharks, turtles (*tortues*) and sea birds. As well as affluent gourmet Japanese, tuna supply nutrition to far needier people. "If the current level of fishing continues or increases, then, sooner rather than later, tuna stocks will collapse," the wildlife conservation group WWF said in a report. "The result will be a huge loss of revenue, and the worrying prospect in some parts of the world of reduced food security for the world's poorest people."
Richard Lloyd Parry, *The Times*, March 11, 2010

a natural disaster	une catastrophe naturelle
a tragedy.	un drame, une tragédie
tragic	dramatique, tragique
a catastrophe [kəˈtæstrəfɪ]	une catastrophe, un sinistre
to affect a region	toucher une région
to devastate, to ravage a region	dévaster, ravager une région
to wreak havoc [riːk ˈhævək]	faire des ravages
to avert [əˈvɜːt] a disaster	éviter, prévenir une catastrophe
the scope, the extent of the disaster	l'étendue, l'ampleur du sinistre
severe, extreme weather	très mauvais temps

to predict, to forecast the weather	prévoir le temps
the weather forecast	les prévisions météo(rologiques)

Water seems to be getting more and more scarce. But it's not. The amount of water on Earth isn't changing, and as a planet we're in no danger of running out. One of the most misleading "facts" we learn about water, starting in the second grade or so, is that 97.5 percent of the water on Earth is unusable by humans, because it's salty ocean water. Actually, the oceans are Olympian springs of fresh water — every day, the sun, the sea and evaporation combine to make 45,000 gallons of rainwater for each man, woman and child on Earth. Even in the United States, where we use water with profligacy (*prodigalité*), the oceans are making more fresh water for each of us in a month than we'll use in a decade.
Charles Fishman, *The Washington Post*, April 6, 2012

drought [draʊt]	la sécheresse
a famine ['fæmɪn]	une famine
hunger	la faim
to starve to death	mourir de faim
to die of thirst	mourir de soif
malnutrition	la malnutrition
to be malnourished, undernourished	souffrir de malnutrition
a cold spell, a cold wave	une vague de froid
a heat wave	une canicule
a storm	une tempête, un orage
a tornado, a twister	une tornade
a hurricane ['hʌrɪkən] , a cyclone ['saɪkləʊn]	un ouragan, un cyclone
a typhoon [taɪ'fuːn]	un typhon
torrential rain	des pluies torrentielles, diluviennes
a flood [flʌd]	une inondation
flooding	des inondations
a flash flood	une crue subite
a flood risk area	une zone inondable

Hurricane Katrina formed on August 23, 2005 over the Bahamas and reached southern Louisiana on August 29, causing huge property damage (*dégâts matériels*) in the city of New Orleans, 80% of which flooded as nearly every levee (*digue*) was breached. With over 1,800 deaths and damage estimates (*évaluations des dégâts*) standing at more than $100 billion, Hurricane Katrina was the largest natural disaster in the history of the US.

an earthquake	un tremblement de terre, un séisme
a fault [fɔːlt]	une faille
a fault line	une ligne de faille
the epicentre	l'épicentre
rubble ['rʌbl] , debris ['debriː]	les décombres

to be trapped / buried in rubble	être prisonnier / enterré sous les décombres
ruins ['ruːɪnz]	ruines
to be reported missing	être porté disparu
a tsunami [tsʊ'nɑːmɪ]	un tsunami
a tidal ['ta'dl] wave	un raz-de-marée
a landslide	un glissement de terrain
a mudslide	une coulée de boue
a snowstorm	une tempête de neige
an avalanche ['ævəlɑːnʃ]	une avalanche
a volcano [vɒl'keɪnəʊ]	un volcan
a crater ['kreɪtər]	un cratère
an eruption	une éruption
lava ['lɑːvə]	la lave
a lava flow	une coulée de lave
ash	les cendres
a fire	un incendie

Erin Brockovich is a 2000 biopic movie directed by Steven Soderbergh and starring Julia Robert as the environmental activist who fights a Californian energy corporation after finding it has contaminated the groundwater in a South Californian town with hexavalent chromium, a dangerous chemical. It later turns out that the company's management knew all along about the pollution but chose not to do anything to stop it even if it resulted in many cases of tumors among local residents. Brockovich eventually succeeds in obtaining $ 333 million in compensation for the victims.

to rescue	sauver
a rescuer, a rescue worker	un secouriste, un sauveteur
a rescue party	une équipe de secours
a fireman, a firefighter	un pompier
to evacuate	évacuer
to be safe	être en sécurité, hors de danger
to survive	survivre
a survivor	un survivant, un rescapé

On a beach in Phuket, Thailand, during Christmas 2004, a 10-year-old British schoolgirl suddenly remembered her geography lesson of two weeks before. The water looked different and was behaving oddly. It was just like the signs she'd been taught were the messengers of an impending (*imminent*) tsunami. Everyone else was out for a good time on a sunny day on the beach — who wanted to listen to a young, increasingly desperate girl? But she trusted her judgement, the best knowledge she had gained from her science lesson, and finally persuaded her mother who had helped with her geography homework. In turn, they persuaded the lifeguard and the beach was cleared, saving about 100 lives on a day when possibly a quarter of a million died.
The Guardian, Friday 1, October 2010

a relief agency, a relief organization	une organisation humanitaire
a relief worker	un travailleur humanitaire
humanitarian aid, assistance	aide, assistance humanitaire
emergency aid, emergency relief	secours, aide d'urgence
to insure sth [ɪn'ʃʊər]	assurer qch
an insurance company	une compagnie d'assurances
compensation	une indemnité, des indemnités
to compensate sb for sth	indemniser qn de qch
to get compensation, to get reimbursed	se faire indemniser

LANGUAGE PRACTICE

1. **Find synonyms for the following words.**

malnourished	....
to jeopardize	to ....
to devastate	to ....
rubble	....

2. **Underline the appropriate words.**

You had better (assure / insure) your house against the risk of flooding.

It was decided to send (emergency / urgency) relief hours after the earthquake struck.

The heavy rains resulted in a (mudslide / landslide) which wiped the whole village off the map.

Several people died immediately and dozens more were reported (lacking / missing).

3. **The spelling of the following words is very close to the French one.**

une espèce	....
évacuer	....
prédire	....
un volcan	....

4. **All the missing words are based on the same root.**

In Britain, the Department of the .... is responsible for the protection of the countryside, the quality of the air and water but also, the building of new roads.

The shrinking of the Aral Sea is one of the planet's worst .... disasters.

Not all .... are in favour of biofuels.

We need to promote more .... friendly modes of transport.

5. **Find the appropriate endings to form the missing words.**

survivre	to survive	....	*un survivant*
avoir faim	to be hungry	....	*la faim*
rare	scarce	....	*la rareté*
sec	dry	....	*la sécheresse*

6. **Translate into French.**

An earthquake of magnitude 6 on the Richter scale hit Indonesia last night.

....

In the drought-stricken areas, children are threatened with starvation.

....

The volcano erupted during the night while the hurricane swept across the island.

....

Fortunately, the villagers were able to escape unscathed.

....

The coast was declared a disaster area so the victims got compensation.

....

7. **Translate into English.**

L'équipe de secours a fourni une aide alimentaire aux rescapés.

....

Comme les gorilles, les ours polaires sont une espèce en voie de disparition.

....

Les consommateurs ont déjà été sensibilisés aux dangers de la déforestation.

....

Des pluies diluviennes se sont abattues sur les zones les plus durement frappées.

....

Le choléra qui s'est propagé à la suite du séisme a fait des centaines de morts.

....

Questions

Sustainable development.
Is it possible to avert natural disasters?
Is eco-tourism no more than a fad?

WRITING TIP N° 16: Passive voice

You may already have noticed that the passive voice is used much more often in English than in French. For instance, set phrases* like "*Cela reste à voir*" or "*À suivre*" are rendered almost literally but in the passive: "This remains to be seen" and "To be continued".

The passive is often the most appropriate equivalent for the French pronoun "*on*", which should not be translated by "we" when there is no identifiable antecedent. Thus,

- « *On peut remarquer que...* » should be "It may be noted that..."
- « *On peut affirmer que...* » should be "It may be argued that..."
- « *On doit reconnaître que...* » corresponds to "It has to be admitted that..."
- « *On croit souvent que...* » to "It is widely believed that..."
- « *Il ne faut pas oublier que...* » → "It should be kept in mind that...",
- « *On pourrait aussi soutenir que...* » → "It could also be argued that...",
- « *Dans quelle mesure peut-on prétendre que...* » → "How far can it be claimed that..."

The passive is also the best equivalent for the French conditional every time it is used to describe what is perceived not as a fact, but as a debatable* opinion, or a piece of news that has not been confirmed yet. For instance: "*D'après certains, le libéralisme serait la solution miracle*" cannot be translated with "would". You have to say "To some, the free-market is thought to be a magic bullet". "*Saddam Hussein aurait eu des armes de destruction massive*" must be translated as "Saddam Hussein was believed / alleged to have weapons of mass destruction".

When you use the passive voice with a phrasal verb (a verb requring* a preposition and / or an adverbial particle), make sure that you do not forget the preposition or the particle at the end. For instance: "Women have always been discriminated against" → "*Les femmes ont toujours été victimes de discrimination*", "The problem has never been dealt with" → "*On ne s'est jamais occupé de ce problème*", "The waste has been disposed of" → "*Les déchets ont été éliminés.*"

Remember also that with verbs such as "give, grant, award, teach..." which have two complements, both complements can be used as subjects of a passive verb form (e.g. "He was awarded the Nobel Prize in 2010", "The Nobel Prize was awarded to him in 2010"). In many cases, it is preferable or even indispensable to choose the human complement as the subject of the passive (e.g. "Children should be taught how to use a computer from an early age").

set phrases: *expressions toutes faites* • **debatable**: *discutable* • **requiring**: *demandant*

17. POLLUTION

9/11 • abortion • advertising • AIDS • alcohol abuse • armed forces •
bonuses • BRICS • CIA • cloning • CO_2 • computers •
consumer **asbestos** society • couch potatoes • creationism • credit
bubble • cultural exception • dating • DEA • death
penalty • deforestation • dictatorship • digital piracy • diplomacy • domestic
violence • drought • drug trafficking • eating disorders • endangered
species • English-speaking world • epidemics • euthanasia • fanaticism •
food scares • **oil slicks** fossil fuels • free speech • free trade •
gender gap • glass ceiling • greenhouse gases • guinea
pigs • gun control • health care • hijacking • human rights • immigration
policy • intercourse • ISPs • IVF • justice system • labour • multiculturalism •
NASA • natural disasters • NGOs
• nuclear • **ozone layer** nuclear deterrent **recycling**
• on parole • outsourcing
• overfishing • PC • pension system • philanthropy • physics • pidgin •
prevention • racial profiling • renewables • RP • salad bowl • same-sex
marriage • second-hand smoking • serial killers
• sex industry • slump • social divide **waste disposal** • social
networks • Spanglish • standard English
• STDs • stem-cell research • suffragettes • suicide bombers • surrogacy •
surveillance • technophobia • teenage violence • truancy • United Nations •
uprisings • video games • welfare state • WMDs • working poor • WTO

to pollute [pə'luːt]	polluer
noise pollution	la pollution sonore
a polluter	un pollueur
a pollutant	un polluant, une substance polluante
polluting	polluant
to pollute little / a lot	être peu / très polluant
non-polluting, eco-friendly products	produits non polluants
to reduce, curb pollution	diminuer la pollution
to waste	gaspiller
harmful	nocif

According to the "**polluter pays principle**", which was adopted at the Earth Summit of 1992 in Rio, a polluter should bear (*supporter*) the cost of pollution.

air pollution	la pollution de l'air, la pollution atmosphérique
smog	le smog
a pollution peak	un pic de pollution
factory smoke, factory fumes [fjuːmz]	les fumées d'usine
car exhausts [ɪg'zɔːsts], exhaust fumes	les gaz d'échappement
unleaded petrol, lead-free petrol	l'essence sans plomb
a catalytic converter	un pot catalytique
to monitor air quality	surveiller la qualité de l'air
asthma ['æsmə]	l'asthme

China will ban shops from giving out free plastic bags and has called on consumers to use baskets and cloth sacks instead to reduce environmental pollution. The regulation, effective in June, was decided on about 15 years after shopkeepers started handing out cheap, flimsy plastic bags to customers. "White pollution," a reference to the color of many bags, has cluttered landfills. "Our country consumes a huge amount of plastic shopping bags each year," said the State Council, China's cabinet. "While plastic shopping bags provide convenience to consumers, this has caused a serious waste of energy and resources and environmental pollution because of excessive usage, inadequate recycling and other reasons."
The Associated Press, January 9, 2008

water pollution	la pollution de l'eau
nitrates ['naɪtreɪts]	les nitrates
fertilizers ['fɜːtɪlaɪzəʳz]	les engrais
groundwater	la nappe phréatique
to poison ['pɔɪzn] rivers	contaminer les rivières
to contaminate	contaminer
a contaminant	un polluant, une substance polluante
a toxic chemical	un produit chimique toxique
dioxin [daɪ'ɒksɪn]	la dioxine
a sewer ['sjʊəʳ]	un égout

sewage ['suːɪdʒ, 'sjuːɪdʒ], waste water	les eaux usées
the sewage system	les égouts
a sewage works	une station d'épuration des eaux

The **Bhopal gas tragedy** is considered one of the worst industrial catastrophes in history. It took place in December 1984 at the Union Carbide pesticide plant in Bhopal, in India. A leak of various chemicals resulted in the exposure of hundreds of thousands of people in the shantytowns (*bidonvilles*) to toxic gases. Between 3,000 and 8,000 are thought to have died in the accident, while many thousands suffered injuries.

asbestos [æz'bestəs]	l'amiante
the ozone layer ['əʊzəʊn 'leɪər]	la couche d'ozone
CFCs	les gaz CFC
ozone depletion	la diminution de la couche d'ozone
ozone-friendly	respectueux de la couche d'ozone
ultra-violet rays	les rayons ultra-violets
acid rains	les pluies acides
lead poisoning [led 'pɔɪznɪŋ]	le saturnisme
PCBs	les PCB

CFCs (abbreviation for chlorofluorocarbon) are a type of gas that is used especially in aerosols (containers in which liquids such as paints are kept under pressure and released as a spray). CFCs damage the ozone layer. **PCBs** (abbreviation for polychlorinated biphenyls) are often formed as waste in industrial processes.

an oil slick	une marée noire
an oil spill	un déversement accidentel de pétrole
oil-covered birds	des oiseaux mazoutés
to empty one's tanks, to flush out one's tanks	dégazer

An **oil spill** is the release of a certain amount of petroleum into the environment, most often the sea, due to human activity such as shipping. An **oil slick** is an area of oil floating on the surface of the sea, usually as a result of an oil spill. Both expressions are translated as "*marée noire*".

waste, rubbish (GB), garbage (US), trash (US)	les ordures, les détritus, les déchets
toxic / organic waste	les déchets toxiques / organiques
hazardous waste	les déchets dangereux
household refuse, household rubbish	les ordures ménagères
to collect waste	ramasser des déchets
waste collection	le ramassage des ordures
a waste collection centre	une déchetterie
an incinerator	un incinérateur

a dustman (GB), a garbage man (US)	un éboueur
litter	les detritus
to dispose of waste	éliminer des déchets
disposable [dɪs'pəʊzəbl]	jetable
biodegradable	biodégradable
a dustbin, a bin (GB), a garbage can (US)	une poubelle
a bin lorry (GB), a garbage truck (US)	un camion poubelle

More and more, the environmental harm that ministers discuss is global or regional, not national. Acid rain and marine pollution hurt neighbouring countries; ozone depletion and global warming threaten the entire planet. Just after the environment ministers return from the OECD, their officials go to Washington to start negotiating a treaty on climate change. Their toughest problem will be that of free riders (*profiteurs*): countries that want to enjoy the benefits of an agreement without curbing their own output (*production*) of global-warming gases. Free-riders risk damaging not just their own climates but, perhaps irreversibly, the climate of every other country — indeed, the very existence of some tiny countries. On ozone depletion, which harms everyone, the Montreal agreement accepted that trade sanctions could be used against free riders. It provided for (prévoir) a ban on imports of ozone-gobbling chlorofluorocarbons (CFCs), of products containing CFCs, and of products which used CFCs in their manufacturing process.
The Economist, December 2011

PCBs (polychlorinated biphenyls) are highly toxic substances used mainly in electric transformers and motors. They may cause skin conditions and liver damage, among other harmful effects.

a rubbish dump (GB), a garbage dump (US)	une décharge, un dépotoir
an illicit rubbish dump	une décharge sauvage
to dump rubbish	déposer, jeter des ordures
a landfill	un site d'enfouissement des ordures
to throw away	jeter
to bury	enterrer, enfouir
to burn	brûler
to destroy	détruire
to melt	fondre

According to the European Commission, "electro-scrap is the fastest growing waste stream [in the EU], growing at 3-5% per year", three times faster than domestic waste in general. In 2002, a European directive was issued requiring member countries to ensure the "re-use, recovery and recycling" of discarded electronic goods. Some retail analysts think the directive — especially its sections on the "financial obligations of producers" to be environmentally responsible, and on how "consumers will be able to take discarded products back to shops for free" — will have a significant effect on the cheap electronics market.
The Guardian, Tuesday February 28, 2006

nuclear waste	les déchets nucléaires
radioactivity	la radioactivité
carcinogenic [ˌkɑːsɪnəˈdʒenɪk]	cancérigène
to dispose of nuclear waste	éliminer les déchets nucléaires
nuclear waste disposal	l'élimination des déchets nucléaires
a container	un conteneur
to store	stocker
storage	le stockage
hermetically sealed containers	des conteneurs hermétiquement fermés
a leak [liːk]	une fuite
the storage of nuclear waste	le stockage des déchets radioactifs

The most serious case of pollution by the nuclear industry is the disaster that took place in **Fukushima** (Japan) in March 2011, when a tsunami caused several explosions in a nuclear plant. Until then, the worst nuclear catastrophe had taken place at the **Chernobyl** nuclear plant (Ukraine) in April 1986 when the core of a reactor melted down. In March 1979, a malfunction in the cooling system of a reactor at the **Three Mile Island** facility (USA), caused a partial meltdown and the release of significant amount of radioactivity. In all three cases, the extent of the damage caused is still in dispute.

recycling	le recyclage
to recycle plastic	recycler le plastique
recyclable	recyclable
a recycling plant	une usine de recyclage
recycling costs	les coûts de recyclage
to process waste	traiter, transformer des déchets
to sort	trier
sorting, waste separation	le tri sélectif
a bottle bank	un conteneur de verre
rags	des chiffons
cardboard	le carton
scrap metal	la ferraille
packaging	les emballages
a can of beer, a beer can	une boîte de bière

WALL-E is a 2008 American computer-animated science fiction film produced by Pixar Animation Studios. WALL-E is a solar-powered robot designed to clean up the Earth which is covered in garbage due to decades of mass consumerism. It scoops up garbage, shovels it into his belly, compresses it into a square and climbs up to the top of a skyscraper (which is in fact made of neatly compacted squares of trash piled on top of one another) to place it on the pile. The film is an explicit critique of American society, which recycles less than a third of the 400 million tons of solid waste it produces every year.

LANGUAGE PRACTICE

1. Find the missing words to complete the sentences.

The new regulations require the use of catalytic converters and lead-.................... petrol.

Particles from domestic heating installations, car .... and factory chimneys pollute the urban atmosphere.

The spectacle of oil-.................... sea birds helplessly attempting to preen themselves was enough to make you sick.

Nuclear waste has to be stored in hermetically .... containers before it is transported.

2. Associate the following words to form compound nouns and translate.

chemical, depletion, oil, ozone, metal, toxic, scrap, slick

....	....
....	....
....	....
....	....

3. Translate the following words, which are both verbs and nouns.

	NOUN	VERB
poison	....	....
waste	....	....
dump	....	....
spill	....	....

4. Find the verbs corresponding to the following definitions.

When a liquid or a gas .... from a container or a pipe, it escapes through a small hole or crack.

To .... waste is to hide it in the ground.

To .... waste is to treat and transform it as part of an industrial operation.

To .... is to arrange things in groups or to separate things of one type from others.

5. Find the appropriate suffix to complete.

polluer	to pollute	a pollu _ _ _	*un pollueur*
polluer	to pollute	a pollu _ _ _ _	*un polluant*
risque, danger	hazard	hazard _ _ _	*dangereux*
nuire	to harm	harm _ _ _	*nocif*

6. Translate into French.

The cost of removing asbestos from the building had been underestimated.

....

Shipowners whose oil tankers discharge waste oil into the sea should be fined.

....

The scourge of plastic bags is afflicting China in unprecedented proportions.

....

The production of disposable diapers requires 200 times more energy than to wash reusable ones.

....

The release of untreated sewage into the Great Lakes has now been banned.

....

7. Translate into English.

En ville, beaucoup de personnes âgées souffrent d'asthme et ont du mal à respirer.

....

On dit que les gaz CFC sont responsables du trou dans la couche d'ozone.

....

Il faut encourager les constructeurs automobiles à produire des véhicules moins polluants.

....

Des produits chimiques toxiques ont contaminé le sol, ce qui fait que les plantes ne poussent plus.

....

La marée noire dans le Golfe du Mexique a eu des conséquences dramatiques sur la pêche et le tourisme.

....

Questions

Economic growth without environmental damage — mirage or reality?
The scourge of plastic bags.
Waste, waste, waste.

WRITING TIP N° 17: Pronouns

Personal pronouns ("I, you, them"…) and relative pronouns ("who, which, whose, that"…) make it possible to avoid awkward* repetitions and thus improve concision.

But even more importantly, they help reinforce* the cohesion of a text. For instance if you write: "Crime is a major concern* for most voters. People feel unsafe* as a result.", you produce two independent sentences reflecting two independent ideas. If you write "Crime is a major concern for most voters. They feel unsafe as a result.", you link the two ideas by referring back to the first sentence. If you write "Crime is a major concern for most voters, who feel unsafe* as a result.", you not only connect the two ideas, but you merge them into a single, more complex, unit. Remember that the word "text" is etymologically linked to "textile": both come from the Latin word "*texere*" meaning "to weave*". Thought is a thread*, and a writer is a weaver who binds words together into strands* of ideas.

The translation of some pronouns from French into English poses a problem:

• While in a French *dissertation*, you may use a rhetorical "*nous*", as in the following introduction: "*Dans un premier temps, nous analyserons…*", you must use "I" when you refer to yourself in an English essay.

• Beware of* uncountable nouns such as "information, evidence, progress, news, waste…". Since they are singular, the pronoun corresponding to them is "it", not "they" and the verb that follows must be in the singular. Thus, the translation of "*Elles (les preuves) sont écrasantes.*" will be "It is overwhelming." The same goes for* "the United States". The translation of "*Ils ont décidé de retirer leurs troupes d'Irak.*" is "It has decided to withdraw its troops from Iraq."

• The best translation of "*on*" is usually the passive form, unless "*on*" refers to a precise group of people — for example, you and your parents: "We went to Spain last year." But when "*on*" refers to people generally, do not use "we": think of the passive voice (e.g. "*On devrait légaliser l'euthanasie*" → "Euthanasia should be legalized.") or "you" (e.g. "*On ne sait jamais.*" → "You never know.") or in a more formal way, "one" (e.g. "*One ne peut pas tourner à droite quand le feu est rouge en France comme souvent aux États-Unis*" → "One cannot turn right on red in France as one often does in the U.S.").

• Remember to use "who" instead of "which" whenever the referent is a person or a group of persons (e.g. "The people who think that…"). Remember also that "whose" is used with both people *and* objects (e.g. "Solar energy is an idea whose time has come").

awkward: *maladroit* • **reinforce**: *renforcer* • **concern**: *préoccupation* • **unsafe**: *en danger* • **weave**: *tisser* • **thread**: *fil* • **strands**: *enchaînements* • **weaver**: *tisserand* • **beware of**: *méfiez-vous* • **The same goes for**: *Il en va de même pour*

18. CLIMATE CHANGE & ENERGY

9/11 • abortion • advertising • AIDS • alcohol abuse • armed forces • asbestos • bonuses • BRICS • CIA • cloning • computers • consumer society • couch potatoes • creationism • credit bubble • cultural exception • dating • DEA • death penalty • deforestation • dictatorship • digital piracy • diplomacy • domestic violence • drought • drug trafficking • eating disorders • endangered species • English-speaking world • epidemics • euthanasia • fanaticism • food scares • free speech • free trade • gender gap • glass ceiling • guinea pigs • gun control • health care • hijacking • human rights • immigration policy • intercourse • ISPs • IVF • justice system • labour • multiculturalism • NASA • natural disasters • NGOs • nuclear deterrent • oil slicks • on parole • outsourcing • overfishing • ozone layer • PC • pension system • philanthropy • physics • pidgin • prevention • racial profiling • recycling • RP • salad bowl • same-sex marriage • second-hand smoking • serial killers • sex industry • slump • social divide • social networks • Spanglish • standard English • STDs • stem-cell research • suffragettes • suicide bombers • surrogacy • surveillance • technophobia • teenage violence • truancy • United Nations • uprisings • video games • waste disposal • welfare state • WMDs • working poor • WTO

CO_2 **fossil fuels** **greenhouse gases** **nuclear** **renewables**

climatology [klaɪmə'tɒlədʒɪ], climate ['klaɪmɪt] science	la climatologie
a climate scientist, a climatologist	un climatologue
global warming	le réchauffement de l'atmosphère, de la planète
man-made, anthropogenic	anthropogénique
carbon dioxide [daɪ'ɒksaɪd], CO_2	le dioxyde de carbone, CO_2
to emit carbon dioxide	émettre, rejeter du CO_2
the greenhouse effect [ɪ'fekt]	l'effet de serre
greenhouse gases [gæsɪs]	les gaz à effet de serre
greenhouse gas emissions	les émissions, les rejets de gaz à effet de serre
carbon emissions	les émissions de dioxyde de carbone

Greenhouse gases (GHGs) are gases such as carbon dioxide, methane, ozone, or nitrous oxide which are emitted into the Earth's atmosphere mainly as a result of the burning of fossil fuels and which are responsible for the greenhouse effect.

a rise in temperatures ['temprɪtʃəʳz]	une augmentation des températures
the sea level	le niveau de la mer
a rise in sea level	une élévation du niveau de la mer
to flood [flʌd]	inonder
a flood	une inondation
above / below sea level	au-dessus / en-dessous du niveau de la mer

The **Kyōto Protocol** (1997) is a treaty that sets targets for developed countries to reduce greenhouse gas emissions. 191 have signed and ratified the treaty and one, the US, signed it but did not ratify it. Canada withdrew from the treaty in 2011.

The **Intergovernmental Panel on Climate Change** (IPCC; in French "*Groupe d'experts intergouvernemental sur l'évolution du climat*", GIEC) is a scientific intergovernmental body set up by the UN in 1988 to evaluate the risk of climate change caused by human activity. It does not do any research of its own, but collects information and investigates man-made climate change and its consequences.

a glacier ['glæsɪəʳ]	un glacier
the polar icecap	la calotte glaciaire, polaire
the North / South Pole	le pôle Nord / Sud
icefield, ice floe [fləʊ]	la banquise
a polar bear	un ours polaire, un ours blanc
to thaw	dégeler, fondre
thaw [θɔː]	dégel
to melt	fondre
fresh water, freshwater	l'eau douce

sea water	eau de mer
groundwater	la nappe phréatique

An Inconvenient Truth (2006) is a documentary film about former Vice-President Al Gore's campaign to raise global awareness of the issues posed by climate change. The film is adapted from a slide show in which he uses detailed graphs and dramatic visuals to describe the consequences he believes global climate change will produce if the amount of human-generated greenhouse gases is not significantly reduced in the very near future. According to him, action must be taken right now or else there will be "an irreversible slide into destruction". Al Gore won the Nobel Peace Prize in 2007, jointly with the IPCC.

to cut, to curb carbon emissions	réduire les émissions de carbone
to reduce one's carbon imprint	reduire son empreinte carbone
to introduce a carbon tax	instaurer une taxe carbone
low-energy lightbulbs	des ampoules basse consommation
to insulate ['ɪnsjʊleɪt] a room	isoler un pièce
insulation	l'isolation (thermique)
a bicyle-sharing scheme, system	un système de vélos en libre-service
to cap carbon emissions	plafonner les rejets de carbone
carbon trading	le commerce des droits d'émission du carbone
cap and trade	plafonner et échanger (les quotas d'émissions)

More complex and less elegant (but politically easier) than a simple carbon tax, a cap-and-trade system limits the emissions of dirty industries and puts a price on their remaining pollution so that market forces, in theory, provide an incentive (*incitation*) for reductions. In California's case, starting in 2013 the government will "cap" the amount of gases (such as carbon dioxide) that industry may emit, and gradually lower that cap (*plafond*). It will also issue permits to companies for their carbon allowance. Firms that reduce their emissions faster than the cap decreases may sell ("trade") their permits and make money. Firms that pollute beyond their quota must buy credits.
The Economist, Oct 29th 2011, Los Angeles

energy policy	politique énergétique
energy production / consumption	la production / consommation d'énergie
energy needs, energy requirements	les besoins en énergie
the energy gap, the energy shortage ['ʃɔːtɪdʒ]	la pénurie d'énergie
an oil crisis, an oil shock	une crise pétrolière, un choc pétrolier
energy savings	les économies d'énergie
energy-saving measures	des mesures d'économie d'énergie
to save / waste energy	économiser / gaspiller l'énergie
a gas-guzzler	une voiture qui consomme beaucoup
an SUV, a sports utility vehicle, a four-wheel drive	un quatre-quatre

> The UK must transform in order to meet the energy needs of the coming decades, warn top engineers. The UK's most eminent engineers have warned that the biggest set of investments and social changes ever seen in peacetime are needed to meet the country's energy needs in the coming decades, while cutting greenhouse gas emissions. The changes include a transformation of the nation's draughty (*mal isolé*) homes and cuts in how far people commute to work, as well as a vast expansion of wind and solar power and dozens of new nuclear or "clean coal" power plants. The authors of the Royal Academy of Engineering report, published today, say the existing level of political will and the market-led approach to energy planning cannot deliver the fundamental restructuring needed.
> *The Guardian*, 18 March 2010

fuel	le combustible OU le carburant
to run out, become depleted	s'épuiser
the depletion of resources [rɪ'sɔːsɪz]	l'épuisement des ressources
oil supplies, oil reserves [rɪ'zɜːvz]	les réserves de pétrole
the exhaustion of oil supplies	l'épuisement des réserves de pétrole

The word **petrol** (GB) is a faux-ami: it does not refer to the thick, black liquid found in rock underground but to the liquid used as fuel in car engines. Petrol is produced from **oil**, which is synonymous with **petroleum**, a technical term. But in the United States, petrol is called **gasoline** (often abbreviated as **gas**). In both Great Britain and the US, the word **gas** also refers to one of the three main **fossil fuels**, together with oil and **coal**.

fossil fuels ['fɒsl fjʊəlz]	les énergies fossiles
hydrocarbons	les hydrocarbures
oil, petroleum	le pétrole
crude oil	le pétrole brut
gas [gæs]	le gaz, (en anglais américain: l'essence)
coal [kəʊl]	le charbon
oil shale [ʃeɪl]	les schistes bitumineux
shale oil / gas	l'huile / le gaz de schiste
tar sands	les sables bitumineux
fracking	l'hydrofracturation

When a fracking well is drilled (*forer*), the initial well extends hundreds of metres below the surface. Thousands of litres of water mixed with sand and chemicals are then blasted through to open up small fractures in the dense rock at the base of the well. This shale rock contains tiny bubbles of natural gas that are released by the fracturing process, and which eventually — over the course of years — find their way to the surface to be collected in pipelines. Shale gas is now one of the major sources of energy in the US, but critics point to ravaged landscapes and contaminated water supplies, as well as concerns over the long-term safety of the wells. Although natural gas is supposed to be a "cleaner" fuel than coal, releasing less carbon when burned, evidence also suggests fracking produces more carbon than exploring for conventional gas supplies, making the fuel less attractive from an environmental point of view.
The Guardian, Tuesday 17, April 2012

an oil well	un puits de pétrole
an oil rig, an oil platform	une plateforme pétrolière
an oil pipeline	un oléoduc
a gas pipeline	un gazoduc
an oil tanker	un pétrolier
oil prices	le prix du pétrole
an oil refinery [rɪ'faɪnərɪ]	une raffinerie de pétrole
oil products	les dérivés du pétrole
petrol (GB), gas (US)	l'essence
heating oil	le fioul, le mazout
a power station, a power plant	une centrale électrique, thermique
an oil-fired power station / a coal-fired power station	une centrale fonctionnant au pétrole / au charbon
to generate electricity	produire de l'électricité

The **Organization of the Petroleum Exporting Countries** (OPEC) is a cartel of 12 countries mostly located in the Arab world but which also includes Venezuela, Ecuador, Algeria and Nigeria. It was founded in 1960 and aims to secure (*assurer*) a steady income to its members as well as eliminate harmful fluctuations in oil prices. After the Six Day War of 1967, the Arab members of OPEC formed a separate group called the Organization of Arab Petroleum Exporting Countries in order to exert pressure on (*faire pression sur*) Western nations. This led to the oil embargo in October 1973 and the first **oil shock** or **oil crisis**.

renewable [rɪ'nju:əbl]	renouvelable
renewable energy sources, renewables	les sources d'énergie renouvelable
wind power	l'énergie éolienne
a wind turbine ['tɜ:baɪn], a windmill, a windpump	une éolienne
a windfarm	un parc d'éoliennes, un parc éolien, une ferme éolienne, un champ d'éoliennes
solar ['səʊlə^r] power, solar energy	l'énergie solaire

a photovoltaic cell	une cellule photovoltaïque, une photopile
a solar panel ['pænəl]	un panneau solaire

"America's sensible fuel," reads a TV advertisement, while a soothing melody plays in the background. Other ads tout (*font de la réclame pour*) a fuel that promotes peace and is economical, home-produced, clean and renewable. So what is this magic potion? Ethanol, of course. Growth Energy, a lobby group, is spending $2.5m on America's first national television campaign for the stuff. "No beaches have been closed due to ethanol spills," one ad notes. Growth Energy planned the campaign before the BP disaster, but the push (*campagne de promotion*) could hardly be better timed. After the oil spill Barack Obama declared that "the time to embrace a clean energy future is now." Biofuels will be part of that future.
The Economist, July 1st 2010

biofuels ['baɪəʊfjʊəlz]	les bio-carburants, les agro-carburants
biomass	la biomasse
bioethanol [ˌbaɪəʊ'eθənɒl]	le bioéthanol
palm oil [pɑːm ɔɪl]	huile de palme
geothermal [ˌdʒiːəʊ'θɜːməl] energy, geothermal power	énergie géothermique
a heat pump	une pompe à chaleur
nuclear power	l'énergie nucléaire
a nuclear plant	une centrale nucléaire
a fast breeder (reactor)	un (réacteur) surgénérateur
uranium [jʊə'reɪnɪəm] enrichment	l'enrichissement de l'uranium
fusion / fission	fusion / fission
the nuclear industry	le nucléaire
to go nuclear	se convertir au nucléaire
to abandon, phase out nuclear energy	sortir du nucléaire
nuclear waste disposal	l'élimination des déchets nucléaires
a meltdown	fusion (du cœur d'un réacteur nucléaire)
hydroelectricity, hydropower	l'hydroélectricité
a dam, a barrage	un barrage
tidal ['taɪdl] energy, tidal power	l'énergie marémotrice, la houille bleue
a tidal power station	une usine marémotrice
a tidal turbine, a marine turbine	une hydrolienne
a battery-powered car, an electric car	une voiture électrique
a hybrid ['haɪbrɪd] car	une voiture hybride
the electric grid, the power grid	le réseau électrique
domestic appliances	les appareils électroménagers
a smart meter ['miːtəʳ]	un compteur intelligent

Tidal turbines are used to produce **tidal power**, a form of **hydropower**. Turbines are placed under water to convert the energy produced by tides to generate electricity.

LANGUAGE PRACTICE

1. The spelling of the following words is very close to the French one.

le dioxyde de carbone	carbon ....
la calotte polaire	the .... icecap
les hydrocarbures	....
une raffinerie de pétrole	an oil ....
une plateforme pétrolière	an oil ....

2. Find the translations of the following faux-amis.

The sun's rays are captured, converted thanks to photovoltaic cells and then used to generate electricity.

After Fukushima, several governments decided to stop building nuclear plants.

Despite a significant drop in crude oil prices, petrol prices are still very high.

The purpose of carbon trading is to curb greenhouse gas emissions as quickly as possible.

A smart meter does not only measure and record the amount of electricity you use, but also when your consumption fluctuates.

3. Find synonyms for the following words.

a climate scientist	a ....
a wind turbine	a ....
a tidal turbine	a ....
a dam	a ....
a four-wheel drive	a ....

4. All the following compounds include the word "energy".

la consommation d'énergie	....
les besoins en énergie	....
la pénurie d'énergie	....
la politique énergétique	....
les économies d'énergie	....

5. Translate into French.

Most scientists agree that the increase in global temperatures is due to the burning of fossil fuels.

……………………………………………………………………………………………

If oil supplies run out in about 30 years, economic growth will come to an end, unless…

……………………………………………………………………………………………

The main argument in favour of nuclear power is that it does not generate greenhouse gases.

……………………………………………………………………………………………

In the 19th century, Malthusians already predicted the world would run out of energy within a few decades.

……………………………………………………………………………………………

Last week's floods would have taken place even without global warming.

……………………………………………………………………………………………

6. Translate into English.

Je vais au travail en vélo pour sauver la planète sur laquelle je vis.

……………………………………………………………………………………………

L'hydrofracturation devient rentable quand le prix du pétrole dépasse 100 dollars le baril.

……………………………………………………………………………………………

Si on avait arrêté de gaspiller le pétrole il y a trente ans, on n'en serait pas là.

……………………………………………………………………………………………

La demande mondiale d'énergie a explosé avec la montée des pays émergents.

……………………………………………………………………………………………

Suffira-t-il de d'éteindre les appareils électriques pour réduire la consommation d'énergie de façon significative ?

……………………………………………………………………………………………

Questions

Energy saved is money saved. Discuss.
What is the future of the oil industry?
Is nuclear energy the solution to the energy gap?

WRITING TIP N° 18: Auxiliaries

English has two kinds of auxiliaries: the basic auxiliairies "be, have, do" and the modal auxiliaries "can, may, must, will, shall" and their past forms: "could, might, would, should". Both are used extensively in idiomatic ways that French speakers often do not use enough.

• "Be, have, do" are used to form questions and negative statements but also to complete a sentence in an elliptical way (e.g. "Google is expanding very fast and so is Facebook.", "Portugal does not have a strong manufacturing basis and neither does Spain.")

• Auxiliairies are used in particular to avoid the repetition of a verb (e.g. "Some young people seem to think they do not really harm* their health when they smoke. They do.") The refutation in the last sentence is all the more effective* because it is short.

• Auxiliairies are used to form "question tags", that is to say short phrases such as "isn't it?" or "do they?" that you add at the end of a sentence to turn it into a question. In a written text, "question tags" are useful to form rhetorical questions, and thus to engage your reader. Watch out*: since a question tag is a sort of question, it cannot follow another question. Thus, the following sentence: "Is the monarchy still popular in Britain, is it?" does not make sense.

• "Do" is sometimes used to emphasize* a statement, in particular to mark a contrast: "Nuclear energy does not emit greenhouse gases, but it does have another nasty by-product: nuclear waste." In French you would have to add an adverb to translate this use of "do": "*L'énergie nucléaire n'émet pas de gaz à effet de serre mais elle a cependant un sous-produit dangereux: les déchets nucléaires*". Sometimes the contrast is not mentioned explicitly. When you say "I do think that it would be a good idea to..." you imply* that there is something else that you think is not a good idea. You may also imply that you think that it's a good one on the whole even if there may be arguments against it.

• Remember that the modal verb "may" is often a good translation for "*peut-être*". Instead of: "The government has maybe made mistakes.", it would be better to write "The government may have made mistakes."

• When discussing policies, the modal "should" is often a better translation of "*devoir*" than "must". For example: "*Doit-on autoriser les policiers à contrôler qui ils veulent, quand ils veulent ?*" → "Should police officers be allowed to check the identity of whoever they want, whenever they want?".

extensively: *très souvent* • **harm**: *faire du tort à* • **effective**: *qui a de l'effet, frappant* • **watch out**: *faites attention* • **emphasize**: *accentuer* • **imply**: *sous-entendez*

19. SCIENCE

9/11 • abortion • advertising • AIDS • alcohol abuse • armed forces • asbestos • bonuses • BRICS • CIA • cloning • CO_2 • computers • consumer society • couch potatoes • credit bubble • cultural exception • dating • DEA • death penalty • deforestation • dictatorship • digital piracy • diplomacy • domestic violence • drought • drug trafficking • eating disorders • endangered species • English-speaking world • epidemics • euthanasia • fanaticism • food scares • fossil fuels • free speech • free trade • gender gap • glass ceiling • greenhouse gases • gun control • health care • hijacking • human rights • immigration policy • intercourse • ISPs • IVF • justice system • labour • multiculturalism • natural disasters • NGOs • nuclear • nuclear deterrent • oil slicks • on parole • outsourcing • overfishing • ozone layer • PC • pension system • philanthropy • pidgin • prevention • racial profiling • recycling • renewables • RP • salad bowl • same-sex marriage • second-hand smoking • serial killers • sex industry • slump • social divide • social networks • Spanglish • standard English • STDs • stem-cell research • suffragettes • suicide bombers • surrogacy • surveillance • teenage violence • truancy • United Nations • uprisings • video games • waste disposal • welfare state • WMDs • working poor • WTO

creationism

guinea pigs

NASA

physics

technophobia

a scientist ['saɪəntɪst]	un scientifique, un savant
scientific progress ['prəʊgres]	les progrès scientifiques
medical / technological advances	les progrès médicaux / technologiques
scientifically proven ['pruːvən, 'prəʊvən]	prouvé scientifiquement
scientism	le scientisme
physics	la physique
a physicist	un physicien
chemistry ['kemɪstrɪ]	la chimie
a chemist ['kemɪst]	un chimiste
computer science	l'informatique
a computer scientist	un informaticien

Pi is an American thriller (1998) about a number theorist (a mathematician who studies the properties of prime numbers) who can do arithmetic calculations involving large numbers in his head but also suffers from paranoia and hallucinations. He first uses his skills as a mathematician to predict share prices (*le cours des actions en bourse*). After meeting a man who explains to him how the Hebrew alphabet can be translated into numbers and who believes the Torah is a string of numbers that form a code sent by God, he starts doing research on the Torah (the Jewish Bible). He is thus led to believe that there are patterns everywhere in nature and that understanding them will allow him to find the mathematical key to everything, from God to stock prices, the weather and baseball results. Finally his paranoia gets worse and he has to perform a lobotomy on himself to avoid becoming completely mad.

knowledge ['nɒlɪdʒ]	la connaissance, le savoir
theoretical	théorique
a hypothesis [ˌhaɪ'pɒθɪsɪs]	une hypothèse
data ['deɪtə, 'dɑːtə]	des données
evidence	des preuves
to have proof of sth	avoir la preuve de qch
to test a theory	mettre une théorie à l'épreuve
to challenge, to question, to dispute an idea	contester une idée

The first fellows (*membres*) of the **Royal Society**, (in full: The Royal Society of London for Improving Natural Knowledge), were followers of Sir Francis Bacon, a 17th-century statesman and philosopher who argued that knowledge could be gained by testing ideas through experiments. On a damp and murky night in November 1660, a dozen of them met to hear a lecture by a 28-year-old astronomer called Christopher Wren, who would later become the architect who designed St Paul's Cathedral. Inspired, they determined to meet every week to discuss scientific matters and to witness experiments conducted by different members of the group. In so doing, they invented the processes on which modern science rests, including scientific publishing and peer review, and made English the primary language of scientific discourse. Sir Isaac Newton, who defined the laws of gravity, became president of the Royal Society in 1703. No more than 44 outstanding British scientists are elected to fellowship each year, along with up to eight foreign members.

basic, fundamental / applied research	la recherche fondamentale / appliquée
to carry out research into / on a subject	faire des recherches sur un sujet
cutting-edge research	la recherche de pointe
a researcher, a research worker	un chercheur
to revolutionize	révolutionner
a patent ['pætənt, 'peɪtənt]	un brevet
to innovate	innover
a pioneer [ˌpaɪə'nɪəʳ]	un pionnier
findings	des conclusions, des résultats
a discovery	une découverte
a breakthrough	une percée
a study ['stʌdɪ]	une étude
a paper	un article
a journal ['dʒɜːnl]	une revue scientifique

The Lancet is one of the world's oldest and most respected medical journals. It was founded in 1823 by an English surgeon who named it after the surgical instrument called a "lancet" (*bistouri*).

an experiment	une expérience
a phenomenon (plural: -na)	un phénomène
to conduct, carry out, make an experiment	faire une expérience
to experiment on mice	faires des expériences sur des souris
a laboratory [lə'bɒrətərɪ], a lab	un laboratoire
a guinea pig ['gɪnɪ pɪg]	un cobaye

Biologists, chemists, physicists…, in other words specialists of experimental sciences conduct **experiments** in their labs. What happens to you in daily life is **experiences** (e.g. unforgettable experiences), and what you gain from these experiences is **experience**. The two words, 'experiment' and 'experience', are often confused also because both of them are used as verbs too. Thus some scientists **experiment on** animals; people **experiment with** new ideas when they test them for instance. You may also **experience** problems or a particular feeling (e.g. Pregnant women may experience nausea in the first few months).

research and development	recherche et développement
to develop [dɪ'veləp]	mettre au point, élaborer
to devise [dɪ'vaɪz]	concevoir
a device [dɪ'vaɪs]	un appareil, un dispositif, un mécanisme
to design	concevoir, élaborer

Steve Jobs insisted that even the innards (*entrailles*) of Apple's machines, which customers normally would never see, should be as well designed as the exterior. "For you to sleep well at night," he said, "the aesthetic, the quality, has to be carried all the way through." In pursuit of perfection, he could hold up (*retarder*) the release of products for years — as he did with the iPad — or demand expensive last-minute changes. A few weeks before its launch, the first iPhone had to have its plastic screen replaced with glass because Jobs thought the plastic scratched too easily… This fetishism, this intense focus on the aesthetic delights and usability, the erotica of the machines, was underpinned by a very ungeeky faith in their benign social significance. "It is in Apple's DNA that technology alone is not enough," Jobs said when he launched the iPad 2. "It's technology married with liberal arts, married with the humanities, that yields us the results that make our hearts sing."
Bryan Appelyard, "The Brain Is Wider Than the Sky", Weidenfeld & Nicolson, 2011

technique [tek'ni:k]	technique
technical	technique
a technician	un technicien
a science park, a technology park	une technopole
technophobia	la technophobie
an engine ['endʒɪn]	un moteur
an engineer	un ingénieur
engineering	le génie, l'ingénierie
civil engineering	le génie civil
robotics	la robotique
electronics	l'électronique
state-of-the-art	dernier cri
a mobile phone, a cell phone (US)	un téléphone portable
a wireless ['waɪəlɪs] device	un appareil sans fil

The communications tool of choice [during the riots of August 2011 in London] has been the BlackBerry. Young people like its BlackBerry Messenger (BBM) feature, which allows users to send free messages to individuals, or to all their contacts at once. It was used to summon mobs (*foule*) to particular venues. The rioters use BBM against the police. But can the police use it against the rioters? Research in Motion (RIM), the firm behind the BlackBerry, and the mobile operators hold at least one, and probably two, sorts of useful information. The first is traffic data: who messaged whom, when and from where. Used in conjunction with CCTV pictures, that could well help police put names to faces.
The Economist, August 13th 2011

a gene [dʒi:n]	un gène
the human genome ['dʒi:nəʊm]	le génome humain
genome mapping	la cartographie du génome
gene map, genetic map	carte génétique

a geneticist	un généticien
eugenics [juːˈdʒenɪks]	l'eugénisme
DNA [ˌdiːenˈeɪ]	l'ADN
a DNA print, genetic print	une empreinte génétique
a DNA sample	un prélèvement d'ADN
DNA analysis	l'analyse ADN
genetic make-up, genetic profile	profil génétique
genetic screening	le dépistage génétique
to be DNA-swabbed	subir un prélèvement d'ADN
gene therapy	la thérapie génique
cloning [ˈkləʊnɪŋ]	le clonage

A **Luddite** is someone who opposes technological change, in other words a "technophobe". The word is derived from the name of a 19th-century weaver (*tisserand*), Ned Ludd, who is said to have broken a weaving machine in order to protest against the unemployment that the new machines were causing.

a genetically modified organism	un organisme génétiquement modifié
GMOs [ˌdʒiːemˈəʊz]	les OGM
a crop	un culture
a GM crop	une culture OGM
seed [siːd]	la semence, les graines
yield [jiːld]	le rendement
a label [ˈleɪbl]	une étiquette
to label	étiquetter
labelling	l'étiquetage
a warning	un avertissement
traceability	la traçabilité
the food chain	la chaîne alimentaire

The **human genome** is all the genetic information in a person. The Human Genome Project is an international research project which started in 1990 and whose purpose is to determine the sequence of chemical base pairs which make up DNA and to identify and map the 25,000 genes of the human genome.

the conquest of space	la conquête de l'espace
NASA [ˈnæsə] (National Aeronautics and Space Administration)	la NASA
the ESA (European Space Agency)	l'Agence spatiale européenne
a manned flight / an unmanned flight	un vol habité / inhabité
a rocket	une fusée
a probe [prəʊb]	une sonde
a spaceship, a rocket ship, spacecraft	un vaisseau spatial
a shuttle	une navette
a space station	une station spatiale
to launch [lɔːntʃ]	lancer
the countdown	le compte à rebours

to propel [prə'pel]	propulser
propellant	le combustible pour fusée, le propergol
to be in orbit / go into orbit	être en orbite / se mettre en orbite
to put a satellite in(to) orbit	mettre, placer un satellite en orbite
to land, to touch down	atterrir
to land on the moon	alunir

When the United States entered the space race in the late 1950s to catch and ultimately beat the then-Soviet Union, national leaders probably never contemplated this: with the end of NASA's space shuttle program this summer, U.S. astronauts are hitchhiking to the International Space Station on Russian rockets. Once a symbol of America's limitless future, NASA seems to be floundering (*patauger*), indecisive and aimless, without clear, cohesive goals. If the agency expects Congress and the American taxpayer to continue investing in space exploration, the agency needs to spell out where it wants to go, why it wants to go there and what getting there could mean for the United States.
Omaha World Herald, Monday October 10, 2011

weightlessness, zero gravity	l'apesanteur
microgravity ['maɪkrəʊ'grævɪtɪ]	la micro-gravité
a spin-off	une retombée
space tourism	le tourisme dans l'espace
satnav, global positioning system, GPS [dʒiːpiː'es]	le GPS
an unidentified flying object, a UFO [ˌjuːe'fəʊ, 'juːfəʊ]	un OVNI

Creationism (also called **intelligent design**) is the belief that the universe was created by a supernatural being, a God. It is therefore incompatible with the theory of evolution and natural selection, which was first described by the naturalist Charles Darwin in *On the Origin of Species* (1859). Creationism is promoted mostly by fundamentalist Christians — Evangelists in the US but also in Great Britain, for example — who want it to be taught in schools alongside or even instead of Darwinism.

LANGUAGE PRACTICE

1. All the words needed to complete these sentences are based on the same root word.

In the comic books *The Adventures of Tintin,* Professor Calculus is the typical mad ....

.... discoveries were the starting point of the Industrial Revolution.

This theory has never been .... proven.

....................., which was widespread in the late 19th century, is complete belief in the reliability of science.

2. What do the letters in these abbreviations stand for?

The GPS is the G..................... P..................... S.....................

GMOs are g..................... m..................... o.....................

The ESA is the E..................... S..................... A.....................

A UFO is an u..................... f..................... o.....................

3. Find the words that are missing in the following contexts.

More government funding is necessary for our team to undertake cutting .... research in areas of strategic importance.

The police are light-years behind the state-of-the-..................... technology used by some criminal gangs.

In 1783, the French Montgolfier brothers launched the first hot air balloon with several people on board: it was the first balloon capable of .... flight.

A guinea .... is someone who is used in a test to see how successful or safe a product is.

4. Find the appropriate prepositions or particles.

Animal rights groups deny labs the right to experiment .... any animals, including mice, rats or rabbits.

South Africa's new communications satellite will go .... orbit at 5. 20 am tomorrow.

The spacecraft managed to touch .... safely after a nerve-racking 15 minutes.

Your genetic make........... is the same as your genetic profile.

5. What are the words corresponding to these definitions?

A .... is a document that protects your right to make or sell an invention or product that others are not allowed to copy.

.... is fear of modern machines and technology.

A .... is an area where there are a lot of companies or organizations involved in scientific research and development.

.... is the signs, facts or data that enable you to conclude that something is true.

6. Translate into French.

I've heard that Samsung has been experimenting with a new touchscreen.

....

The recent field trials on soyabeans and rapeseed are inconclusive.

....

The airlock on the new multi-stage rocket is remote-controlled.

....

Hardly anything is known about the long-term effects of mobile phone radiations.

....

Computer buffs or more generally tech-savvy youngsters always talk in jargon.

....

7. Translate into English.

Le clonage peut être utilisé à des fins thérapeutiques ou reproductives.

....

Cette technique révolutionnaire a servi pour effectuer une étude sur les pommes de terre génétiquement modifiées.

....

La course dans l'espace a débuté avec le lancement du premier Spoutnik en octobre 57.

....

Les satellites espions ont joué un rôle crucial durant la guerre du Golfe.

....

La recherche fondamentale peut-elle se passer de fonds publics ?

....

Questions

Should research be funded with public money?
Is it possible to reconcile public opinion with science?
Is science a threat to humanity?

WRITING TIP N° 19: Phrases

To become a better writer, you must of course practise writing but you should also read and listen to as much good English as you can. Moreover, to make the most of* what you read, highlight* the passages you feel are worth memorizing*. Learning by heart sentences that you think are particularly well-written is often helpful, because they will become patterns* that stick in your mind* even after you've forgotten the phrases themselves.

Whenever you read, make a note of phrases you think will come in handy* when you have to express yourself. Focus first on words or expressions that may be used in various contexts: you will of course need to know the vocabulary about unemployment when writing an essay about unemployment, but you will need to talk about cause and effect, advantages and drawbacks, problems and solutions etc. to write about *any* issue.

It is important that you should build up your own databank* of such phrases. By way of illustration*, here is a sample* of constructions with their French equivalents that you may find useful.

- "The important thing / interesting thing / strange thing is that ..." → *"Ce qu'il y a d'important / d'intéressant / de bizarre, c'est que..."*
- "The fact remains that..." → *"Il n'en reste pas moins que..."*
- "There is no / little / hardly any doubt that..." → *"Il n'y pas /guère de doute que..."*
- "There is no denying that... / no knowing what may happen / no predicting the consequences of..." → *"On ne peut pas nier que... / On ne peut savoir ce qui peut arriver / prédire les conséquences de..."*
- "What remains to be seen is whether... → *"Ce qui reste à voir, c'est si..."*
- "Contrary to popular belief / Contrary to what is often thought / Contrary to what is sometimes claimed,... → *"Contrairement à ce que croient les gens / à ce que l'on croit souvent / ce que l'on prétend parfois, ...*
- "It is sometimes said / claimed / that..." → *"On dit parfois / prétend que..."*
- "It may be noted / argued that..." → *"On peut noter / soutenir que..."*
- "Let's face it / Let's consider the first example" → *"Regardons les choses en face / Considérons le premier exemple..."*
- "Surprisingly / Unsurprisingly / More importantly, Brazil seems to have..." → *"Ce qui est surprenant / Ce qui n'est pas surprenant / Ce qui est plus important, c'est que le Brésil semble avoir..."*

make the most of: *tirer le meilleur parti de* • **highlight**: *surligner* • **are worth memorizing**: *méritent d'être retenus* • **patterns**: *modèles* • **stick in your mind**: *vous restent en mémoire* • **will come in handy**: *seront utiles* • **databank**: *banque de données* • **By way of illustration**: *En guise d'illustration* • **sample**: *échantillon*

20. INFORMATION TECHNOLOGY

9/11 • abortion • advertising • AIDS • alcohol abuse • armed forces • asbestos • bonuses • BRICS • CIA • cloning • CO_2 • consumer society • couch potatoes • creationism • credit bubble • cultural exception • dating • DEA • death penalty • deforestation • dictatorship • diplomacy • domestic violence • drought • drug trafficking • eating disorders • endangered species • English-speaking world • epidemics • euthanasia • fanaticism • food scares • fossil fuels • free speech • free trade • gender gap • glass ceiling • greenhouse gases • guinea pigs • gun control • health care • hijacking • human rights • immigration policy • intercourse • IVF • justice system • labour • multiculturalism • NASA • natural disasters • NGOs • nuclear • nuclear deterrent • oil slicks • on parole • outsourcing • overfishing • ozone layer • PC • pension system • philanthropy • physics • pidgin • prevention • racial profiling • recycling • renewables • RP • salad bowl • same-sex marriage • second-hand smoking • serial killers • sex industry • slump • social divide • Spanglish • standard English • STDs • stem-cell research • suffragettes • suicide bombers • surrogacy • surveillance • technophobia • teenage violence • truancy • United Nations • uprisings • waste disposal • welfare state • WMDs • working poor • WTO

computers

ISPs

digital piracy

social networks

video games

computer science, computing	l'informatique
information technology, IT	technologie de l'information, informatique
a computer scientist, an IT specialist	un informaticien
to be computer literate ['lɪtərɪt]	savoir utiliser un ordinateur
the computer age, the information age	l'ère de l'informatique
a programmer, a programer (US)	un programmeur
to computerize	informatiser
computerization	l'informatisation
a computer geek, a computer nerd [nɜːd]	un mordu d'informatique, un fana d'informatique, un geek
Information and Communication Technologies, ICT	technologies de l'information et de la communication, TIC

Bio, 28, a single mother living with her parents, set up her first internet cafe in the Sierra Leone capital, Freetown, only a year ago. She has expanded with two more branches, and plans to go national if she can secure a bank loan [...] The swell (*accroissement*) of internet users in her cafe tells Bio she is on a winning road. Access to the internet and computer literacy is an area of much needed growth and investment. Only around 0.3% of the population are described as internet users, while fibre-optic broadband will not arrive until next year. Bio offers women evening computer courses "to make them stronger".
The Guardian, 30 Aug., 2011

digital ['dɪdʒɪtəl]	digital
to digitize ['dɪdʒɪtaɪz], to digitalize	numériser, digitaliser
digitization	numérisation
the digital era ['ɪərə]	l'ère numérique
the digital divide	le fossé numérique

The **digital divide** is the gap between those who have access to computers and the internet and those who don't. There is a digital divide between rich and poor countries, and a digital divide between rich and poor people within a given country.

hardware	le matériel
a PC, a personal computer	un PC, un ordinateur personnel
a (micro-)processor	un (micro-)processeur
a chip	une puce (électronique)
a hard disk	un disque dur
a key	une touche
a keyboard	un clavier
a mousepad	un tapis de souris
a desktop (computer)	un ordinateur de bureau
a laptop (computer)	un ordinateur portable
a tablet computer	un ordinateur tablette
a memory stick, a USB key	une clé USB
a screen	un écran

a touchscreen	un écran tactile
a printer	une imprimante

Moore's Law (1965) states that the power of semiconductors doubles roughly every two years.

software	des logiciels
a software programme, a piece of software, an application	un logiciel
to upgrade, to update	mettre à jour
a word processor	un traitement de texte
a spreadsheet ['spredʃiːt]	un tableur
a database ['deɪtəbeɪs]	une base de données
user-friendly	convivial
freeware, shareware	des logiciels gratuits

The Social Network (2010) explains how Mark Zuckerberg, a Harvard student, created Facebook and became a billionaire in his early 20s. After a spat (*querelle*) with his girlfriend, Zuckerberg decided to get his own back on (*se venger de*) all the women at Harvard University. To do so, he hacked into the "facebooks" (*trombinoscope*) of the university to collect their pictures and create a page on which the girls could be rated (*évaluer*) for their beauty. The site was totally illegal, but it turned out to be immensely popular and its success was the starting-point of the Facebook adventure. The movie goes on to explain how Sean Parker, the founder of Napster, helped M. Zuckerberg turn Facebook into big business.

to cut and paste [peɪst], to copy and paste	copier-coller
to delete [dɪ'liːt], to erase [ɪ'reɪz]	effacer
to save	sauvegarder, enregistrer
to store information	stocker des données
to enter a word, to type in a word	saisir, entrer un mot
a backup copy	une copie de sauvegarde
to print	imprimer, tirer
a print-out	une sortie imprimante

The phrase **data smog** is used to refer to the fact that as a result of the information revolution, the massive amount of data available on the internet may be counterproductive: we are so overwhelmed with information that we cannot process it adequately and may therefore suffer from **information overload**. Another, synonymous, phrase, is **information glut** [glʌt] (a glut is an excessive supply of something on a market). A British psychologist coined the phrase **information fatigue syndrome** to describe the symptoms resulting from information overload: paralysis of analytical capacity, anxiety and self-doubt, leading to foolish decisions and flawed conclusions. All these expressions may be translated as "*surinformation*" or "*surabondance d'information*".

a videogame	un jeu vidéo
a network game	un jeu en réseau
a videogame console	une console de jeu vidéo
a massively multiplayer online role-playing game, MMORPG	un MMORPG
an avatar ['ævətɑː(r)]	un avatar

> What does playing computer games do to us? According to a YouGov poll, one in six children under the age of seven in England has difficulty talking — a problem that will have many worried parents looking at games consoles and wondering how far their children's onscreen delights are implicated in this decline. Overbusy parents can spend dangerously little time talking to their children. Far easier to plonk (*planter*) them down in front of a mesmerising (*hypnotisant*) screen. A lack of parental time and engagement is self-evidently a bad thing, as is the excessive use of any one medium. Yet this vision of gaming as a passive, inert activity does little to help struggling parents. For perhaps the most remarkable thing about modern video games is the degree to which they offer not a sullen and silent unreality, but a realm that's thick with difficulties, obligations, judgments and allegiances.
> Tom Chatfield, *Fun Inc: Why Games are the 21st Century's Most Serious Business* (2010)

the internet, the web	internet, la toile
information highways	les autoroutes de l'information
to go online, to browse the net	aller sur internet
an Internet user, a web user, a web surfer	un internaute
a browser ['braʊzər]	un navigateur
a search engine	un moteur de recherche
cyberspace ['saɪbəspeɪs]	le cyberespace
a hyperlink	un lien hypertexte
a portal ['pɔːtl]	un portail
a server	un serveur
to host [həʊst] a site	héberger un site
high-speed internet access	le haut débit
ADSL [ˌeɪdiːes'el], broadband access	ADSL
a service provider, an Internet access provider, an ISP [ˌaɪes'piː]	un fournisseur d'accès (internet)

Be careful: there are two translations in English for the French verb "*télécharger*". What people do most of the time is **downloading**, whether it be software, films or music files, sometimes illegally. But when you want to post photos on Flickr or a video on YouTube, you **upload** them, from your computer to a server.

a user name, a login (name)	un identifiant, un nom d'utilisateur
to have access to a website	avoir accès à un site
to access a website	accéder, avoir accès à un site
to download	télécharger
to upload	télécharger (vers un serveur)

a password	un mot de passe
a nickname	un pseudo(nyme)
to type in, to enter one's password	taper son mot de passe
to visit, to check a website	aller sur, visiter un site internet
to log in to a site, to log on to a site	se connecter à un site
to log off	se déconnecter
to check one's mail	regarder, vérifier son courrier
to forward ['fɔːwəd] a message	faire suivre un message
to send an attachment	envoyer une pièce jointe

The **Pirate** ['paɪərɪt] **Party** is a political party which advocates unrestricted access to the Internet and campaigns for the reform of copyrights and patents (*brevets*) laws as well as for a strengthening (*renforcement*) of the right to privacy. There are now officially registered Pirate Parties in twenty countries.

> The Pirates, whose core agenda is to increase people's privacy on the Internet and protect freedom of speech, are now active in more than 50 countries, from Europe to Australia, Belarus, Nepal, and Tunisia… Accounting for much of the Pirates' spectacular rise, supporters say, is the lack of political debate on moral issues raised by the development of new technologies. The Pirate parties fill a gap keenly felt by many Internet-savvy voters. The Pirates' belief that culture and knowledge should be shared free of charge appeals to a large portion of what Troberg describes as "the generation that grew up with [the] Internet." The bulk of followers are between 15 and 30 years old.
> Claire Bigg, *Radio Free Europe*, April 19, 2012

a social networking site	un réseau de socialisation, un réseau social
a video-sharing site	un site d'hébergement de vidéos
an auction ['ɔːkʃən] site	un site de vente aux enchères
an internet recruitment site	un site de recrutement sur internet
a chat room	un salon de discussion, un forum
a messaging service	une messagerie
a dating site	un site de rencontres
to post a video	mettre une vidéo en ligne
to meet sb face to face, meet sb offline	rencontrer qn physiquement
e-business	l'e-commerce, le commerce electronique
online shopping	le commerce en ligne

The **Anti-Counterfeiting Trade Agreement** (ACTA, *Accord commercial anti-contrefaçon, ACAC*), is a multinational treaty which aims to protect intellectual property rights and to fight digital piracy as well as the trade of counterfeit goods or generic medicines. This controversial agreement was signed in 2011 but is opposed by many who think it may infringe on fundamental rights such as freedom of expression, privacy or access to medicines in developing countries.

digital piracy ['paɪərəsɪ]	le piratage sur Internet
a hacker, a cracker	un hacker, un pirate informatique
to hack into a system	s'introduire dans un système informatique
to deface [dɪ'feɪs] a site	dégrader un site
to disable, to crash a site	mettre un site hors d'état
cybercrime	la cybercriminalité
cybertheft	le vol de données électroniques
identity theft	le vol d'identité
a bug [bʌg]	un bogue
a virus (pl: viruses) ['vaɪərəs, 'vaɪərəsɪz]	un virus
cyberwar	la guerre informatique, cybernétique

Hacktivism (hacker + activism) is a portmanteau word that refers to the use of hacking to further (*faire avancer*) political or social causes. Wikileaks, which has released a large number of classified documents on its site, is probably the best-known such initiative. Hacktivist groups such as "Anonymous" oppose Internet censorship and anti-digital piracy legislation. **Slacktivism** (slacker + activism) consists in signing internet petitions, copying and pasting messages on a social network etc. in other words doing things that require little effort but give "slacktivists" the impression they are supporting social causes. In fact their action has little impact other than make them feel good about themselves.

a filesharing site	un site de partage de fichiers
to swap [swɒp]	échanger
a music file / an MP3 file	un fichier de musique / un fichier MP3
an MP3 player	un lecteur MP3, un baladeur MP3
intellectual property	la propriété intellectuelle
copyrights	les droits d'auteur, le copyright
to charge sb for sth	faire payer qn pour qch
to infringe on sb's rights	léser les droits de qn, porter atteinte aux droits de quelqu'un
to disconnect a user	priver un internaute d'accès internet

A **P2P** (or peer-to-peer) computer system is one in which each participating computer has access to the files in the other computers without the need for a central server.

LANGUAGE PRACTICE

1. Insert the appropriate preposition or particle, or write Ø if no word is needed.

Today's tech-savvy criminals can hack .... your computer system to gain access to sensitive information about your customers.

To complete your application, print .... the form, fill it in and post it to us with a copy of your ID card.

You need to type in your password so as to access .... the ministry's website.

After you've transferred the money from your account, do remember to log .... from the bank's website.

2. Find the appropriate prefixes or suffixes to form the following words.

charger	to load	to	*télécharger (vers un serveur)*
surfer	to browse	a	*un navigateur*
pouvoir	to be able	to	*mettre un site hors d'état*
numérique	digital	to	*numériser*

3. Form four compound nouns with the following elements and translate.

digital, divide, engine, identity, provider, search, service, theft.

....

....

....

....

4. Only one of the following words is not a faux ami Translate.

Telephone operators charge their subscribers when they listen to music.

A cracker is someone who manages to steal information on someone else's computer.

An avatar is a picture of you that is supposed to represent you when you play online videogames or chat on the web.

You need to register on the site before you can post a message.

5. What are these websites called?

A .... site will help you find a job.

A .... site enables you to exchange messages and to share activities and interests with people called "friends".

An .... site is a site where you can sell your old bike or a Christmas present you don't like.

A .... site is a site you browse to find a lover or someone to marry.

6. Translate into French

You need to update your software to improve its performance.

....

Digital natives are supposed to prefer watching videos on YouTube to reading books.

....

I was able to retrieve my parents' confidential data in a few clicks.

....

Their website went down last week and has been off-line since then.

....

Should the authorities crack down on illegal downloading?

....

7. Translate into English

Il suffit de double-cliquer sur l'icône en haut à gauche pour accéder au site.

....

Tu risques d'avoir une amende si tu télécharges illégalement des films ou des clips.

....

De plus en plus de gens vont sur internet pour réserver des billets d'avion.

....

La quantité d'informations disponibles est telle que l'on finit par se sentir complètement perdu.

....

La plupart des réseaux dont nous dépendons sont conçus par des entreprises privées.

....

Questions

How dangerous are video games?
Why are social networking sites so popular?
Does the internet encourage democracy?

WRITING TIP N° 20: Dos and don'ts*

- Always keep in mind* that clarity is the main quality of good writing.
- You cannot write clearly if:

  a) you don't know how to say what you mean,

  but also if

  b) you don't know what you mean.

  So try to dissociate content from form as far as this is possible: first think about the question (content), then focus on the words (form).
- Keep your reader in mind. For instance, make sure your handwriting is legible*. Do not waste the examiner's time with pointless repetitions or extraneous* words. Do not be too assertive* — you might sound unpleasant or naïve.
- Writing good English does not consist in embellishing sloppy* English with a few idiomatic expressions or sophisticated link-words.
- Beware* of literal translations from the French.
- Re-read yourself (several times if possible), and do not hesitate to cut out* anything that is ambiguous or does not lead your reader forward.
- Pay attention to minutiae* like punctuation, spelling, prepositions, articles… Every single detail counts in a language exam. Besides, writers who do not bother to get the little things right give the impression they cannot be trusted on the big ones.
- Do not try to pass off* someone else's words as your own.
- Do not believe that the longer an essay, the better the mark: quality matters more than quantity.
- Bear in mind that learning to write is learning to think. The amount of time and effort you spend on the quest* for the right word or the right sentence is time well-spent since it will help you understand your subject better: writing is how we think our way into a subject and make it our own.

Dos and don'ts: *A faire et à ne pas faire* • **Always keep in mind**: *N'oubliez jamais* • **legible**: *lisible* • **assertive**: *affirmatif, dogmatique* • **extraneous**: *sans rapport avec le sujet* • **sloppy**: *négligé* • **beware**: *méfiez-vous* • **cut out**: *supprimer* • **minutiae**: *détails* • **pass off**: *faire passer* • **quest**: *recherche*

CORRIGÉS

1. HEALTH

1.

un chirurgien	a surgeon	surg**ery**	*chirurgie*
contagion	contagion	contagi**ous**	*contagieux*
cancer	cancer	carcino**genic**	*cancérigène*
se rétablir	to recover	recov**ery**	*guérison*
retrouver	to trace	trace**ability**	*traçabilité*

2.

The NHS is the National Health Service
The WHO is World Health Organization
STDs are sexually transmitted diseases
A GP is a general practitioner
AIDS means Acquired Immune Deficiency Syndrome

3.

binge drinking	*excès de boisson*
breast cancer	*cancer du sein*
vaccination campaign	*campagne de vaccination*
fatty foods	*aliments riches en graisses*
screening test	*test de dépistage*

4.

to go **on** a diet : *faire un régime*
to come **down** with the flu : *attraper la grippe*
to suffer **from** a disease : *souffrir d'une maladie*
to put **on** weight : *gagner du poids*
to be screened **for** AIDS : *subir un test de dépistage du SIDA*

5.

Anorexia is estimated to affect 1% of adolescent girls.
On estime que l'anorexie touche 1% des adolescentes.

My uncle, a heavy smoker, was diagnosed with lung cancer last year.
L'an dernier on a diagnostiqué un cancer du poumon à mon oncle, un gros fumeur.

Ivor will have to be operated on if his heath doesn't improve.
Il faudra qu'Ivor se fasse opérer si sa santé ne s'améliore pas.

Sophie's husband is at least ten kilos overweight.
Le mari de Sophie pèse au moins dix kilos de trop.

Some young people don't realize how dangerous unprotected sex is.
Il y a des jeunes qui ne se rendent pas compte à quel point c'est dangereux d'avoir des rapports non protégés.

6.

Les soins médicaux représentent une part énorme de notre budget.
Health care accounts for a huge share of our budget.

L'épidémie s'est déclarée il y a trois jours et se propage rapidement.
The epidemic broke out three days ago and is spreading fast.

Il faudra changer tes habitudes alimentaires si tu veux perdre du poids.
You will have to change your eating habits if you want to lose weight.

On ne sert pas d'aliments diététiques dans les fast foods.
Health foods aren't served in fast food restaurants.

Les effets secondaires de ce nouveau vaccin sont encore mal compris.
The side effects of this new vaccine are still poorly understood.

2. DRUGS

1.

to **experiment** with psychoactive substances : *essayer des psychotropes*
to get **drunk** : *se saoûler*
the **pros** of a policy : *les arguments pour, les avantages d'une politique*
hard drugs : *drogues dures*
a **heavy** cannabis user : *un gros consommateur de cannabis*

2.

la toxicomanie	drug abuse, drug addiction
un toxicomane	a drug user, drug abuser, drug addict
une drogue de synthèse	a designer drug, a synthetic drug
un trafiquant de drogue	a drug-trafficker
un réseau de trafiquants	a drug ring, a drug cartel

3.

to cut down **on** one's consumption : *réduire sa consommation*
to phase **out** : *éliminer progressivement*
to deter people **from** smoking : *dissuader les gens de fumer*
to resist **Ø** temptation : *résister à la tentation*
to become hooked **on** crack cocaine : *devenir accro à la cocaïne*

4.

drug-**related** charges : *infractions liées à la drogue*
driving **while** intoxicated : *conduite en état d'ébriété, d'ivresse*
second-**hand** smoking : *le tabagisme passif*
a smoke-**filled** environment : *un endroit enfumé*
to quit cold **turkey** : *arrêter d'un seul coup*

5.

He was a chain-smoker and eventually died of throat cancer.
Il fumait cigarette sur cigarette et et il a fini par mourir du cancer de la gorge.

They used mules to smuggle LSD and amphetamines into the country.
Ils se servaient de mules pour faire entrer du LSD et des amphétamines dans le pays.

You can become addicted even if you don't inhale the smoke.
On peut devenir accro même si on n'avale pas la fumée.

Prohibition encouraged the spread of guns and crime.
La Prohibition a favorisé la dissémination des armes à feu et stimulé la criminalité.

Turning to crime may be the only solution some addicts have to pay for their daily dose.
Il arrive que devenir criminel soit le seul moyen pour certains drogués de financer leur dose quotidienne.

6.

Il faut aussi réduire la demande de drogue dans les pays riches.
The demand for drugs in rich countries also needs to be curbed.

Le tabac et l'alcool sont responsables de milliers de morts chaque année.
Smoking and alcohol abuse are responsible for thousands of deaths every year.

La cocaïne s'est beaucoup banalisée ces dernières années.
Cocaine use has become very common over the last few years.

Il faut sensibiliser les jeunes aux dangers du cannabis.
Young people must be made aware of the dangers of cannabis.

Devrait-on dépénaliser les drogues douces ? Faut-il criminaliser l'abus d'alcool ?
Should soft drugs be decriminalized? Should alcohol abuse be criminalized?

3. SEX & LOVE

1.

érotique	erotic	eroti**cism**	*l'érotisme*
sexuel	sexual	to be sexu**ally** aroused	*être excité sexuellement*
compagnon	partner	civil partner**ship**	*PACS*
homophobe (n)	homophobe (n)	homophob**ic**	*homophobe (adj)*

2.

one-night **stand** : *une liaison sans lendemain*
same-sex parenting : *homoparentalité*
to be sex-**starved** : *être frustré sexuellement*
to set up **house** : *se mettre en ménage avec qn*

3.

nymphomane : nymphoman**iac**
homophobie : homophob**ia**
fidélité : fid**e**lit**y**
mariage : ma**rr**iage

4.

to be unfaithful to sb = **to cheat on sb, to deceive sb** : *tromper qn*
to fall for sb = **to fall in love with sb** : *tomber amoureux de qn*
to court sb = **to woo sb** : *faire la cour à qn*
to get married to sb = **to marry sb** : *se marier avec qn*

5.

sperm count	*nombre de spermatozoïdes*
dating site	*site de rencontres*
sex offender	*délinquant sexuel*
pedophile ring	*réseau pédophile*

6.

The most common age of consent worldwide is 16.
L'âge de la majorité sexuelle le plus fréquent dans le monde est de 16 ans.

Hard-line Catholics have always taken a tough line on gay marriage.
Les catholiques purs et durs ont toujours été inflexibles au sujet du mariage homosexuel.

Copenhagen is described as the world's most gay-friendly city.
Copenhague a la réputation d'être la ville la plus accueillante pour les homosexuels.

Anthony made a pass at the waitress, but she did not respond.
Anthony a fait des avances à la serveuse, mais elle n'a pas réagi.

They were deeply in love and decided to tie the knot straight away.
C'était le grand amour et ils ont décidé de convoler aussitôt.

7.

Cela fait plusieurs années qu'il n'a pas eu quelqu'un dans sa vie.
He hasn't been in a relationship for several years.

Il faut avoir des rapports protégés pour éviter d'attraper la syphilis.
You must have protected sex to avoid catching syphilis.

Elle a été agressée sexuellement à deux reprises par son employeur.
She was sexually assaulted by her employer on two occasions.

Aux Etats-Unis, un homme politique n'est pas censé avoir des aventures.
In the US, politicians are not supposed to have affairs.

Les opposants au mariage homosexuel voudraient qu'il soit interdit pour toujours.
Opponents of same-sex marriage would like it to be banned for ever.

4. WOMEN

1.

une mère	a mother	mother**hood**	*maternité*
harceler	to harass	harass**ment**	*harcèlement*
être en enceinte	to be pregnant	pregn**ancy**	*grossesse*
contraception	contraception	a contracept**ive**	*un contraceptif*
terminer	to terminate	a termina**tion**	*une IVG*

2.

a **dowry** : *une dot*

a **midwife** : *une sage-femme*

a **nanny** : *une nourrice* • a **childminder** : *une assistante maternelle, une nourrice*

a **pill** : *une pillule*

coil : *un stérilet*

3.

female circumcision	*excision*
male preserve	*chasse gardée pour les hommes*
parental leave	*congé parental*
equal opportunity	*égalité des chances*
menial job	*emploi subalterne*

4.

a pro-**life** activist : *un militant contre l'avortement*

female employment : *l'emploi des femmes*

domestic appliances : *appareils électro-ménagers*

to do the housework : *faire le ménage*

egalitarian : *égalitaire*

5.

Women have always been discriminated against.
Les femmes ont toujours été victimes de discriminations.

My daughter's been on the pill since she was 17.
Ma fille prend la pilule depuis qu'elle a 17 ans.

Women now make up nearly half the workforce.
Les femmes représentent maintenant près de la moitié de la main d'œuvre.

There are still many barriers to female advancement.
Il y a encore beaucoup d'obstacles à la promotion des femmes.

In the US, pro-life activists are a vocal minority.
Aux États-Unis, les militants contre l'avortement forment une minorité qui se fait beaucoup entendre.

6.

Aux États-Unis, les femmes ont le droit de vote depuis près d'un siècle.
In the US, women have had the right to vote for nearly a century.

Serena a dû aller à la maternité à pied depuis chez elle.
Serena had to walk to the maternity hospital from her home.

Elle travaille à mi-temps pour pouvoir s'occuper de ses enfants.
She works part-time to be able to look after her children.

La plupart d'entre elles ont du mal à trouver un équilibre entre travail et famille.
Most of them have difficulty balancing work and family.

Elles sont encore loin d'avoir atteint l'égalité avec les hommes.
They are still a long way from achieving equality with men.

5. BIOETHICS

1.

a code of **ethics** : *déontologie, code de conduite* (also **code of conduct**)
ethical : *éthique*
ethically : *d'un point de vue éthique, sur le plan éthique*
unethical : *moralement contestable, contraire à l'éthique*

2.

a **terminal** disease : *une maladie incurable*
an organ **recipient** : *un receveur d'organe*
agony : *douleur atroce*
to provide **relief** : *apporter un soulagement*

3.

a surrogate mother	surrog**acy**	*gestation pour autrui*
to bear	**un**bear**able**	*insupportable*
to donate	an egg don**or**	*un donneuse d'ovule*
sacred	the sacred**ness** of life	*le caractère sacré de la vie*

4.

semen = **sperm** : *du sperme*
palliative treatment = palliative **care** : *soins palliatifs*
to withdraw treatment = to **stop, withhold, cease** treatment : *arrêter les soins*
womb = **uterus** : *utérus*

5.

l'eugénisme : eugen**ics**
controversé : controvers**ial**
le clonage : clon**ing**
la paralysie : paralys**is**

6.

After the crash, my uncle remained paralyzed from the waist down.
Après l'accident, mon oncle est resté paraplégique.

The decision of the British Medical Association caused an uproar.
La décision de l'Association des médecins britanniques (*équivalent du Conseil de l'Ordre des médecins*) a provoqué une tempête de protestations.

Therapeutic cloning consists in replacing damaged organs with genetically identical cells.
Le clonage thérapeutique consiste à remplacer des organes abîmés par des cellules génétiquement identiques.

Scientists may be tempted to play God.
Les scientifiques peuvent être tentés de jouer à l'apprenti sorcier.

I agree that morally questionable practices should be outlawed.
Je suis d'accord pour dire que les pratiques moralement discutables devraient être interdites.

7.

Les partisans de l'euthanasie voudraient qu'elle soit dépénalisée.
Supporters of euthanasia would like it to be decriminalized.

On a dû mettre le jeune garçon sous assistance respiratoire.
The young boy had to be hooked up to a respirator.

Ma voisine est dans le coma depuis qu'elle a tenté de se suicider.
My neighbour has been in a coma since she attempted suicide.

La fécondation in vitro a permis à des milliers de parents d'avoir un enfant.
In vitro fertilization has enabled thousands of parents to have children.

La plupart des infirmières sont-elles opposées au suicide médicalement assisté ?
Do most nurses oppose doctor-assisted suicide?

6. ENGLISH

1.

mother **tongue** : *langue maternelle*
in **other** words : *en d'autres termes*
to express **oneself** (ici : themselves) : *s'exprimer*
an **understatement** : *une litote*

2.

to translate the Bible **into** English : *traduire la bible en anglais*
to brush **up** one's Hungarian : *rafraîchir son hongrois*
to be good **at** languages : *être bon en langues*
proficiency **in** Italian : *compétence en italien*

3.

	NOM	VERBE
spread	*propagation, diffusion*	*se propager, se diffuser*
phrase	*expression*	*formuler, exprimer*
coin	*pièce (de monnaie)*	*inventer (un mot)*
quote	*citation*	*citer*

4.

to make oneself **understood** : *se faire comprendre*
Do you know what the word « pidgin » **means**? : *Savez-vous ce que veut dire le mot « pidgin » ?*
broken English : *mauvais anglais*
written English : *anglais écrit*

5.

buzz word	*mot à la mode*
mumbo jumbo	*charabia*
working language	*langue de travail*
native speaker	*locuteur natif*

6.

When I said your father was a coward it was only a figure of speech.
Quand j'ai dit que ton père était un lâche, c'était seulement une figure de style.

What's the English for « boulot »?
Comment dit-on « boulot » en anglais ?

Rita is... how shall I put it?... not always easy-going.
Rita est... comment dirais-je ? ... pas toujours commode.

In 1990 the Netherlands considered making English the sole language of university education.
En 1990, les Pays-Bas ont envisagé de faire de l'anglais la seule langue de l'enseignement supérieur.

Some think the days of English as the world's lingua-franca may be numbered.
Certains pensent que les jours de l'anglais en tant que lingua franca du monde entier sont peut-être comptés.

7.

Que veut dire l'expression « recreational drug » ?
What does the phrase « recreational drug » mean?

Je ne sais pas vraiment ce que veut dire le mot «indigent ».
I don't really know what the word « indigent » means.

Ivor parle déjà couramment l'arabe et le japonais.
Ivor already speaks Arabic and Japanese fluently.

Vous aurez du mal à parler le mandarin sans accent.
You will have trouble speaking Mandarin without an accent.

Il faut être un homme politique chevronné pour manier la langue de bois avec autant de brio.
You need to be a veteran politician to use cant so brilliantly.

7. GLOBALIZATION

1.

fair trade : *le commerce équitable*
economic growth : *croissance économique*
a tax **haven** : *paradis fiscal*
flight of capital : *fuite de capitaux*
trade **surplus** : *excédent commercial*

2.

un pays émergent : an **emerging** country
un pays développé : a **developed** country
déréglementer : to **deregulate**
tarifs douaniers : **tariffs**
un exportateur : an **exporter**

3.

dumping : *dumping* **trading at a loss** : *vendre à perte*
outsourcing, offshoring, relocating : *délocalisations*
competitiveness : *compétitivité*
manufacturing : *le secteur secondaire, l'industrie*
deregulation : *dérèglementation*, **liberalization** : *libéralisation*

4.

être en concurrence	to compete	a compet**itor**	*un concurrent*
norme	standard	standard**ization**	*uniformisation*
marché	market	a free-market**eer**	*partisan du libéralisme*
frontière	border	border**less**	*sans frontières*
subvention	subsidy	to subsid**ize -dise**	*subventionner*

5.

Some claim globalization dates back to the days of Christopher Columbus.
Certains prétendent que la mondialisation remonte à l'époque de Christophe Colomb.

NAFTA is a free trade area between Canada, Mexico and the US.
L'ALENA (Accord de libre-échange nord-américain) est une zone de libre-échange entre le Canada, le Mexique et les Etats-Unis.

Third-World countries need trade barriers to protect their nascent industries.
Les pays du Tiers-Monde ont besoin de barrières douanières pour protéger leurs industries naissantes.

Higher taxation of company profits could lead to more outsourcing.
Une plus forte imposition des bénéfices des entreprises pourrait entraîner davantage de délocalisations.

What measure of protectionism is desirable in the face of unfair trading practices?
Quelle dose de protectionisme est-elle souhaitable face aux pratiques commerciales déloyales?

6.

Les échanges de la Chine ont explosé depuis son admission à l'OMC.
China's trade has soared since it was admitted into the WTO.

Leur but est de profiter la main d'œuvre bon marché au Vietnam.
Their aim is to take advantage of Vietnam's cheap labour.

La baisse du taux de change du dollar est favorable aux importateurs.
The drop in the exchange rate of the dollar favours importers.

Les altermondialistes ne tiennent pas compte des bienfaits du commerce mondial.
Antiglobalists do not take account of the benefits of world trade.

Plus la concurrence devient déloyale, plus on est tenté de rétablir des droits de douane.
The more unfair competition becomes, the more one is tempted to re-introduce customs duties.

8. THE ECONOMIC CRISIS

1.

a skilled **worker** : *un travailleur qualifié* (ici **workers**)
the **workplace** : *le lieu de travail*
the **working** population : *la population active*
Thailand's **workforce** : *la main d'œuvre thailandaise*

2.

	VERB	NOUN
collapse	*s'effondrer*	*effondrement*
claim	*revendiquer*	*revendication*
share	*partager*	*une action*
recruit	*recruter*	*une recrue*

3.

a **shop steward** : *un délégué syndical*
a **hedge fund** : *un fonds spéculatif*
fringe benefits : *avantages en nature*
insider dealing, insider trading : *délit d'initié*

4.

to retire : *prendre sa retraite*
to resume work : *reprendre le travail*
to save money : *économiser de l'argent, épargner*
to recover : *se redresser, se rétablir*

5.

offre d'emploi : **job vacancy, job offer, job opportunity**
marché de l'emploi : **job market**
demandeur d'emploi : **job seeker**
sécurité de l'emploi : **job security**

6.

The British economy went through a very bad patch in the 1970s.
L'économie britannique a traversé une passe très difficile dans les années 70.

There were too many people on the payroll of state-owned companies.
Il y avait trop de gens employés dans les entreprises appartenant à l'Etat.

The financialization of the economy is said to be responsible for the global meltdown of 2007.
On dit que la financiarisation de l'économie est responsable de l'effondrement de l'économie mondiale de 2007.

Portugal's economy was in the doldrums as a result of drastic budget cuts.
L'économie portugaise était dans le marasme à la suite de réductions budgétaires draconiennes.

Public-sector employees account for a huge share of the French working population.
Les fonctionnaires représentent une part énorme de la population active en France.

7.

Et ta femme, elle fait quoi, dans la vie ?
What about your wife? What does she do for a living?

L'Administration Obama a été obligée de prendre des mesures d'urgence dès 2009.
The Obama Administration was forced to take emergency measures as early as 2009.

Les petits épargnants ont beaucoup plus perdu que les gros investisseurs.
Small savers lost much more than big investors.

Le chômage des jeunes atteint plus de 50% dans plusieurs pays européens.
Youth unemployment stands at over 50% in several European countries.

Faut-il supprimer les agences de notation ?
Should credit-rating agencies be done away with?

9. INEQUALITIES

1.

housing **benefit** : *allocation logement*

to support a charitable cause : *soutenir une bonne cause*

a volunteer : *une bénévole*

destitution : *dénuement, misère noire*

a charity : *une organisation caritative, une œuvre de charité*

2.

lifestyle = **way of life** : *mode de vie*

a not-for profit organization = a **non-profit-making** organization : *une organisation à but non lucratif*

dire poverty = **extreme** poverty : *misère*

underprivileged = **deprived, disadvantaged** : *défavorisé*

to pledge $1 million in aid = to **promise** $1 million in aid : *promettre 1 million de dollars d'aide*

3.

to be entitled **to** legal aid : *avoir droit à l'aide juridique*

to write **off** a debt : *effacer, annuler une dette*

to sink **into** poverty : *sombrer dans la pauvreté*

to share **out** : *distribuer, répartir*

to scrape **by** : *vivoter*

4.

tax break	*réduction d'impôts*
health coverage	*couverture médicale*
life expectancy	*espérance de vie*
soup kitchen	*soupe populaire*
welfare state	*Etat-providence*

5.

Homelessness has been on the rise over the past few years.
Il y a de plus en plus de sans-abri depuis quelques années.

Without work, you may have to live on state handouts.
Sans travail, il se peut que vous soyez obligés de vivre de l'aide sociale.

Even today, more than one American in six lives below the poverty line.
Encore aujourd'hui, plus d'un Américain sur six vit en dessous du seuil de pauvreté.

Even bright students have difficulty moving up the social ladder.
Même des étudiants brillants ont du mal à grimper dans l'échelle sociale.

My ex-wife will spend €500 on a handbag but won't make a €10 donation.
Mon ex-femme est prête à dépenser 500 euros pour un sac à main, mais ne veut pas faire un don de 10 euros.

6.

Le fossé entre les pauvres et les riches ne cesse de se creuser.
The gap between rich and poor keeps widening.

De plus en plus de personnes ont du mal à joindre les deux bouts.
More and more people find it hard to make ends meet.

Vous ne toucherez votre retraite qu'après avoir travaillé 42 ans.
You will receive your pension only after you have worked for forty-two years.

C'est un philanthrope qui a fondé une organisation humanitaire.
He is a philanthropist who has founded a relief agency.

Pourquoi la répartition de la richesse ne pourrait-elle pas être plus juste ?
Why couldn't the distribution of wealth be fairer?

10. SOCIAL ILLS

1.

custody : *garde (des enfants)*
a **scholarship,** a **grant** : *une bourse*
shoplifting : *vol à l'étalage*
a **hoarding** (GB), a **billboard** (US) : *un panneau publicitaire*

2.

matériel	material	material**istic**	*matérialiste (adj)*
agressif	aggressive	aggressive**ness**	*agressivité*
tromper	to deceive	dece**ptive**	*trompeur*
ordre	order	**dis**order**ly** conduct	*incivilités*

3.

anti-social behaviour : *comportement anti-social*
to **play** truant (*ici* played) : *faire l'école buissonnière*
to be born out of **wedlock** : *naître hors mariage*
a no-**go** zone : *une zone de non-droit*

4.

blended family	*famille recomposée*
reality television	*télé-réalité*
young offender	*délinquant juvénile*
childhood obesity	*obésité chez les enfants*

5.

consumer society : *société de consommation*
youth unemployment : *chômage des jeunes*
advertising : *publicité (secteur économique)*
single-parent families : *familles monoparentales*

6.

Money can't buy happiness… or can It?
L'argent ne fait pas le bonheur… ou bien le fait-il ?

Many dropouts come from broken homes.
Beaucoup de jeunes qui abandonnent leurs études viennent de familles désunies.

The integration of young people into the world of work is a major issue of the presidential campaign.
L'insertion professionnelle des jeunes est un enjeu majeur de la campagne présidentielle.

Consumers are brainwashed into buying gadgets they don't need.
On fait un lavage de cerveau aux consommateurs pour qu'ils achètent des gadgets dont ils n'ont pas besoin.

She was a successful executive but she grew tired of the rat race.
Elle était cadre et elle réussissait mais elle s'est lassée de la compétition acharnée de la vie moderne.

7.

Le problème de beaucoup de jeunes, c'est qu'ils n'ont pas de repères.
The problem of many young people is that they have no points of reference.

Ils ignorent tout des valeurs familiales traditionnelles.
They know nothing about traditional family values.

La télé-réalité fait croire à certains qu'il suffit d'être jeune et beau pour devenir riche.
Reality TV makes some believe that being young and good-looking is enough to become rich.

La méritocratie récompense les gens en fonction de leurs performances.
Meritocracy rewards people according to their performance

L'ascenseur social est-il en panne dans les quartiers défavorisés ?
Is the social ladder broken in underprivileged areas?

11. CULTURAL DIVERSITY

1.

un passeport : **a passport**
l'asile poltique : **political asylum**
exclure : **to exclude**
l'antisémitisme : **anti-Semitism**

2.

to **emigrate** : *émigrer*
migrant / immigrant workers : *travailleurs migrants*
immigrate : *immigrer*
immigration / migration policy : *politique migratoire*

3.

	VERB	NOUN
mistrust	*se méfier*	*méfiance*
fuel	*alimenter, nourrir, entretenir*	*combustible, carburant*
shelter	*abriter*	*refuge, abri*
abuse	*insulter, injurier*	*insultes, injures* OU *abus*

4.

racist attack : *agression raciste*
family reunion : *regroupement familial*
a secular society : *une société laique*
to deport sb : *expulser qn*

5.

citoyen	citizen	citizen**ship**	*citoyenneté*
inciter	to incite	incite**ment** to racial hatred	*incitation à la haine raciale*
contrôler	to control	**unc**ontro**lled** immigration	*immigration sauvage*
profil	profile	racial profil**ing**	*délit de faciès*

6.

Most of my friends have at least one foreign-born grandparent.
La plupart de mes amis ont au moins un grand-parent né à l'étranger.

He was turned away at the border because his papers were not in order.
Il a été refoulé à la frontière parce qu'il était en situation irrégulière.

It could take you years before you are granted British citizenship.
Il te faudra peut-être des années avant d'obtenir la nationalité britannique.

Every citizen regardless of race or ethnicity must have access to education.
Tous les citoyens, quelles que soient leur race ou appartenance ethnique, doivent avoir accès à l'éducation.

There is no evidence that immigration hurts indigenous workers.
Rien ne prouve que l'immigration fait du tort aux travailleurs autochtones.

7.

On quitte généralement son pays natal à la recherche de meilleures conditions de vie.
People generally leave their native country in search of better living conditions.

Si sa femme n'apprend pas la langue, elle risque d'être coupée du reste de la société.
If his wife doesn't learn the language, she risks being cut off from the rest of society.

Les partis d'extrême-droite distinguent entre les Français « de souche » et les autres.
Far-right parties distinguish between people « of French extraction » and the others.

Plusieurs Musulmans d'origine pakistanaise ont été la cible d'insultes à caractère racial.
Several Muslims of Pakistani origin suffered racist abuse.

L'élection d'un président métis signifie-t-elle que la société américaine est devenue « post-raciale » ?
Does the election of a mixed-race president mean that US society has become "post-racial"?

12. DEMOCRACY

1.

political **system** : *régime politique*
single-party system : *système de parti unique*
to declare **a** state of emergency : *déclarer l'état d'urgence*
to come into **office** (= come to power) *arriver au pouvoir*
stop and **search** : *interpeller et fouiller*

2.

closed **circuit** TV : *télévision en circuit fermé*
freedom of **worship**, of **religion** : *liberté de culte* ou *religieuse*
military **junta** : *junte militaire*
to detain a suspect without **charge** : *détenir un suspect sans l'inculper*
to hold a leader to **account** : *tenir un dirigeant pour responsable*

3.

to overthrow a dictator = **to topple,** to **oust** a dictator : *renverser, évincer un dictateur*
a protester = **a demonstrator** : *un manifestant*
a crackdown = **a clampdown** : *mesures de répression*
sleaze = **corruption, bribery** : *corruption*
a breach of privacy = **a violation of privacy, a privacy violation** : *une atteinte à la vie privée*

4.

to snoop **on** people : *espionner les gens*
to be **in** power : *être au pouvoir*
an infringement **on** sb's rights : *une atteinte, une entorse aux droits de qn*
the right **to** vote : *le droit de vote*
a crime **against** humanity **:** *un crime contre l'humanité*

5.

In a parliamentary system, the prime minister is accoutable to an elected assembly.
Dans un régime parlementaire, le premier ministre est responsable devant une assemblée élue.

It became clear that the election had been rigged when the outgoing president was re-elected with 97.6% of the vote.
Il devint évident que l'élection avait été truquée lorsque le président sortant fut réélu avec 97,6% des voix.

After the murder, several suspects were DNA-swabbed, to no avail.
Après le meurtre, plusieurs suspects ont subi un test ADN, en vain.

It took the French Republic decades to admit the Vichy regime had deported Jews.
Il a fallu des décennies à la République française pour reconnaître que le régime de Vichy avait déporté des Juifs.

Which country has the worse human-rights record, North Korea or Iran?
Quel pays a le pire bilan en matière de droits de l'homme, la Corée du Nord ou l'Iran ?

6.

La plupart des pays d'Amérique Latine se sont démocratisés dans les années 70.
Most Latin American countries became more democratic in the 70s.

Les émeutes ont éclaté peu après la chute du gouvernement de gauche.
The riots broke out soon after the downfall of the left-wing government.

La police a le droit de ficher qui elle veut et de conserver ces informations pendant des années
The police have the right to put whoever they want on file and to store this information for years.

Les dirigeants élus démocratiquement du Mali ont été renversés avant-hier.
Mali's democratically elected leaders were overthrown the day before yesterday.

Il aurait fallu surveiller les frontières de plus près.
The borders should have been more closely monitored.

13. CRIME

1.

to charge sb : *inculper, accuser qn*
to confess : *avouer*
to pardon sb : *grâcier qn*
a corpse : *un cadavre*

2.

to **steal** a wallet : *voler un portefeuille*
a **life** sentence : *une condamnation à perpétuité*
manslaughter : *homicide*
to **sue** sb : *engager des poursuites contre qn, intenter un procès à qn*

3.

un voleur	a thief	th**eft**	*le vol*
une arme à feu	a gun	a gun**man**	*un homme armé*
juger	to try	a tr**ial**	*un procès*
assassiner	to murder	a murder**er**	*un assassin, un meurtrier*

4.

a **slaughter** : *massacre*
a **vigilante** : *membre d'un groupe d'auto-défense*
a **bullet** : *une balle*
a **defendant** : *un accusé*

5.

la petite délinquance	petty crime
la criminalité organisée	organized crime
le taux de criminalité	crime rate
la criminalité en col blanc	white-collar crime

6.

In Antiquity, it was very common to demand an eye for an eye and a tooth for a tooth.
Dans l'Antiquité, la loi du talion était très répandue.

According to the Declaration of Human Rights, a defendant is innocent until proven guilty.
D'après la Déclaration des droits de l'homme, un accusé est présumé innocent jusqu'à ce que sa culpabilité soit établie.

Many convicts on death row spend decades in jail.
Beaucoup de condamnés à mort passent des dizaines d'années en prison.

If you own a gun, you may be tempted to take the law into your own hands.
Si l'on possède une arme, on peut être tenté de se faire justice.

Dozens of convicts have now been cleared by DNA analysis.
Des dizaines de condamnés ont maintenant été innocentés grâce aux analyses ADN.

7.

Le comptable a avoué avoir détourné 40 000 euros l'an dernier.
The accountant confessed to embezzling 40,000 euros last year.

C'est pourquoi il a été condamné à six mois de prison.
That is why he was sentenced to six months' imprisonment.

Proportionnellement, les Etats-Unis ont la population carcérale la plus importante du monde entier.
Proportionally, the US has the largest prison population in the whole world.

Eric agissait en état de légitime défense et il a donc plaidé non coupable.
Eric was acting in self-defence and so pleaded not guilty.

La peine de mort a-t-elle vraiment un effet dissuasif ?
Does the death penalty really act as a deterrent?

14. TERRORISM

1.

to **defuse** a bomb : *désamorcer une bombe*
to **hijack** a plane : *détourner un avion*
to **blackmail** sb : *faire chanter qn*
to **eradicate** terrorism : *éradiquer le terrorisme*

2.

	NOUN	VERB
plot	*complot*	*comploter, conspirer*
fear	*peur*	*craindre, avoir peur*
harbour	*port*	*héberger, abriter*
target	*cible*	*avoir pour cible, viser*

3.

une conspiration : **a conspiracy**
le fanatisme : **fanaticism**
un otage : **a hostage**
démanteler : **to dismantle**

4.

a **suicide** bomber : *kamikaze*
a **rogue** state : *un État-voyou*
a bomb **hoax** : *une fausse alerter à la bombe*
the death **toll** : *le nombre des victimes*

5.

to foil a plot = **to thwart** a plot : *déjouer, faire échouer un compot*
to scare people = **to frighten** people : *effrayer, faire peur aux gens*
to combat terrorism = **to fight, to tackle** terrorism : *lutter contre le terrorisme*
to yield to a threat = **to give in** to a threat : *céder à une menace*

6.

No-one has claimed responsibility for last week's bomb attack yet.
Personne n'a encore revendiqué l'attentat de la semaine dernière.

A spate of bombings hit Paris in the late eighties.
Une vague d'attentats a frappé Paris vers la fin des années 80.

A dozen people were killed in the attack which took place last night.
L'attentat qui a eu lieu hier soir a fait une douzaine de victimes.

Many analysts think that terrorism is here to stay.
Nombreux sont les experts qui pensent que le terrorisme n'est pas près de disparaître.

The hijackers attempted to blackmail the Israeli authorities into freeing some prisoners.
Les pirates de l'air ont tenté de faire chanter les autorités israeliennes pour qu'elles libèrent quelques prisonniers.

7.

Ils ne se rendent pas compte qu'en recourant à la violence, ils discréditent leur cause.
They don't realize that by resorting to violence they discredit their cause.

Un groupe d'extrême-droite a fait sauter plusieurs bâtiments officiels.
A far-right organization blew up several government buildings.

La CIA a pu démanteler plusieurs réseaux terroristes islamistes en 2010.
The CIA was able to dismantle several Islamic terrorist networks in 2010.

L'expression de l'Administration Bush, « la guerre contre la terreur », ne veut pas dire grand-chose.
The Bush Administration's phrase, "war on terror", does not mean much.

Le terrorisme sera-t-il jamais éradiqué ?
Will terrorism ever be eradicated?

15. INTERNATIONAL RELATIONS

1.

NGO : **non-governmental organization** : *une ONG*
POW : **prisoner of war** : *un prisonnier de guerre*
WMD : **weapon of mass destruction** : *arme de destruction massive*
PTSD : **post-traumatic stress disorder** : *névrose post-traumatique*
ICBM : **intercontinental ballistic missile** : *missile ballistique intercontinental*

2.

nuclear **fallout** : *retombées nucléaires*
nuclear **deterrent** : *dissuasion nucléaire*
nuclear **warfare** : *guerre nucléaire*
nuclear **testing** : *essais nucléaires*
nuclear **facilities** : *installations nucléaires*

3.

	NOUN	VERB
bomb	*bombe*	*bombarder*
spy	*espion*	*espionner*
defeat	*défaite*	*vaincre, battre*
veto	*véto*	*mettre son véto*
compromise	*compromis*	*transiger* OU *compromettre*

4.

to withdraw troops **from** a country : *retirer des troupes d'un pays*
to wage a war **on, against** a country : *faire la guerre à un pays*
to retaliate **against** an enemy : *exercer des représailles contre un ennemi*
the balance **of** power : *équilibre des forces*
to impose sanctions **on** a country : *imposer des sanctions à un pays*

5.

Russia did not hesitate to flex its muscles and issue threats.
La Russie n'a pas hésité à faire étalage de sa force et à proférer des menaces.

Iran's new plutonium-processing facility is unlikely to make the world a safer place.
Il est peu probable que la nouvelle usine d'enrichissement du plutonium de l'Iran rende le monde plus sûr.

The liberation of the prisoners was indispensable to the resumption of talks.
La libération des prisonniers était indispensable à la reprise des discussions.

Will the deployment of troops at the border deter the dictator from attacking?
Le déploiement de troupes à la frontière dissuadera-t-il le dictateur d'attaquer ?

A two-thirds majority is required before EU membership negotiations start.
Une majorité des deux-tiers est nécessaire avant que ne commencent les négociations d'adhésion à l'U.E.

6.

Les membres du Conseil de sécurité de l'ONU se sont engagés à aider le nouvel Etat.
The members of the UN Security Council pledged to help the new state.

La Pologne joue un rôle croissant sur la scène internationale.
Poland plays an increasing role on the international stage.

En définitive, les Etats-Unis ont ramené Israël à la table des négociations.
Eventually, the United States brought Israel back to the negotiating table.

La Grande-Bretagne a fait pression sur l'Afrique du Sud dès les années 1960.
Great Britain put pressure on South Africa as early as the 1960s.

Cela sert-il à quelque chose de voter des résolutions que l'on ne pourra pas faire respecter ?
Is there any point in voting resolutions that it will be impossible to enforce?

16. ENVIRONMENTAL ISSUES

1.

to be malnourished = to be **undernourished** (also: underfed) : *souffrir de malnutrition*

to jeopardize sth = **to endanger sth, to put sth at risk** : *mettre qch en danger*

to devastate = **to ravage** : *dévaster, ravager*

rubble = **debris** : *décombres*

2.

to **insure** a house : *assurer une maison*

emergency relief : *des secours d'urgence*

a **mudslide** : *une coulée de boue*

to be reported **missing** : *être porté disparu*

3.

une espèce : **a species**

évacuer : **to evacuate**

prédire : **to predict**

un volcan : **a volcano**

4.

the Department of the **Environment** : *le Ministère de l'environnement*

an **environmental** disaster : *une catastrophe écologique*

an **environmentalist** : *un écologiste* (here: environmentalists)

environmentally friendly, **environment-friendly** : *respectueux de l'environnement*

5.

survivre	to survive	a surviv**or**	*un survivant*
avoir faim	to be hungry	hung**er**	*la faim*
rare	scarce	scarc**ity**	*la rareté*
sec	dry	dr**ought**	*la sécheresse*

6.

An earthquake of magnitude 6 on the Richter scale hit Indonesia last night.
Un séisme de magnitude 6 sur l'échelle de Richter a frappé l'Indonésie hier soir.

In the drought-stricken areas, children are threatened with starvation.
Dans les zones frappées par la sécheresse, les enfants risquent de mourir de faim.

The volcano erupted during the night while the hurricane swept across the island.
Le volcan est entré en éruption pendant la nuit alors que l'ouragan balayait l'île.

Fortunately, the villagers were able to escape unscathed.
Heureusement, les villageois ont pu s'échapper sains et saufs.

The coast was declared a disaster area so the victims got compensation.
La côte a été déclarée zone sinistrée si bien que les victimes ont été indemnisées.

7.

L'équipe de secours a fourni une aide alimentaire aux rescapés.
The rescue team supplied the survivors with food aid.

Comme les gorilles, les ours polaires sont une espèce en voie de disparition.
Like gorillas, polar bears are an endangered species.

Les consommateurs ont déjà été sensibilisés aux dangers de la déforestation.
Consumers have already been made aware of the dangers of deforestation.

Des pluies diluviennes se sont abattues sur les zones les plus durement frappées.
Torrential rain fell on the worst-hit areas.

Le choléra qui s'est propagé à la suite du séisme a fait des centaines de morts.
The cholera which spread in the aftermath of the earthquake claimed hundreds of lives.

17. POLLUTION

1.

lead-**free** petrol : *essence sans plomb*
car **exhausts, exhaust fumes** : *gaz d'échappement*
oil-**covered** birds : *oiseaux mazoutés*
hermetically **sealed** containers : *containers hermétiquement fermés*

2.

toxic chemical	*produit chimique toxique*
ozone depletion	*diminution de la couche d'ozone*
oil slick	*marée noire*
scrap metal	*ferraille*

3.

	NOM	VERBE
poison	*poison*	*contaminer (une rivière)*
waste	*déchets*	*gaspiller (des ressources)*
dump	*décharge, dépotoir*	*déposer, jeter (des ordures)*
spill	*déversement (de pétrole)*	*renverser, déverser*

4.

to **leak** (here: leaks) : *fuir*
bury : *enterrer*
to **process**, to **recycle** waste : *traiter, recycler des déchets*
to **sort** : *trier*

5.

polluer	to pollute	a pollu**ter**	*un pollueur*
polluer	to pollute	a pollu**tant**	*un polluant*
risque, danger	hazard	hazard**ous**	*dangereux*
nuire	to harm	harm**ful**	*nocif*

6.

The cost of removing asbestos from the building had been underestimated.
Le coût du désamiantage du batîment avait été sous-évalué.

Shipowners whose oil tankers discharge waste oil into the sea should be fined.
On devrait faire payer une amende aux armateurs dont les pétroliers dégazent en mer.

The scourge of plastic bags is afflicting China in unprecedented proportions.
Le fléau des sacs en plastique touche la Chine dans des proportions sans précédent.

The production of disposable diapers requires 200 times more energy than to wash reusable ones.
La production de couches jetables consomme 200 fois plus d'énergie que le lavage de couches ré-utilisables.

The release of untreated sewage into the Great Lakes has now been banned.
Le déversement d'eaux usées non traitées dans les Grands Lacs a maintenant été interdit.

7

En ville, beaucoup de personnes âgées souffrent d'asthme et ont du mal à respirer.
In towns, many elderly people suffer from asthma and have difficulty breathing.

On dit que les gaz CFC sont responsables du trou dans la couche d'ozone.
CFCs are said to be responsible for the hole in the ozone layer.

Il faut encourager les constructeurs automobiles à produire des véhicules moins polluants.
Car-makers must be encouraged to produce vehicles that pollute less.

Des produits chimiques toxiques ont contaminé le sol, ce qui fait que les plantes ne poussent plus.
Toxic chemicals have contaminated the soil, with the result that plants do not grow any more.

La marée noire dans le Golfe du Mexique a eu des conséquences dramatiques sur la pêche et le tourisme.
The oil spill in the Gulf of Mexico had tragic consequences on fishing and tourism.

18. CLIMATE CHANGE & ENERGY

1.

le dioxyde de carbone : carbon **dioxide**
la calotte polaire : the **polar** icecap
les hydrocarbures : **hydrocarbons**
une raffinerie de pétrole : an oil **refinery**
une plateforme pétrolière : an oil **platform** (also : oil rig)

2.

to generate electricity : *produire de l'électricité*
a nuclear plant : *une centrale nucléaire*
crude oil prices : *le prix du pétrole brut*
to curb greenhouse gas emissions : *réduire les émissions de gaz à effet de serre*
a smart meter : *un compteur intelligent*

3.

a climate scientist = a **climatologist** : *un climatologue*
a wind turbine = a **windmill**, a **windpump** : *une éolienne*
a tidal turbine = a **marine turbine** : *une hydrolienne*
a dam = a **barrage** : *un barrage*
a four-wheel drive = a **sports utility vehicle**, an **SUV** : *un quatre-quatre*

4.

la consommation d'énergie	energy consumption
les besoins en énergie	energy needs, requirements
la pénurie d'énergie	energy gap, shortage, shortfall
la politique énergétique	energy policy
les économies d'énergie	energy savings

5.

Most scientists agree that the increase in global temperatures is due to the burning of fossil fuels.
La plupart des scientifiques sont d'accord pour dire que l'augmentation de la température de la planète est due à la combustion d'énergies fossiles.

If oil supplies run out in about 30 years, economic growth will come to an end, unless…
Si les réserves de pétrole s'épuisent dans une trentaine d'années, la croissance économique prendra fin, à moins que…

The main argument in favour of nuclear power is that it does not generate greenhouse gases.
Le principal argument en faveur de l'énergie nucléaire est qu'elle ne produit pas de gaz à effet de serre.

In the 19th century, Malthusians already predicted the world would run out of energy within a few decades.
Au dix-neuvième siècle, les Malthusiens prédisaient déjà que l'on viendrait à manquer d'énergie en l'espace de quelques décennies.

Last week's floods would have taken place even without global warming.
Les inondations de la semaine dernière auraient eu lieu même sans le réchauffement climatique.

6.

Je vais au travail en vélo pour sauver la planète sur laquelle je vis.
I cycle to work in order to save the planet I live on.

L'hydrofracturation devient rentable quand le prix du pétrole dépasse 100 dollars le baril.
Fracking becomes profitable when oil prices top $ 100 a barrel.

Si on avait arrêté de gaspiller le pétrole il y a trente ans, on n'en serait pas là.
If we had stopped wasting oil thirty years ago, we wouldn't be in this situation.

La demande mondiale d'énergie a explosé avec la montée des pays émergents.
The global demand for energy sky-rocketed with the rise of emerging countries.

Suffira-t-il de d'éteindre les appareils électriques pour réduire la consommation d'énergie de façon significative ?
Will it be enough to switch off electrical appliances to curb energy consumption significantly?

19. SCIENCE

1.

a **scientist** : *un scientifique*
scientific : *scientifique*
scientifically : *scientifiquement*
scientism : *scientisme*

2.

GPS = **global positioning system** : *GPS*
GMO = **genetically modified organism** : *organisme génétiquement modifié*
ESA = **European Space Agency** : *Agence spatiale européenne*
UFO = **unidentified flying object** : *objet volant non identifié, OVNI*

3.

cutting **edge** research : *recherche de pointe*
state-of-the-**art** technology : *technologie dernier cri*
manned flight : *vol habité*
a guinea **pig** : *un cobaye*

4.

to experiment **on** mice : *faire des expériences sur des souris*
to go **into** orbit : *entrer en orbite*
to touch **down** : *se poser*
genetic make-**up** : *profil génétique*

5.

a patent : *un brevet*
technophobia, **technofear** : *technophobie*
a science park, **a technology park** : *une technopole*
evidence : *preuves, données*

6.

I've heard that Samsung has been experimenting with a new touchscreen.
J'ai entendu dire que Samsung expérimentait un nouvel écran tactile.

The recent field trials on soyabeans and rapeseed are inconclusive.
Les récents essais en champ sur le soja et le colza sont peu concluants.

The airlock on the new multi-stage rocket is remote-controlled.
Le sas de la nouvelle fusée à étages est télécommandé.

Hardly anything is known about the long-term effects of mobile phone radiations.
On ne sait presque rien des effets à long terme des radiations émises par les téléphones portables.

Computer buffs or more generally tech-savvy youngsters always talk in jargon.
Les fanas d'informatique et autres jeunes gens calés en matière de technologie ne cessent de jargonner.

7.

Le clonage peut être utilisé à des fins thérapeutiques ou reproductives.
Cloning can be used for therapeutic or reproductive purposes.

Cette technique révolutionnaire a servi pour effectuer une étude sur les pommes de terre génétiquement modifiées.
This revolutionary technique was used to conduct a study on GM potatoes.

La course dans l'espace a commencé avec le lancement du premier Spoutnik en octobre 1957.
The space race started with the launching of the first Sputnik in October 1957.

Les satellites espions ont joué un rôle crucial durant la guerre du Golfe.
Spy satellites played a crucial role during the Gulf War.

La recherche fondamentale peut-elle se passer de fonds publics ?
Can basic research do without public funding?

20. INFORMATION TECHNOLOGY

1.

to hack **into** a computer system : *s'introduire dans un système informatique*
to print **out, print ø** : *imprimer*
to access **ø** a website : *accéder à un site*
to log **off, log out** : *se déconnecter*

2.

charger	to load	to **up**load	*télécharger (vers un serveur)*
surfer	to browse	a brows**er**	*un navigateur*
pouvoir	to be able	to **dis**able a site	*mettre un site hors d'état*
numérique	digital	to digit**ize**, to digit**alize**	*numériser*

3.

digital divide	*fossé numérique*
search engine	*moteur de recherche*
identity theft	*vol d'identité*
service provider	*fournisseur d'accès (internet)*

4.

to charge sb : *faire payer qn*
a cracker : *un hacker / un pirate (informatique)*
an avatar : *un avatar*
to post a message : *mettre en ligne, publier un message*

5.

a **recruitment site** : *un site de recrutement*
a **social networking site** : *un reseau social, de socialisation*
an **auction site** : *un site de vente aux enchères*
a **dating site** : *un site de rencontres*

6.

You need to update your software to improve its performance.
Il faut que tu mettes à jour ton logiciel pour améliorer ses performances.

Digital natives are supposed to prefer watching videos on YouTube to reading books.
La « génération numérique » est censée préférer regarder des vidéos sur YouTube plutôt que lire des livres.

I was able to retrieve my parents' confidential data in a few clicks.
J'ai pu récupérer les informations confidentielles de mes parents en quelques clics.

Their website went down last week and has been off-line since then.
Leur site a fermé la semaine dernière et n'est plus accessible depuis.

Should the authorities crack down on illegal downloading?
Les autorités devraient-elles réprimer le téléchargement illégal ?

7.

Il suffit de double-cliquer sur l'icône dans le coin en haut à gauche pour accéder au site.
To access the site, you simply need to double-click on the icon in the top left corner.

Tu risques d'avoir une amende si tu télécharges illégalement des films ou des clips.
You may get fined if you download movies or video clips illegally.

De plus en plus de gens vont sur internet pour réserver des billets d'avion.
More and more people go online to book plane tickets.

La quantité d'informations disponibles est telle que l'on finit par se sentir complètement perdu.
The amount of available information is such that you end up feeling completely lost.

La plupart des réseaux dont nous dépendons sont conçus par des entreprises privées.
Most of the networks we depend on are designed by private companies.

ANNEXES

1. ORAL PRESENTATIONS

The advice in the following pages is meant first of all for students taking the entrance exams to the "grandes écoles" (business or engineering schools) but also for all those who take an oral exam which consists in first presenting, then commenting on a newspaper article or an audio document. The typical preparation time is twenty minutes.

➲ GENERAL ADVICE

⇨ First, remember it is best to address the examiner in English right from the start. You might say for instance: "May I sit down?" or "Shall I sit here?" "Do you want me to start now?".

⇨ Throughout the interview, it is essential that **you should not read your notes**: you are taking an oral exam and you must do your best to express yourself as naturally, as spontaneously as possible. You must never give the impression that you are reciting something.

⇨ It follows from this* that **you must not write complete sentences** when you prepare your presentation: a plan and a few key-words should be enough, with possibly a few sentences for a conclusion so that you have a clear idea of where you are heading*. But if you write every word down, you will be tempted* to read. In addition, writing complete sentences would use up too much of your time, with the result that you would not have enough time left to *think* about the issue. In particular, writing introductory sentences such as "This is an article taken from *The Washington Post*..." is a total waste of time.

⇨ A few grammar mistakes will not prevent you from getting a good or even very good mark as long as* you get your meaning across*. If you realize you've just made a mistake, however, correct it immediately. (e.g. "The United States are responsible for the crisis that started... sorry: The United States *is* responsible for the crisis that ...").

⇨ If you are stuck* because you don't remember the English word for something, say "How shall I put it?" or something similar. You may also say: 'I'm sorry but I can't remember the English for "*sondage*".' But of course, you cannot do this too often. Remember there are almost always several ways of expressing a particular idea, so instead of making a long pause trying to remember *the* translation that escapes you, reformulate the context.

⇨ If you get stuck in the middle of a long, complicated sentence you don't know how to finish, you should say "Sorry, I'll start again" or "Sorry, I'll put that differently" ... and start again.

➲ INTRODUCTION

⇨ If you are talking about a newspaper article, use the word "article" (rather than "text", which sounds rather academic*) or, if you happen to know what kind of article you have read, "leading article, editorial": *éditorial*, "feature article": *article de fond*, "column": *chronique*, "opinion piece": *tribune*, "book review": *critique de livre*. Also remember that, unlike people, articles do not 'speak' or 'talk' about something: they 'deal with' or 'are about' something. You may also explain that in the article, the writer 'tackles' or 'addresses' the issue of...

⇨ You must **identify the issue** as clearly as possible. Remember to mention the country (or countries) involved if necessary. There is usually no point in reading the title of the article (since the examiner has already read it) but you might do so if you have something to say about it (for instance, if you want to point out that it contains a pun* or an allusion to a historical event). Examples:

- "This is an article about a bicycle-sharing scheme which has just been inaugurated in London..."
- "The article I have read concerns a new bill now under discussion in the US Congress..."

⇨ You are usually expected to **mention the source** (that is to say the name of the publication from which your document is taken). It may be a good idea to add a comment on the newspaper if it can help your listener understand something about the article. Examples:

- "It was published in *The Economist*, a well-known British weekly magazine."
- "This is taken from *The New York Times*, a major American daily."

The fact that the newspaper is British or American may be of interest. Mentioning its political orientation — if you happen to know what it is— may be helpful too.

⇨ You are also expected to **mention the time of publication**. But instead of saying " the article was published on March 23, 2012" — which sounds rather artificial — it is usually preferable to mention this date in connection with the present moment, for instance "last week" or "about six months ago." If possible, you should connect the date of publication with an event related to the issue dealt with in the article. Examples:

- "This article was published a month ago, shortly before a meeting of the G8 summit in Naples..."
- "This article is taken from *The Independent* and was published on the occasion of a demonstration two weeks ago by French farmers protesting against..."

- "In this article published last April, the writer reflects on the possible consequences of a measure adopted by the British government four months ago…"

In most cases, it is a good idea to ask yourself **on what occasion the article was published**.

⇨ There is no point in mentioning **the name of the writer** if you have never heard of him. But if the article is about feminism, for instance, the fact that the writer is a man (or a woman) may be significant.
Remember that the writer may not be a journalist. So as a rule, use the word "writer" instead of "journalist". Avoid "author" too, because an author is usually someone who writes books rather than newspaper articles.
He or she may be a politician, a scientist, a novelist, a political expert… If so, *do* mention his or her function, because this may shed some light* on what he or she says. By contrast, the name itself does not mean anything unless the person is a well-known personality. Examples:

- "The article was written by Shirin Ebadi, an Iranian lawyer who was awarded the Nobel Peace Prize in 2003."
- "… by John Major, a former leader of the Conservative Party who was Britain's Prime Minister in the 1990s"
- "The writer is Director of UNICEF, a United Nations agency which provides aid for children in difficulty."

If the writer is not well-known, the job title matters more than the name.

⊃ ANALYSIS / SUMMARY

In many exams, students are required to present the article and then to comment on it. It is important not to confuse these two parts. In the first part, **you should not comment** on the writer's position or include any information that is not given in the article.

⇨ Do not repeat the text word for word. Instead, **reformulate.** In this way you prove:

a) that you have really understood what you have read.
b) that you can actually express yourself using your own words.

and this is the whole point of the exam. However, you may quote a few words from the article which you think are worth commenting on — for example if the word is a neologism or an interesting image or metaphor.

⇨ Do not summarize one paragraph after another. Try and have a more synthetic approach (what is called a bird's eye view*) right from the beginning, and do not worry too much if you don't understand a detail here and there.

- Do not say: "In the first paragraph / At the begining of the article the journalist says..., in the second / third paragraph, she says...". Instead go straight to the point: "A law was passed by the American Congress last year, and now..." or "DNA analysis now makes it possible to identify..." Talk about the issue under consideration, not the article as such.
- It is usually needless to mention the names of the people involved or quoted in the article or to give details of specific cases described or anecdotes told by the writer. But if a personality is quoted, *do* say who they are (e.g. an economist, a political scientist...) when you report their opinion.
- There are often repetitions in newspaper articles or passages that are not worth mentioning because they contain little information. Do not do the same. You *can*, and in fact quite often you *should*, **re-organize the information** given in the article in a logical way.
- If the tone of the article is **polemical** — if the writer wants to convince the reader that a particular decision or policy is good or bad — you must say so in your analysis and clearly identify the position of the writer. Remarks about **the style or tone** used by the writer (e.g. irony, humour, aggressiveness...) are welcome.
- Make sure that your account of the article is well-balanced, in other words that you do not devote half of your time to the first paragraph, for instance.

TRANSITION

The transition between the first and the second parts must be **clear but smooth**.

- Never say: "This is the end of my summary... And now for the commentary": in fact, avoid using the words "summary" or "commentary" at any point in your presentation.
- However you must make it clear to the examiner that you are now starting the second part of your presentation. You can make a brief pause —10 seconds is more than enough. But more importantly, start off with a sentence including the pronoun 'I'. In this way, you show that you are no longer simply reporting, but adding something of your own. Here are a few examples:
  - "What I would like to comment on now is the ..."
  - "I will now focus on one aspect..."
  - "What struck me in this article is the fact that...
  - "What I found particularly interesting about this new scheme is that..."

Please note that you should not say: "~~We~~ can ~~try~~ to study the problem of...", because *you* will do the talking, not the examiner: so use the pronoun *I*. And then, you are not going to *try* to analyse the problem, you are going to analyse it.

➲ COMMENTARY

⇨ In the second part **do not paraphrase** what you have just said in the analysis. If you are tempted to read the article over and over again when you prepare your presentation, turn the page over* and do not look at it again, except briefly to check a detail.

⇨ You don't *have to* start your commentary with "I think that... ". Instead, start by explaining, describing, comparing. A commentary is not only a personal opinion.
What's more, remember that "according to" cannot be followed by "me" because "according to" implies that you distance yourself from the opinion that follows (you cannot distance yourself from yourself!).

⇨ Make sure that **at least part of your commentary** (the beginning) is closely connected with the specific issue dealt with in the article. For instance, if you're given an article about measures to reduce alcohol consumption on the New York public transport system, do not immediately embark on general considerations about the threat posed by alcohol abuse in today's society. You might give the impression that you are just reciting something you prepared before the exam.

⇨ Make the most of your general knowledge, what you have been taught in your French, history or philosophy classes. You won't be able to discuss every single aspect of the problem, however, so **choose the ones you know best**. Here are a few hints on how to find something to say:

- **generalizing**: start from the problem dealt with in the article and move on to a more general problem. With an article concerning the situation of the black minority in the US, you can move on to the situation of other minorities in the US, and then to minorities in other countries.
- **illustrating**: find examples illustrating the general ideas presented in the article, if possible examples in English-speaking countries.
- **comparing**: if the article is about a particular problem in Great Britain, try and see if it is posed in the same terms in France or Germany. Compare the situation today with what it was like 50 years ago.
- **commenting**: if there is a phrase or a sentence you think is particularly interesting because it has important implications, explain what it suggests, what it reveals about the writer's bias*.
- **debating**: examine the pros and cons of various policies (How far should the state intervene in the economy? Should we bring back

the death penalty? Should animal experiments be prohibited? If not, under what conditions should they be tolerated?)

- **taking sides**: if you feel strongly about a particular issue, then do explain your position. The important thing is that you should be able to present a number of arguments, not simply a value judgment such as 'I'm against this or that' or 'I think that X is good or bad'. Take the arguments of those who disagree with you into account, and more generally, make sure you won't antagonize* your examiner if he or she does not share your views.
- **commenting on the pictures,** photographs, cartoons, or diagrams if there are any.

⇨ In some cases, your personal experience may be a good starting point, especially if you mention experiences you may have had in English-speaking countries.

⇨ Avoid stereotypes and clichés, challenge conventional wisdom. You will be more likely to retain your listener's attention.

⇨ If you are *not* interested in the topic you have to deal with, pretend that you are and play the game.

➲ CONCLUSION

⇨ You must always make a concluding remark so that your listener is in no doubt that you have finished and that he or she can now start asking you a few questions.

⇨ However, avoid repeating in your conclusion what you have already said.

As in any oral exam, your **ability to communicate**, irrespective of* the language you are using, also comes into play. This means in particular that:

⇨ you should not look at your notes all the time but instead make eye-contact with the examiner... but of course remember that staring* at people is rude.

⇨ you should make sure that you speak loud enough and that you articulate so that the examiner does not have to strain his or her ears* to hear what you are saying.

⇨ you should not speak too fast, and not speak too slowly either. Accelerate when you are saying something that is simple and obvious, slow down when it is more complex, subtle, original...

Remember that examiners are human beings, and that they may be tired because they have just listened to ten other candidates like you: anything you can do to make your presentation clearer, easier to follow, more lively, more interesting may earn you a bonus… Remember also that your intonation, and not only the words you use, is important for communicating in English. You will be more convincing if the tone of your voice follows what you are saying. Make sure in particular that your conclusion sounds conclusive!

where you are heading: *là où vous vous* dirigez
tempted: *tenté*
as long as: *du moment* que
get your meaning across: *vous faire comprendre*
stuck: *en panne*
academic: *scolaire*
pun: *jeu de mots*
shed some light: *éclairer*
bird's eye view: *vue d'ensemble*
punctuation mark: *signe de ponctuation*
take a stand: *prendre parti*
turn the page over: *retournez la page*
bias: *préjugé(s)*
antagonize: *contrarier, indisposer*
irrespective of: *indépendamment de*
staring: *fixer*
strain one's ears: *tendre l'oreille*

2. ALL-PURPOSE VOCABULARY

This is a list of words that you will find useful when writing about or debating current issues, whatever the topic. Read the examples carefully and pay special attention to the way these words are used. In particular, make sure you do not confuse expressions that include the same words, for instance "on the contrary", an adverbial phrase, and "contrary to" a prepositional phrase — therefore followed by a noun or noun group.

➲ PREPOSITIONS AND PREPOSITIONAL PHRASES

in spite of, despite a ⇨ *malgré*

The law was passed despite its many flaws.
La loi a été votée malgré ses nombreux défauts.

contrary to ⇨ *contrairement à*

Contrary to expectations, oil prices kept rising.
Contrairement aux attentes, le prix du pétrole continuait d'augmenter.

unlike ⇨ *contrairement à*

Unlike his predecessor, the Labour leader speaks several foreign languages.
Contrairement à son prédécesseur, le chef du Parti travailliste parle plusieurs langues étrangères.

according to ⇨ *d'après, selon*

According to the rebel leaders, the days of the regime are numbered.
D'après les dirigeants rebelles, les jours du régime sont comptés.

NB : "according to" *n'est jamais suivi de* « me ».

as opposed to, in contrast with ⇨ *par opposition à*

At the time inflation was around 10% a year, as opposed to 2.5% today.
À l'époque, l'inflation s'élevait à environ 10% par an, contre 2,5 aujourd'hui.

compared to, in comparison with ⇨ *en comparaison de, par rapport à*

There have been substantial changes compared to the situation described in the report published a year ago.
Il y a eu des changements importants par rapport à la situation décrite dans le rapport publié il y a un an.

considering, given ⇨ *étant donné*

Considering the tremendous difficulties faced by the country, the party in power did not do so badly.

Étant donné les énormes difficultés auxquelles le pays était confronté, le parti au pouvoir ne s'en est pas si mal sorti.

as a result of ⇨ *en conséquence de, par suite de*

Imports fell as a result of the rise of the US dollar.

Les importations ont chuté par suite de la hausse du dollar américain.

in terms of ⇨ *sur le plan de*

Huge progress has been made in terms of transparency and access to official documents.

D'énormes progrès ont été réalisés sur le plan de la transparence et de l'accès aux documents officiels.

as regards ⇨ *pour ce qui concerne, s'agissant de, en matière de*

There are no significant differences between the two countries as regards employment and economic growth.

Il n'y a pas de différences significatives entre les deux pays en ce qui concerne l'emploi et la croissance économique.

➲ SUBORDINATING CONJUNCTIONS

whereas, while ⇨ *tandis que, alors que*

Some studies suggest that boys score higher in abstract reasoning whereas girls have greater language skills.

Certaines études semblent indiquer que les garçons ont de meilleurs résultats pour le raisonnement abstrait tandis que les filles ont de plus grandes compétences linguistiques.

although, though, even though ⇨ *bien que, quoique*

He amassed a fortune even though he had had no formal education.

Il a fait fortune bien qu'il n'ait pas fait de vraies études.

as, since, considering that ⇨ *puisque*

How come so few people give up smoking since they know it is bad for them?

Comment se fait-il que si peu de gens arrêtent de fumer puisqu'ils savent que c'est mauvais pour eux ?

whether ⇨ *si*

No-one knows for sure whether gender differences are rooted in biology.

Personne ne sait avec certitude si les différences entre les sexes ont un fondement biologique.

supposing ⇨ *à supposer que*

Supposing the Left wins the election, how would the stock market respond?

En supposant que la Gauche gagne les élections, comment réagirait la Bourse ?

unless ⇨ *à moins que*

The conference is bound to end in failure unless the Israelis make some concessions.

La conférence va forcément se terminer par un échec si les Israéliens ne font pas de concessions.

⮊ ADVERBS AND ADVERBIAL PHRASES

in my opinion, in my view, to my mind ⇨ *à mon avis, selon moi*

Everyone seems to agree that recycling can help, but in my view, it is often counter-productive.

Tout le monde semble être d'accord sur le fait que le recyclage est utile, mais à mon avis, c'est souvent contre-productif.

as a result, as a consequence ⇨ *en conséquence*

They dropped the reform, and as a result, the situation got worse and worse.

Ils ont laissé tomber la réforme et en conséquence, la situation n'a cessé d'empirer.

even so, for all that ⇨ *pourtant, tout de même, malgré tout*

He failed his first two exams, but even so he went on to become first in his class.

Il a raté ses deux premiers examens, mais par la suite il est tout de même devenu major de sa promo.

on the contrary ⇨ *au contraire*

There's nothing wrong with your suggestion; on the contrary, I think it's excellent.

Ta proposition ne pose aucun problème ; au contraire, je crois qu'elle est excellente.

by contrast, by comparison ⇨ *par contraste, par comparaison*

Unemployment here is on the rise while, by contrast, it is declining in Germany.

Ici le chômage est en hausse tandis que par comparaison, il recule en Allemagne.

meanwhile, at the same time ⇨ *cependant, dans le même temps*

Most mothers have jobs now. Meanwhile they still do most of the household chores.

La plupart des mères travaillent maintenant. Dans le même temps, elles continuent d'assumer la plupart des tâches ménagères.

on the whole, by and large ⇨ *dans l'ensemble, globalement*

The plan may not be flawless but on the whole, it looks satisfactory.

Le plan n'est peut-être pas parfait, mais dans l'ensemble, il a l'air satisfaisant.

at first sight / on closer inspection ⇨ *à première vue / si l'on y regarde de plus près*

At first sight the new policy seemed to be working fine, but on closer inspection, it turned out to pose several difficulties.

À première vue, la nouvelle politique semblait bien fonctionner, mais en y regardant de plus près, il s'est avéré qu'elle présentait plusieurs difficultés.

granted, admittedly, true ⇨ *certes*

I think the first candidate was the best by far. Granted, his English is not perfect but his presentation was impressive all the same.

Je trouve que le premier candidat était de loin le meilleur. Certes, son anglais n'est pas parfait, mais sa présentation était quand même impressionnante.

likewise, similarly ⇨ *de la même façon*

Boys under twenty spend an average of two hours a day using social networks. Similarly, most girls say they enjoy using them too.

Les garçons de moins de vingt ans passent en moyenne deux heures par jour sur les réseaux sociaux. De la même façon, la plupart des filles déclarent qu'elles les apprécient aussi.

politically / economically etc. speaking ⇨ *d'un point de vue politique / économique etc.*

The country hasn't yet taken off economically speaking. No wonder it is still immature politically speaking.

D'un point de vue économique, le pays n'a pas encore décollé. Pas étonnant qu'il manque de maturité, politiquement parlant.

paradoxically ⇨ *paradoxalement*

Paradoxically, drinking only water can pose risks.

Paradoxalement, ne boire que de l'eau peut présenter des risques.

surprisingly ⇨ *de façon suprenante*

Surprisingly, a majority of voters agrees with the new tax.

Ce qui est surprenant, c'est qu'une majorité d'électeurs est d'accord avec le nouvel impôt.

arguably ⇨ *sans doute*

His latest movie is arguably the best he's ever done.

Son dernier film est sans doute le meilleur qu'il ait jamais fait.

➲ SAYING VERBS

to argue that... ⇨ *soutenir, avancer que...*

Critics of the scheme argue it would be too costly.

Les opposants au projet soutiennent qu'il serait trop coûteux.

to claim, to maintain that... ⇨ *prétendre que*

It is sometimes claimed that in future, renewables will cover our energy needs.

On prétend parfois qu'à l'avenir, les énergies renouvelables couvriront nos besoins énergétiques.

to imply, to suggest that... ⇨ *laisser entendre, sous-entendre suggérer que*

The writer offers several solutions but at the same time implies that the problem posed is intractable.

L'auteur propose plusieurs solutions mais en même temps laisse entendre que le problème est insoluble.

to add that... ⇨ *préciser que*

The Secretary of State explained that the situation in Iraq had improved and added that the troops would be withdrawn by next December.

Le secrétaire d'Etat a expliqué que la situation en Irak s'était améliorée et a précisé que les troupes seraient retirées d'ici décembre prochain.

to admit that... ⇨ *reconnaître que*

Some pro-lifers admit that abortion should be legal in case of rape or incest.

Certains opposants à l'avortement reconnaissent qu'il devrait être permis en cas de viol ou d'inceste.

to stress, to emphasize, to insist that... ⇨ *souligner, insister sur le fait que...*

In their book *The Spirit Level*, the authors stress that higher levels of inequality have drastic consequences.

Dans leur livre « L'égalité, c'est la santé », les auteurs soulignent que l'accroissement des inégalités a des conséquences dramatiques.

to agree that... ⇨ *être d'accord sur le fait que*

Most experts agree that affirmative action policies have serious drawbacks.

La plupart des experts sont d'accord pour dire que les mesures de discrimination positive présentent de graves inconvénients.

➲ OTHER VERBS

to deal with, to be about ⇨ *parler de*

The article deals with the attitude of the gun lobby in the wake of the Virginia Tech massacre.

L'article parle de l'attitude du lobby des armes au lendemain du massacre de Virginia Tech.

to be confronted with, to be faced with ⇨ *être confronté à*

The country is confronted with an unprecedented spate of racially motivated attacks.

Le pays est confronté à une vague sans précédent d'agressions à caractère racial.

to tackle, to combat ⇨ *s'attaquer à*

The opposition accused the government of not doing enough to tackle climate change.

L'opposition a accusé le gouvernement de ne pas assez faire pour s'attaquer au changement climatique.

to raise an issue ⇨ *soulever un problème*

Will the problem be raised at the next summit?

Le problème sera-t-il soulevé au prochain sommet ?

to discuss an issue ⇨ *débattre d'un problème*

The House of Commons is expected to discuss the issue next week.

La Chambre des Communes est censée débattre du problème la semaine prochaine.

to take sth into account, into consideration ⇨ *tenir compte de qch*

The minister had not taken the grim economic situation into account.

Le ministre n'avait pas tenu compte de la mauvaise conjoncture.

to be in favour of, to favour, to support, to back ⇨ *soutenir*

Big business backed the initiative but it fell through all the same.

Les grandes entreprises ont soutenu cette initiative mais elle est tout de même tombée à l'eau.

to advocate, to recommend ⇨ *préconiser, prôner, recommander*

The committeed advocated a moratorium.

La commission a préconisé un moratoire.

to object to, to oppose ⇨ *s'opposer à, être contre, s'élever contre*

The Greens are sure to object to the construction of a new bridge.

Les Verts vont certainement s'opposer à la construction d'un nouveau pont.

⊃ NOUNS

a controversy ⇨ *une polémique, une controverse, un débat*

The president's remarks on anti-white racism sparked off a fierce controversy.

Les remarques du président sur le racisme anti-blanc ont provoqué une vive polémique.

a bone of contention ⇨ *une pomme de discorde.*

EU membership has long been a bone of contention within the Conservative Party.

L'appartenance à l'UE est depuis longtemps une pomme de discorde au sein du Parti conservateur.

an advantage, a benefit ⇨ *un avantage, un bienfait*

The reform will bring benefits to patients and doctors alike.

La réforme bénéficiera aux patients comme aux médecins.

a disadvantage, a drawback ⇨ *un inconvénient, un désavantage*

The drawbacks of the scheme far outweigh its advantages.

Les inconvénients du projet pèsent bien plus lourd que ses avantages.

the case for / the case against ⇨ *les arguments pour / contre*

In his book, the writer argues the case for a new sort of carbon tax.

Dans son livre, l'auteur présente les arguments en faveur d'un nouveau genre de taxe carbone.

the upside / the downside ⇨ *le bon côté / le mauvais côté*

Taxing the rich is a good idea; the downside is that it will scare them away.

C'est une bonne idée de taxer les riches ; l'inconvénient, c'est que cela les fera fuir.

the pros and the cons ⇨ *le pour et le contre*

Work out the pros and cons of the options you are considering before making a decision.

Réfléchissez bien aux avantages et inconvénients des différentes options que vous envisagez avant de prendre une décision.

an outcry, an uproar ⇨ *un tollé, une levée de boucliers*

The unexpected ruling of the Supreme Court caused an outcry.

La décision inattendue de la Cour suprême a suscité un tollé.

a supporter, an advocate ⇨ *un défenseur, un partisan*

Supporters of a tax on financial transactions agree that its introduction requires careful planning.

Les partisans d'une taxe sur les transactions financières sont d'accord pour dire que sa mise en œuvre doit être soigneusement planifiée.

a critic, an opponent ⇨ *un opposant, un adversaire*

Opponents of euthanasia argue that life is sacred.

Ceux qui s'opposent à l'euthanasie soutiennent que la vie est sacrée.

➲ ADJECTIVES

topical ⇨ *d'actualité*

She is more interested in history than in topical issues.

Elle s'intéresse davantage à l'histoire qu'aux questions d'actualité.

hot button (US) ⇨ *brûlant*

The decriminalization of prostitution is a hot-button issue in some countries.

La dépénalisation de la prostitution est une question brûlante dans certains pays.

controversial, contentious, divisive ⇨ *controversé*

Abortion is still a very contentious issue in much of the US while it is non-controversial in most of Europe.

L'avortement est encore un sujet très controversé dans une grande partie des Etats-Unis alors qu'il ne prête pas à controverse dans la plupart des pays européens.

questionable ⇨ *discutable, contestable*

True the conclusions of the study are thought-provoking, but its methodology is questionable.

Certes, les conclusions de l'étude font réfléchir, mais sa méthodologie est contestable.

beneficial ⇨ *bénéfique*

The policy will have beneficial effects in the long term.

La politique aura des effets bénéfiques sur le long terme.

detrimental ⇨ *préjudiciable, nuisible*

Paradoxically, the introduction of quotas might have detrimental effects on the way women are perceived.

Paradoxalement, l'instauration de quotas pourrait nuire à la façon dont les femmes sont perçues.

CPI
AUBIN IMPRIMEUR

Achevé d'imprimer en avril 2013
N° d'impression 1304.0066
Dépôt légal, avril 2013
Imprimé en France